# Rambling Recollections

MACMILLAN AND CO., Limited
LONDON · BOMBAY · CALCUTTA
MELBOURNE

THE MACMILLAN COMPANY
NEW YORK · BOSTON · CHICAGO
ATLANTA · SAN FRANCISCO

THE MACMILLAN CO. OF CANADA, Ltd.
TORONTO

*Henry Drummond Wolff*
æt 13½
from a drawing by H. B. Ziegler

Emery Walker Ph. Sc.

# Rambling Recollections

BY

THE RIGHT HONOURABLE

## SIR HENRY DRUMMOND WOLFF

G.C.B., G.C.M.G.

LATE BRITISH AMBASSADOR IN SPAIN

Ut, quocunque loco fueris, vixisse libenter
Te dicas.                          Hor. Epis. I. xi.

IN TWO VOLUMES

VOL. I

MACMILLAN AND CO., LIMITED
ST. MARTIN'S STREET, LONDON
1908

*First Edition January* 1908
*Reprinted February and March* 1908

TO MY WIFE

LADY WOLFF

FOR SO MANY YEARS MY CONSTANT COMRADE

# PREFACE

THE title of this book conveys my meaning clearly.
It is not an autobiography, nor even a continuous
narrative. It is founded on no diary or record.
Whatever the contents of the book—whether
narrative or anecdotic—they are given just as
they come unbidden into my memory, which is
not a bad one, though possibly not so exact as I
could wish. I have not attempted to be strictly
accurate as to chronological order, though the
events described harmonise with the period in
connection with which they appear. By anticipa-
tion, therefore, I fully recognise the defects arising
from want of premeditation.

Any apologies that may be required of me, I
make at once. I am prepared to accept criticism
without remonstrance.

There are many points omitted. I have not
even alluded to the great change in English society
caused by the influx of American notables. I
believe that this peculiar feature of recent years
is likely to bring great improvement and advantage

to both countries. Unfortunately, what are called my declining years have not been overcrowded with enjoyment; but among my pleasanter recollections are those of Americans like Consuelo, Duchess of Manchester; her sister, Lady Lister-Kaye; Mrs. Adair, and Lady Randolph Churchill. These friends being still alive—let us hope for many years to come—I venture neither to eulogise nor to criticise.

I have also much to say of gratitude to the family of the late Duke and Duchess of Marlborough, to Lord and Lady Londonderry, to Lady Chesterfield, and to Mr. and Mrs. George Bankes and their family, from all of whom I have received many acts of kindness. I may say the same of the late Duke of Wellington—a man of extraordinary common sense and irresistible humour. If it were my misfortune to write any sequel to this book, I should have much to say that space has now forced me to omit.

I feel under great obligations to Sir Edward Grey and to other members of the Foreign Office for the facilities they have given me in connection with this work. My warm thanks are also due to the Russian Ambassador and to the Persian chargé d'affaires.

# CONTENTS

## CHAPTER I

## CHAPTER II

## CHAPTER III

## CHAPTER IV

## CHAPTER V

## CHAPTER VI

## CHAPTER VII

## CHAPTER VIII

## CHAPTER IX

## CHAPTER X

# CONTENTS

## CHAPTER XI

## CHAPTER XII

## CHAPTER XIII

## CHAPTER XIV

## CHAPTER XV

## CHAPTER XVI

## CHAPTER XVII

# CHAPTER XXIII

# CHAPTER XXIV

# CHAPTER XXV

# CHAPTER XXVI

# CHAPTER XXVII

# ILLUSTRATIONS

# CHAPTER I

Malta—Mr. Hookham Frere—Naval friends—Sir Frederick Ponsonby —His family—Other acquaintances—Arrival of Turkish ladies— Giraffes—Malta transferred to Europe by Act of Parliament— Government—Summers in Malta.

My first recollections began at Malta, in a large garden at the Pietà.   Here I used to play of a morning, when a door would open in the wall from another garden, admitting a gentleman in a skull-cap, who said, " Good-morning, little boy."   It was Mr. Hookham Frere, the uncle of the first Sir Bartle.   He had retired to Malta after leaving the Embassy in Spain, where he had some misunderstanding with the Government of the day in connection with the battle of Corunna and the retreat of Sir John Moore.   After leaving Spain I do not think he was ever employed again.   In earlier life he had been the great friend and associate of George Canning, and many anecdotes are told of their powers of repartee.   There is one, I believe, well known, and which many years ago I read in a book—I think Mr. Samuel Rogers' *Table-talk*.   Amongst other friends of Mr. Canning and Mr. Frere was Dr. Legge, who was appointed

Bishop of Oxford.  He invited his two friends to attend his first sermon, which they did accordingly. Afterwards they went to have luncheon with him, and he, full of his newly acquired dignity, asked them what they thought of his sermon.  Mr. Canning replied, "You were short."  The Bishop rejoined, "I am glad you found me short, for I was afraid of being tedious"; whereupon Mr. Frere remarked, "You *were* tedious."

Mr. Frere had a brother whom I knew afterwards in London—Mr. Hatley Frere, who lived in Poets' Corner.  His daughter, I think, had married Bishop Spencer.  He wished to be very kind, and asked me to dine at his house when I chose.  Unfortunately, he dined at four o'clock, in those days not an unusual hour, but one during which I was detained at the Foreign Office, and I fear he was hurt at my constantly refusing his invitations.

Mr. Hookham Frere was the author of a poem called *Whistlecraft*—still almost a classic. In Parliament he had been associated with Mr. Canning and with Mr. Ellis, who was the first among them to be put into office.  This was at the India Board, where he was made to suffer many jokes on the part of his two friends. They were in the habit of writing to him under assumed names on subjects supposed to be connected with his office.  One joke, still remembered, is a letter, purporting to have been written from India by a lady who was born a French Canadian

H. D. W. ÆT. 4½.

and who claimed the intervention of the Home
Government. It was dated from a place, totally
invented by the writers, called the Negudda
Pelangs, where, the lady wrote, she had come with
her husband, "*et où il s'est fait nègre.*" Against
this grievance the lady appealed as a British
subject.

Mr. Frere had been married to the Dowager
Lady Erroll, and in his house there still lived a
niece of that lady, known as Miss Blake, afterwards Lady Hamilton Chichester. I knew later
in London an aunt of hers, an old lady and a great
whist-player, who was irreverently known by the
name of Peggy Blake. On the death of Lady
Erroll, Mr. Frere's sister, Miss Susan Frere, whom
I recollect as a charming elderly lady, took the head
of his household. There was also a young Greek
lady whom Mr. Frere, when yachting in Greek
waters, had rescued as a baby from an island during
some massacre. She was known as Miss Statyra
Livedostro, and married Captain Hope, a son of
the Lord President of the Court of Session, and
grandson of the first Earl of Hopetoun. I still
have in my possession a little New Testament
which she gave me with her autograph. Captain
Hope, whom I also recollect as having been kind
to me in my infancy, was later appointed to some
important post at the Cape of Good Hope, and
there, I believe, he died.

Malta was then, as it is now, a great resort for
the Navy, and I recollect vaguely the great kind-

ness of the different naval officers I met. One
whom I knew to the end of his life was Sir
Rodney Mundy. I met him subsequently at
Corfu and then in England, and always felt for
him a sincere regard. Amongst others was
Captain Halstead, afterwards Admiral Halstead,
Secretary at Lloyd's. Two cousins of mine—Sir
William Hoste and his brother, Theodore Hoste—
were constantly backwards and forwards as mid-
shipmen in the Navy. They were the sons of
the celebrated Sir William Hoste, well known as
the conqueror at the battle of Lissa and the
capture of Cattaro. Theodore Hoste died at
Malta.

Many of the anecdotes current in Maltese
society referred to the Navy. There was one
concerning an Admiral, a man of gruff disposition,
who had come to Malta with his wife, a lady of
great sentimentality. It was related that she
always addressed him as " My Heart," upon which
the Admiral used to rejoin, " Your *what?* "

One must have lived in foreign seaports to
realise the cause of the popularity of the British
Fleet. All ranks are so invariably sociable and
obliging. Many years later at Corfu, when British
ships were in the harbour, I used to see men of the
Fleet helping the inhabitants to dig their gardens
and playing with the children. During the last
scenes, when the Assembly had been dissolved on
the question of annexation to Greece, I found a
lot of sailors shouting and gesticulating in the

town.  When I asked the cause of this apparent
enthusiasm, the reply was, "We were told an
election was going on, and we thought we'd take
part in the fun."

The Governor of Malta was Sir Frederick
Ponsonby.  His wife, Lady Emily Ponsonby, was
a daughter of Lord Bathurst.  Colonel Seymour
Bathurst, grandfather of the present Lord, was
Military Secretary.  His wife, later, as a widow,
had a house in Grosvenor Square, where she entertained a great deal : it was the one now occupied
by Lord Haversham.

I knew the Ponsonby family well, and look
upon it as one of the most personally popular in
the kingdom.  Through life I have met with much
kindness from them.

Sir Frederick had lost an arm at Waterloo, and
I recollect my astonishment at seeing his left
sleeve empty, sewn up to his coat.  His sons were
very distinguished.  One was General Sir Henry
Ponsonby, Private Secretary to Queen Victoria ;
and the other, Colonel Arthur Ponsonby, who,
having been *aide-de-camp* to Sir George Brown, and
afterwards holding a similar appointment with Sir
George Buller at Corfu, commanded a regiment,
and died when in that capacity.  Both brothers
had, to a great degree, the family predilection for
private theatricals and cricket.

They had an uncle, Lord de Mauley, who was
fond of telling the story of King William IV.
going to dissolve the Parliament which refused

to ratify the Reform Bill. He told me that William IV. had found himself opposed by being told that there was no time to prepare the royal carriages, to which he replied, " Then I will go down in a hackney coach."

I find in a letter of Lady Emily Ponsonby's to my mother the following passage relative to Lord de Mauley, who had even more than the usual kindly nature of his family :—

I am very grateful to you for your sympathy. Poor dear Lord M. — he is indeed a *very* great loss to me. I miss him in all my thoughts. No incident ever occurred to me and mine that I did not find him liking me to communicate with him. Losing such a brother-in-law is a most sorrowful event to me, and I am now the last as belonging to them. His dear boy Ashley had only left him forty-eight hours before for the Crimea. Lord M. had been ill for three weeks, but was supposed to be getting much better, and there were no apprehensions at all about him, when in twenty minutes all was over. Most fortunately his daughter and Lord Kinnaird were in the room when his fainting came on, which ended in death. The doctor considers it was suppressed feeling.

Lord de Mauley had been the owner of Canford, now the property of Lord Wimborne. When he sold it to Sir John Guest for £200,000, it is said that the latter sent an ordinary cheque for that amount to him by post.

Lady Emily Ponsonby, on returning to England, was granted apartments in Hampton Court Palace, and there for many years I was constantly invited. I often met her sister there—Lady Georgiana Bathurst—and one of her brothers, Mr. William

Bathurst, Clerk of the Council, who afterwards became Lord Bathurst.

I have just seen a letter, written lately to a friend by Lady Emily Ponsonby, which says that Malta was associated in her memory with some of her happiest days.

I can recollect the arrival in Malta of Dr. Davy, brother of Sir Humphry Davy, and being very much struck by the medal he wore, which was, in fact, the Waterloo medal.

Amongst other people living at that time at Malta was Mr. Locker, who had been, I think, secretary to Lord Nelson. Mr. C. H. Smith was his deputy in the Victualling Department. I also remember a clergyman, named Le Mesurier, who was afterwards appointed Archdeacon when the Bishopric of Gibraltar and Malta was established. The Chaplain was the Rev. Mr. Cleugh. I met him and his daughter many years afterwards on my way to Corfu, when I was appointed Secretary.

There had always been considerable connection between Malta and Corfu. Sir Thomas Maitland was Governor of Malta and Lord High Commissioner of the Ionian Islands at the same time, as well as Commander-in-Chief of the Mediterranean. I believe that he really started the policy, which I see is now about to be adopted, of having the Mediterranean as a basis. He is known in Mediterranean history as " King Tom."

Among other residents was Miss Hamilton, a

truly charming old lady, whose sister was, I think,
the wife of Lord George Seymour, and who was
either aunt or great-aunt to Sir Hamilton Seymour.
General and Mrs. Wood, who afterwards inhabited
Bath, and General and Miss Forbes all lived at
Malta. Miss Forbes married a French gentleman,
and died at Mont-de-Marsan.

I have a vivid recollection, too, of Prince Puckler-
Muskau, who very properly snubbed me as a forward
child, and of Mr. Schlienz, a kind-hearted German
clergyman, the head of a missionary establishment,
which, I believe, printed books for circulation in
the East.

The only lessons I learnt were from a Sergeant
Kerby, who instructed me, as far as possible, in the
three R's. He had a son, named Jimmy, who used
to accompany me in my lessons.

Two incidents made a great impression on me.
One was the arrival at Malta of some Turkish
ladies, who had, for some reason, sought refuge
there. I was taken to see them, and, having heard
that Turkish ladies could only see persons of their
own sex, was much astonished at their receiving
me. They were, I recollect, very kind and generous
with sugar-plums. The other incident was the
arrival at Malta of four giraffes, the first that had
ever been seen in the West. They were taken to
England, and were for some years at the Zoological
Gardens. One, however, died shortly afterwards, and
the Gardens possessed only the three survivors.
In connection with the recent announcement of

the birth of a giraffe at the Zoological Gardens, it was stated that "most of the zoological gardens in Europe have been supplied with giraffes in the descendants of an original four which reached the London Zoological Gardens from Kordofan in 1835."

Malta was at that time much less known to the English than at present. Strange to say, it had been transformed geographically through its acquisition by England. Previously it had been assigned to Africa, to which it seems naturally to belong, both from its topography and its language, really a dialect of Arabic. Shortly after its annexation by Great Britain, however, it appeared that troops employed out of Europe were entitled to higher pay than for European service. An Act of Parliament was therefore passed declaring that, for this purpose, Malta was to be considered in Europe; otherwise the garrison, in regard of pay, would have been more privileged than the soldiers in the Ionian Islands, who belonged to the same command. It used to be said in joke that Malta had become part of Europe by Act of Parliament— a joke now admitted to be a reality.

The Governor of Malta in those days had only the rank of Lieutenant-Governor, being, I suppose, subordinate to the Lord High Commissioner of the Ionian Islands. Of this, however, I am not quite sure. In those days, and for many years afterwards, the island was governed as a Crown Colony. As will be seen, Sir Thomas Maitland had been instructed to assimilate the Constitution of the Ionian Islands, supposed to be quite free, to the administration of a Crown Colony.

We used to spend the summer occasionally at Gozo, and often went to Sant' Antonio, the summer residence of the Governor, which was memorable for its rich crop of Japan medlars. At Gozo we were once or twice accompanied by Miss Frere and Miss Statyra. The Deputy Governor or Principal Administrator at Gozo was Major Bayley. We lived near or at his house, and I well remember the good-nature of the soldiers of the small garrison in making rough toys for me, and teaching me games.

# CHAPTER II

WHEN I was between six and seven years old we left Malta. I recollect the rather dirty Neapolitan steamer on which we travelled. There was no stewardess, but two good-natured Neapolitan stewards, who made up for the want. They had free access to the ladies' cabins, and used to assist them in their toilet, even lacing their stays.

The first place we stopped at was Naples, which made more impression on my mind than any other town I have ever visited, owing doubtless to its being the first place I had seen out of Malta. I saw Herculaneum and Pompeii, and also Caserta, where the King of Naples had his collection of wild animals, and I remember being very much pleased at chasing some kangaroos which jumped about the garden.

From Naples we proceeded to Leghorn, where Lady Harriet Hoste and her daughters were then residing. We made several excursions, amongst

11

others to Pisa, and I had until lately an alabaster
*presse-papier*, given me at that time, on which was
engraved a picture of the Leaning Tower. Amongst
other things which I recollect very vividly was the
appearance of an elderly gentleman sitting on a
balcony near the Arno. He was pointed out as
being the brother of Napoleon. It was Louis,
ex-King of Holland, and the father of Emperor
Napoleon III.

I also made the acquaintance of some relatives
of mine, Mr. and Mrs. Craufurd. They were the
parents of Mr. Craufurd, for some time Member
for the Ayr Burghs. There were four sons and
two daughters, the whole family being then, and
later, active sympathisers with the Liberal movement in Italy. All spoke Italian in preference to
English. I recollect seeing at their house in
London many years afterwards, at different periods,
Mazzini, Orsini, and once a Garibaldian soldier in
a red shirt.

From Leghorn we had an uneventful journey to
Marseilles, and thence to Geneva, where we lived for
about a year, and where I began my first experience
of school.

Geneva I always look back upon as one of the
pleasantest towns I have seen, and on the Swiss as
a kindly and hospitable people. We used occasionally to visit M. and Mme. Saladin de Cran, who
had a beautiful place some miles from Geneva, and
in whose town-house we had what is now called a
flat.

At that time there was a great Evangelical revival in Switzerland. I still recollect several of the heads of that movement, amongst others M. Merle d'Aubigné, the author of *The History of the Reformation*, who lived at Lausanne, and at Geneva itself, Mr. Gaussen, who had relations, I believe, in England, and who had married a very amiable English lady whose name was Milne. Their son was my schoolfellow. Amongst my other schoolfellows were two boys named Floyd, who were nephews by marriage of Sir Robert Peel, and I believe, though I am not certain, that the celebrated French writer, Monsieur Cherbuliez, went to this same school with us.

Switzerland has great attractions for children. In the winter there was tobogganing, and, in the summer, excursions on the lake and tours throughout the country. At Berne, we saw Mr. David Morier, the British Minister, father of Sir Robert Morier, our late Ambassador at St. Petersburg. Sir Robert was then a boy a few years older than myself.

At Geneva there resided a Swiss clergyman of very great celebrity—Dr. Malan—a gentleman of some age, whose son subsequently entered the Church of England, and had for many years a living in Dorsetshire. Dr. Malan was a great friend of Mr. Henry Drummond, my godfather, whose acquaintance I made at Geneva when he came on a visit to his friend. I recollect going to two large meetings, one at Geneva and the other at Lausanne, held for some religious purpose in connection with the Evangelical movement. I was much impressed also with the appearance of the Swiss army when it came out once a year for exercise. I then found peaceable tradesmen dressed in uniform and with all the appearance of warriors.

We left Geneva somewhere about 1838, and I made my first acquaintance with England. We settled for some time at Richmond, where I had an aunt living—a lady who was born blind. I recollect being very much struck by the gas-lighting in the streets and shops, then recently introduced and still a matter of interest. The master of a lodging-house taught me how gas was made by means of a tobacco-pipe, the bowl of which he filled with coal-dust, covering it over with putty and placing it on the fire. In a short time, gas enough was generated to be lit at the mouthpiece.

Lucifer matches at that time were quite a novelty. All lighting had previously been done by flint and steel. At first there was a complicated arrangement by which the lucifer had to be held in a bottle of some preparation, which lighted it. Rubbing lucifers were of later date.

Whilst at Richmond, I attended two schools successively. I have found through life that my frequent change of schools has had a great influence over me, and while I have collected a good deal of information, yet, in consequence of these frequent changes, none of my knowledge is in a systematic shape. One of my schools at Richmond was kept by Mr. Delafosse, a clergyman of considerable reputation, who had a large house on Richmond Green. He was in some way or other favoured by the father of the late Duke of Cambridge, who used occasionally to dine with him ; but he left Richmond for a living at Shere in Surrey, near Albury, which was the country residence of Mr. Henry Drummond. There I met him frequently.

At Richmond, I constantly visited Lady Shaftesbury, the mother of the well-known philanthropist, Lord Ashley. She was most kind and genial. Macaws and parrots of every kind lived in her conservatory, and she was also the owner of many Persian cats. Through life I had constant proofs of the kindly nature of Lord Ashley, later Lord Shaftesbury, and the communication I frequently enjoyed with his son, Mr. Evelyn Ashley, was one of my chief pleasures in life. While writing I have heard with deep sorrow of the death of my old and much beloved friend.

I then left home for the first time and went to a school at Henley-on-Thames, picturesquely situated on the Fair Mile. It was kept by Mr. and Mrs. Lamb. He, I believe, had been steward to Mr. Childers in the north, and his wife a governess in that family. It was a pleasant school, and as Mr. Lamb, in addition to his scholastic labours, was a farmer, we had twelve acres of fields as playground, and were initiated into agriculture to a certain extent. "Treading the mow" was one of our occupations in summer. Amongst my schoolfellows there was Mr. Spencer Childers, who was killed in the Crimean War, having entered the Artillery. He was very amiable, and, though it is so long ago, I recollect the sorrow with which all his friends heard the news of his death. We generally used to attend the fine old parish church at Henley, but occasionally in the summer we were taken to country churches in the neighbour-hood. One of them was at Remenham, which now belongs to Lady Hambleden. I remember very well a gentleman preaching at Henley Church who had been with Bishop Heber in India ; but naturally our daily life exhibited no great features, though I occasionally visited Oxford to see one or two friends of mine there.

I consider nothing in my recollection irrelevant, and I may therefore here quote an anecdote heard many years ago. A gentleman having a fine place on the Thames, near Henley, had arranged to hold the funeral of an old servant at his house. As the procession was about to leave, another servant came to him and said, " If you please, sir, the corpse's brother would like to say a word to you."

During the period of my early school-life, I made the acquaintance of the late Mr. Milnes Gaskell, who gave me his last frank the day before the privilege was abolished.

Postage up to then was a matter of great con-sideration. Envelopes were not known, and letters were folded up on the paper on which they were written and directed on the outside. The cost of postage was very heavy, amounting, if I recollect rightly, sometimes to a shilling for inland letters. It was considered discourteous to prepay your letters. In consequence the recipients of letters having a heavy postage sometimes declined to take them in, and they were returned to the writers. This was one of the reasons why, in the new Act, letters, when not prepaid, were charged double to the receiver. At first, instead of stamps, which were a later invention, envelopes were sold with a complicated allegorical design, which was much laughed at. Cheap postage began, I think, at fourpence a letter, but it was reduced after a certain date to a penny. For a long time, however, economy was observed, and I find from old correspondence of fifty years ago, and later, that envelopes were remarkably small—many of them not more than four inches long by two wide.

In those days I made the acquaintance of Sir Francis and Lady Doyle. Lady Doyle was a sister of Mrs. Gaskell and a cousin of Sir Watkin Wynn. I often met them in later life.

Sir Francis Doyle was a man of considerable mark as Receiver-General of Customs, and a poet of great merit. Talking of a lady who was in the habit of abusing people with whom she quarrelled, he told me that one of her methods of annoying him was to send him letters to the Custom House with offensive words on the cover. These were naturally delivered to him by the office messengers.

On one occasion she addressed him as "Receiver-General of Customs, however infamous"; but he took all this very kindly, and afterwards the lady was decided to be out of her senses. He was a relation of Mr. Percy Doyle, a gentleman well known in the Diplomatic Service, of Colonel North, and of General Doyle, at one time Governor of Portsmouth—three brothers.

It is needless to recall all the schools I attended. After a move to the Grammar School at Wakefield, I went to Rugby, under Dr. Tait, afterwards Archbishop of Canterbury. I feel it a great honour to have received condign punishment at his hands.

Dr. Tait had only been nominated Head Master about six months before, having then succeeded the celebrated Dr. Arnold. My name had been put down in Dr. Arnold's time, and I was sent to a house, near the Schoolhouse, under the tuition of the Rev. Henry Highton, a special favourite of Dr. Arnold. I see by the papers that Mrs. Highton has only recently died at an advanced age. Mr. Highton was better fitted to be a tutor a few years later than at that period. He was very much what is now called "up-to-date," and paid considerable attention to the scientific acquirements of his pupils. Unfortunately, science in those days obtained no marks, and the time consumed in this study told very little on the examinations. The principal text-book was Joyce's *Dialogues*.

Mr. Highton was a great electrician. A brother

of his became one of the first electrical engineers, and Mr. Highton himself was, I believe, the author of some improvements in the electric telegraph, in those days still undeveloped.   I recollect seeing one of the first models of the invention at work at the Polytechnic Institute in London.   Everything in modern progress attracted Mr. Highton's sympathy, and I remember when Mr.—later Sir Isaac—Pitman, the author of a system of stenography, was on a tour through England to advocate his invention, that he gave a lecture to Mr. Highton's pupils at which our tutor himself was present.

A well-known master at Rugby was a gentleman named Anstey, commonly known as "Donnegan Anstey," as the only punishment he ever gave was to order a boy to write out so many pages of Donnegan's Lexicon.

On the whole holiday which was given on what was called Lawrence Sheriff's Day — Lawrence Sheriff being the founder of the school—the boys were allowed to be absent if any one invited them. I used generally to go to Leamington by stage-coach, passing Kenilworth and Warwick.   I was invited by Mrs. Hook, the mother of Dr. Hook, afterwards Dean of Chichester, and a relative of Theodore Hook.

One of my greatest friends at Rugby was the late Sir Henry Wilmot, who obtained the Victoria Cross in the Crimea, and who was subsequently in the House of Commons at the same time as myself: the other was Mr. Chaffey, who died young.   He

came from Martock, in Somersetshire, and certainly
was one of the most kind-hearted and good-natured
beings I ever came across.   I cannot pass over his
name.

I also made the acquaintance of Lord Bangor
and his brothers, whom since then I have had the
good fortune to meet frequently.

There were some notable pupils at that time at
Rugby.   I am not certain whether Lord Goschen
was there at the same time as myself, but I fancy
he came shortly after me.   Lord Cross had been
there before me.   M. Waddington, afterwards
Prime Minister in France, was there, and I remember that, before French lessons, he used to be
surrounded by a crowd of boys to whom he gave
a translation of the portion set out for the day.
French lessons were of a rather summary description, and very Anglican; in fact, French was even
less cultivated in those days at public schools than
it is now.   It may not be out of place here to
quote some words of Lord Salisbury's, written on
May 23, 1883, in reply to some remarks I made
on the necessity of foreign languages being more
carefully taught in our public schools.

I have been long of the opinion expressed in your letter.
The extreme uselessness of the education of the upper
classes is deplorable, and in this day of keen competition
handicaps them heavily.   It is always humiliating to find
how well Germans of the upper class can talk both English
and French.   But the difficulties in the way of a change are
very formidable.   The men who manage our public schools
have won their distinction in classics and seldom know any-

thing else; and it is of little use to give a high position there to masters of French or German extraction, for the boys will not obey them. At Wellington College, which ought to have been superior to mere traditions, the difficulty of having foreign masters was found to be so great that they gave the French mastership to the English mathematical master—with what results you may imagine.

At Rugby, French was put on the same footing as writing and arithmetic, which were supposed to be acquired before boys joined the school. Arithmetic was taught by an unhappy layman, who was made rather a butt by his pupils. It was said of him that he had asked leave of Dr. Arnold to wear a cap and gown like the other masters, to which Dr. Arnold replied, "That's as *you* like, Mr. Sale." He then asked whether the boys ought not to touch their hats to him and "shirk" him. To this Dr. Arnold replied, "That's as *they* like, Mr. Sale."

It must here be said that "shirking" was an almost classical term adopted in the school. Not only the masters, but members of the Sixth Form, called "præpostors," had the right of being shirked —that is to say, lower boys, when walking out of bounds, on seeing the approach of a præpostor made a feint of running away. Thereupon the Sixth Form man cried "On"; but if the shirking were not properly executed he would cry "Back."

These Sixth Form boys, who were approaching manhood, had very peculiar privileges, amongst others that of thrashing lower boys with a cane which they always carried. The four præpostors of the week kept order whenever the school was being called over. They had their own regular forms of discipline, and on one occasion, when one of their body dissented from an order they had made affecting the lower boys, the Sixth Form held a meeting and censured his conduct as "courting popularity among the rabble fags."

I do not know whether these rules still exist, as, strange to say, I have never been at Rugby since I left the school. When there, I was most lamentably undistinguished. Being very short-sighted, I was unable to take part in any of the games, and that was enough to ensure unpopularity.

I have met many Rugby boys since I left, amongst others Sir Richard Temple, Mr. Lawley, and the late Mr. St. Leger Glyn. The two latter were really the show men of the school, and were generally admired, when walking together, for the brilliant way in which they were dressed. There were three boys at Rugby who were all interesting —Mr. Caillard, Mr. Tycho Wynn, and Mr. Basevi. All three were related to Lord Beaconsfield. Mr. Caillard I met later in life, but I have not heard of the others again.

Owing to my having been at Rugby, though younger than himself, I knew Mr. Matthew Arnold very well in later life, and had the greatest possible regard and admiration for him. In 1869 a question arose which to me was very interesting, and which I do not think I shall be indiscreet in mentioning. A proposal had been made that the

Duke of Genoa should reside with Mr. Arnold, while going through the school course at Harrow. His parents did not wish him to go to an ordinary boarding-house, and Mr. Matthew Arnold was at that time residing at Harrow for the education of his own sons. He did not himself like the task of settling the terms on which the young Prince was to live with him. Count Maffei, the Italian chargé d'affaires, wished to refer the question to Lord Clarendon, or to Lord de Grey, then the head of the Education Department. Neither, for one reason or another, would interfere, but as both Count Maffei and Mr. Arnold were friends of mine, they left the decision to me. This I undertook —I hope conscientiously—collecting such evidence as I could of similar instances. I was told that there was a case admirably in point. The Prince de Condé, son of the Duc d'Aumale, was put to live in the house of one of the professors at Edinburgh, while attending the academical classes. My recommendation was based on this precedent, and I am happy to say it succeeded admirably. Mr. Arnold and his family were much pleased with their inmate, and the royal family of Italy showed great kindness to Mr. Arnold when he went to that country, giving him a high decoration. About that time I received the following letter from him, written in Edinburgh :—

. . . I suggested that he [1] should speak to you as I knew he was acquainted with you, having seen him talking to you

---

[1] Count Maffei.

at the Athenæum.   I have heard nothing from him, but see him if you can. . . .

I tried much to see you last week, but you were away on some of your sinister errands somewhere, and the Athenæum porter said your whereabouts were involved in utter mystery. I hope you are now come back.

I am here to be made a doctor.   In another hour the fatal step will have been taken, and I shall be LL.D. Tremble and adore!

The objection alleged against referring the point to Lord de Grey was the circumstance of his being Head of the Education Department, of which Mr. Arnold was an Inspector.

When Mr. Lowe was Minister of Education, he introduced what was known as the Revised Code.   This elicited vehement opposition in which Mr. Arnold joined with a pamphlet or letter which was conclusive.   On some one asking Mr. Lowe what he thought of Mr. Arnold's pamphlet, he replied, "Had Zimri peace who slew his master?"

Mr. Lowe had a very sardonic wit, and, though rather out of place, I must here instance some of his observations.   We were once speaking together of a friend of ours, Mr. Bailey, who, like Mr. Lowe, had once been a writer in the *Times*, with respect to an appointment he had just received as Governor of the Bahamas.   Mr. Lowe observed, "That is the place where pineapples flourish in such quantities."   I asked, "Is it not a good appointment?"   Mr. Lowe replied, "Man cannot live on pineapples alone."   His jokes were almost always of the same kind.

The night before the defeat of the Government of which he was a member, Mr. Lowe gave a dinner to some friends, reciting, as a grace, the words, "Let us eat and drink, for to-morrow we die."

He was very fond of riding a bicycle, and in the neighbourhood of his country-house at Caterham he unfortunately once ran over a man. It was agreed that he was to give a certain sum of money as compensation, which he did. Shortly afterwards, the man found that the sum was not sufficient for the expenses incurred, and committed suicide. He left a paper whereon was written, "This is all along o' Boblo."

Mr. Lowe, though a Minister of State, at one time had some difficulty in obtaining a seat. Lord Lansdowne therefore recommended him to the electors of Calne, a borough practically under the domination of Lord Lansdowne, and where, for a long time past, there had never been anything like a contest. One day, Mr. Lowe's Committee drove from Calne to Bowood, and said to Lord Lansdowne that Mr. Lowe had told them they were a pack of fools. Lord Lansdowne, when repeating the story, said, "I am convinced that Lowe never made use of any such term, but I am equally convinced that he said something which made them think he had done so."

The story is told of Mr. Lowe attending a Royal wedding at Windsor. I rather think it was that of Prince Leopold. On his return to London, he travelled with his wife and several members of the party in a saloon carriage. He inveighed against the ceremonial and said that some parts of it were absurd. When he married, he had to say, " With all my worldly goods I thee endow," and, he added, " I had not a brass farthing to give my wife." Mrs. Lowe said, " Oh, but, my dear, you forget there is your genius." He replied, " Well, you cannot say that I endowed you with that."

Mr. Lowe was celebrated for his familiarity with various languages. I do not know whether he actually spoke them all, but he undoubtedly had a profound knowledge of many. His friend Mr.— afterwards Sir George—Dasent had penetrated him with the beauty of Scandinavian poems, and Mr. Lowe had studied Icelandic with a view to reading some of them. I recollect being present at a small dinner of Sir George Dasent's to meet Lord Dufferin, after his return from Iceland. The talk turned on Scandinavian literature, and Mr. Lowe discussed some Icelandic poems, evidently knowing them thoroughly and quoting them in the vernacular. Of course I cannot answer for his pronunciation. I have recently been told that, with the object of reading some Jewish newspapers, he set to work and studied Hebrew late in life, and mastered that language, at all events sufficiently for his purpose.

# CHAPTER III

BEING intended for the Foreign Office, which I
was likely to enter early, I was taken away from
Rugby and placed with a tutor in Belgium. The
tutor was the Chaplain at Bruges—a very pleasant
man who had begun life at Worcester, where his
father had been, I think, a canon. His son was
also a canon of Manchester. My tutor had a very
strange reminiscence of his boyhood. On one
occasion, being very small, he had climbed to the
top of the Cathedral tower in company with some
officers in the Army. One of them took him by
the leg and held him suspended outside from the
top of the tower, a tremendous height. This
terrible experience had never left his mind, and it
imbued him through life with a dread of going to
a great height. Another recollection of his was
the opening of the coffin of King John, when the
whole of his body, on being exposed to the air,

27

though perfect for a few minutes, crumbled into dust. Some one, he said, had taken the big toe of the sovereign, and converted it into a tobacco-stopper.

In those days, the steamers from Ostend to Dover took from eight to ten hours, and those from Ostend to London, up the Thames, considerably longer. In order to catch the latter, I used to have to go to Ostend by a late train, as the steamers generally left at about one in the morning. I passed the intervening hours with a gentleman who was in the employment of one of the Steam Companies. I dined with him and his wife, and they were most amiable to me; but, if my host happened to do anything which offended the lady, she would pour out a volume of abuse at him in the strongest language, whereupon he used to address her as follows : " I wonder how you can use such language to me. You know I am a most desirable husband. I am young, good-looking, agreeable, with splendid manners, accomplished, and highly educated! You ought to be on your knees all day thanking Heaven for giving you such a husband. Instead of that, you make use of this language before strangers!" After I had been at their house a few times I became accustomed to this, and it no longer astonished me, but it has always remained impressed on my memory. On one occasion, when going from Dover to Ostend, I was informed that the Comte de Chambord was on board. I think he was then generally known as the Duc de Bordeaux.

The other pupils at this tutor's I have since known very well.   There were Mr. Trevanion, who subsequently married Lady Frances Lyon, and Mr. Thellusson, as well as the late Sir Hedworth Williamson and his brother William, whose parents took a house for a short time in Bruges, so as to be near their sons.   It is impossible to forget the attractive and kindly presence of Lady Williamson.

In summer, we used to take walking tours. I recollect one which lasted three weeks, and cost a most extraordinarily small sum.   We went to the Ardennes, where the hotel prices seem scarcely credible now.   They took us in, gave us comfortable rooms and very good food, consisting of the Ardennes mutton, very like Welsh mutton, bilberry tart and cream, and the trout which we ourselves caught in the river, together with a light French *vin ordinaire*.   For this they charged us at Dinant two and a half francs each per day.   At Neupont the charge was only two francs; while at St. Hubert, which had greater pretensions to being a town, we were charged three francs.   This included a pony for me as the youngest of the party.   We also went to Luxembourg, to Arlon, and then arrived at the Moselle, where we took boat, first to Coblentz, and then on the Rhine to Cologne.   We afterwards joined some friends at Aix-la-Chapelle, and thence home, the whole cost of the journey being 150 francs each.

The winter at Bruges for a youth of my age

was uncommonly pleasant. There were several English families, established there either for economical or educational purposes, who gave frequent dances. One rich English gentleman, Mr. Barron, had a large house, where he and his wife were most hospitable. Mrs. Barron was a sister of Sir Roger Palmer, and Mr. Barron came of a commercial family domiciled in Mexico.

There also lived at Bruges, with his family, a very remarkable man of great wit and versatile disposition, whose name was Addison. He was the author of several plays, and would have written well had he taken a little more pains. Many of the playwriters of the day were his friends; so also was Mr. Charles Lever, who, with his wife, once came to stay with him at Bruges. Later, I saw a great deal of Lever when in Florence, and while he was Consul at Spezzia. He had begun life as a medical man, and was for some time Physician to the Legation at Brussels. Like Colonel Addison, he was an Irishman, and gifted with great intellectual powers. Charles Lever and, in a lesser degree, Colonel Addison would have been greater writers had they been less inclined to amusement. Colonel Addison was always turning up somewhere. At one time he was a banker at Bruges; at another he organised in Ireland a political expedition to the Equator. I believe that he really was the founder of a very considerable bank in London, and he wrote one or two books which were undoubtedly able, but spoilt by haste and carelessness. Colonel Addison was very good company. His conversation was one continuous flow of jokes — some good and some bad—but all making an impression by the rapidity of their conception. I heard some one telling him that within a few days two foremost English brewers had visited Bruges. One, I believe, was Mr. Whitbread, and the other Mr. Barclay. With an exaggerated English accent, Colonel Addison replied, " *Tant mieux.*" He was a most amiable man, and was always treated in a friendly way by Mr. Thackeray and the principal writers of the day. As I am writing, I learn that his son, a King's Counsel and County Court Judge, who was for some time in Parliament, has just died.

At Bruges I made the acquaintance of Dr. Forster, a very remarkable man and a naturalist, but somewhat peculiar. He was a great lover of animals, and was convinced that there was a future state for dogs. His wife was very much liked. She was Miss Angerstein by birth. On one occasion, at dinner, the guests were discussing the origin of names. Dr. Forster, who was rather fond of hearing himself speak, declared that his name was derived from the French. Colonel Addison, who was present, broke in, saying, " Oh, certainly it is : *faut se taire.*"

Our principal amusement was boating. Bruges, which is now being made a seaport, was surrounded by canals. We used to go by water to a town in Holland called Sluys, where they gave us a luncheon consisting principally of brown bread and butter, Dutch beer, and hard-boiled eggs. One of our party had an enormous appetite. I recollect on one occasion he ate fourteen eggs, but I cannot remember how many glasses of beer he drank.

An unique experience of my lifetime occurred while at Bruges. There had been great floods, and all the canals overflowed. Afterwards a hard frost set in, and all the country for miles around was one mass of ice. We used to drive some distance out of the town ; then, putting on our skates, we spread our greatcoats, which served as sails, and the wind would blow us rapidly along the ice, sometimes for several miles, until we reached the town. All we had to do was to stand still on our skates, keeping our feet together.

While at Bruges, I was taken by a connection of mine, General Craufurd, uncle of the late Member for the Ayr Burghs, on a journey to Aix-la-Chapelle, where we associated principally with the family of Mrs. Beaumont, the mother of Mr. Henry Beaumont who was not long ago Member for one of the divisions of Yorkshire. With them we took a short trip as far as Frankfort.

At Aix-la-Chapelle, I received the following letter from Mr. Henry Drummond, whose real kindness has never been sufficiently appreciated. To me it was particularly striking.

*October* 12, 1844.

MY DEAR HENRY—This is your birthday, and I write you a few lines to prove to you that you are not forgotten by your godfather, and to inquire after your welfare. I do not know whether your mother is at Rugby or not. Pray do not forget, when you write, to remember me most kindly to her.

Write to me a few lines, and believe me always, with fervent wishes for many returns of this anniversary to you, yours very affectionately,    HENRY DRUMMOND.

I once stayed with him for a long time at Albury, and well recollect the kindness with which he treated me, teaching me to fish, and advising me as to my studies. His daughters were also kind friends. The only son, Arthur, was ill of consumption, and died young.

It is said of the member of the Drummond family who bought the place, built the house, and began the various improvements that had been carried out in the village, that on one occasion he showed the place to the king — which king I do not recollect. His Majesty asked him what the estate produced. Mr. Drummond replied, "Cheques on Charing Cross, sir."

In Bruges, I passed two very happy years, until the time approached for me to enter the Foreign Office. In those days there were no examinations, and I went to the house of the Rev. Dr. Worthington, rector of a church in Gray's Inn Lane, where I remained six months to study history and matters of that kind, so as not to be quite ignorant of them. While I was there, I developed a desire to learn music, which has not been successful. In fact, my acquirements only consist in being able to play the National Anthem with the forefinger of my right hand. I have found even this useful, however, as a means of giving tedious guests a delicate hint that they had better go. For lessons, I had been introduced by Colonel Addison to Mr. Alexander Lee, a well-known composer, who had written two songs very much sung at that time: *Come where the Aspens quiver*, and *I'd be a Butterfly*. He was leader of the orchestra at the Lyceum under the Keeleys' management, and also leader of the orchestra at Vauxhall. To the latter place I often accompanied him, but at the end of the season of 1846 an explosion took place, and the company exhibited many grievances against the management. A banquet was given to Mr. Lee by the orchestra and the other persons engaged at the Gardens, in order to present him with a watch, and this banquet I attended. All classes of employés had a grievance—even the low comedian related his sufferings, by which, however, he moved us rather to laughter than to tears.

Mr. Alexander Lee was married to a lady who had been an actress, and had retired. Her name was Mrs. Waylett. She had very interesting reminiscences of the stage for many years. They had a cottage in the middle of a nursery-garden at Kennington, and there they were frequently visited by actors of different kinds. In the absence of many of my friends from London, I often visited them and dined, taking with me a portion of the dinner, such as game, or anything beyond their usual fare.

Mrs. Waylett used to sing her husband's compositions, particularly the two I have mentioned, and often gave us songs out of what would now be called "comic operas." I recollect one stanza taken from Theodore Hook's opera, called, I believe, *Teleki*. It ran as follows :—

> Adieu, my Floreski, for ever!
> And welcome the sorrows I prove!
> O Fate! why delight'st thou to sever
> Two bosoms united by love?

A lady who often came to the Lees' house, but whose name I forget, used to sing in what was then called an "arch" manner. This did not go well with her appearance, which was decidedly middle-aged. There was also a very melancholy-looking man who sang comic songs. The contrast between these and the solemn appearance of the singer was most ludicrous. On one occasion, after a sentimental ballad from one of the ladies, he was asked to favour us. Strangers anticipated a most gloomy representation of some painful sentiment, instead of which, with the gravest face, he gave us a song beginning as follows :—

> A little cock-sparrow he sat on a tree,
> He chirped, and he chattered, so merry was he,
> He chirped, and he chattered, so merry was he,
> This little cock-sparrow that sat on a tree!
> There came a little boy, with a bow and an arrow,
> Determined to shoot this little cock-sparrow.
> Determined to shoot this little cock-sparrow
> Was this little boy, with his bow and his arrow.

I forget the rest of this lyric, but it was infinitely

ludicrous, sung by a man with so lugubrious a physiognomy. If the song still exists in the repertoire of children, it may be a satisfaction to know that it dates from, at any rate, the beginning of last century, for it was sung to me in my childhood. I have, unfortunately, lost the words and music, which were given me a great many years ago by a lady, who, had she now been alive, would be about 112 years old. She told me that she could remember it being sung when she was a child, and always in the same gloomy manner.

In my youth there were a number of actors who struck me as remarkably good, and of whom I entertain a vivid recollection. First, Madame Vestris, celebrated for her singing of a very foolish song called *Cherry Ripe*. Then there was a pretty actress, who was very popular, called Miss Julia Bennett. She played at the Haymarket with Miss Priscilla Horton, who subsequently married Mr. German Reed.

At the Adelphi was a mixture of farce and melodrama, and there was then a really remarkable company, the theatre being owned, I believe, by Mr. Webster. Madame Céleste acted the most heartrending parts with a strong French accent, and there was a celebrated man called Mr. Paul Bedford who had made one phrase his own, and it was repeated all over London. This was, " I believe you, my boy," and he was the singer of a song very celebrated in my youth, called *Nix, my*

*dolly, pals, fake away.*   He was supported by one
of the most humorous comedians I think I ever
saw—Mr. Wright—and also by the most gloomy
melodramatic actor, who represented with gusto
and humour the part of an evil spirit, and who was
known as Mr. O. Smith.   Mr. Wright, together
with Mr. Paul Bedford and Madame Céleste, made
the reputation of a piece which for a long time
was running on the stage, called *Green Bushes.*

At the Lyceum, Mr. and Mrs. Keeley used to
draw crowds by their wonderfully comic powers, and
I recollect a piece called *To Parents and Guardians,*
written by Mr. Tom Taylor, which had a most
extraordinary run.   It represented a boys' school
in which Mrs. Keeley was practically the dictator
and Mr. Keeley the fag.   Mr. Tom Taylor was a
most remarkable man and very popular in every
class of society.   He had great humour, and was
a good official, being Secretary to some Board.
At the Lyceum was also Mr. Emery, a versatile
actor, whose descendants, I believe, are still on the
stage.

At that time the plays that were acted were
formed very much on the Georgian model, and in
the play-bills one used often to see "Mr. So-and-
So, with a song."   The song was intruded in the
most irrelevant manner and had nothing to do
with the piece, but was a great attraction.   The
walking gentlemen also were instructed to use
language very much like that of the fops in the old
plays.   I recollect, when I had emerged from the

pupil-stage which had made me seek this society, going one night to the theatre with some ladies whose good opinion I was anxious to secure.   One of the walking gentlemen—a former acquaintance —meeting me going away from the box of a theatre with a lady on my arm, approached me with the fashionable manners of the stage, and, flipping me with his handkerchief, said, "Introduce me, introduce me."   I do not know what answer I gave him.   At any rate he rejoined, in the same fashion as before, "'Sdeath! you kill me, or may I be freckled!"

At Mrs. Waylett's cottage, one frequently met not only theatrical celebrities, but also writers, and occasionally—though very seldom—Mr. Planché, the founder of a new school of burlesque.   I often met him subsequently at Sir John Burgoyne's, and I recollect two of his remarkably graceful and striking compositions.   One was *The Invisible Prince*, in which the chief character was represented by Miss Priscilla Horton, and another was called *The Fair One with the Golden Locks*.   In this Mr. Planché introduced a charming parody of the Italian serenade *Com' è gentil*.   It began " Comb it genteelly."   Another of Mrs. Waylett's guests was Mr. Charles Dance, a rival of Planché. I recollect many lines from his productions also : they were excessively good, and at that time in quite a new style.   In one of Mr. Dance's burlesques, a father, represented by Mr. Keeley, expatiated on the virtues of his son, and ended thus :—

> This hopeful offspring of a doting sire
> Once chanced to thrust his finger in the fire,
> And, finding that by far too hot to hold him,
> He took it out again, though no one told him.

Mr. Talfourd, the son of Justice Talfourd, also wrote some brilliant burlesques, and one pun of his I always remember. Describing the life of a man, he ended by saying :—

> And like a detonator down he goes,
> To pay the debt o' natur that he owes.

Amongst other writers was Mr. Albert Smith, who, I think, afterwards married a daughter of Mr. and Mrs. Keeley. He, with a gentleman called Angus Reach, started a little periodical somewhat on the model of *Punch*. It was called *The Man in the Moon*. In it, on one occasion, they had a forecast of a burlesque likely to be given in the winter. It was the story of King Alfred baking the cakes. He was supposed to have been left in the house of a Mr. and Mrs. Smith to take charge of the baking, which he neglected, and he said :—

> There'll be a row when Mrs. Smith returns
> To this, which seems the land of cakes and Burns.

Mr. Reach used to pronounce his name Re-ach, so Mr. Thackeray, meeting him one day at dinner, said, "Mr. Re-ach, would you give me a pe-ach?"

I recollect at this time how very different were the movements of young ladies from what they are at the present day. None of a certain standing were ever allowed to go out alone. If walking, they were accompanied by a footman or their own maid. They never went in cabs, or, indeed, in any public conveyance. When travelling, they accompanied their parents, either in their own carriage, or in a post-chaise; but they were cut off from all general society by these exclusive habits. I recollect very well when omnibuses were introduced to go to Richmond and Hampton Court, there were great debates among the inhabitants of Hampton Court Palace whether or not they should be made use of by persons of what is called Society. The freedom which now exists, dates, I think, from the development of railways, where it is impossible to be exclusive, and where young ladies sit near any one whom fortune may bring.

I also remember the High Church movement, and then young ladies in Belgravia were allowed to go to church in the morning and to walk about alone. At the same time, the young gentlemen had also taken very much to frequenting the churches at the early services. A lady well known for her wit was told that in that district young ladies walked without a chaperon, and young gentlemen attended the eight o'clock service. She replied, "Yes, Belgravia is a country where all the women are bold, and all the men are virtuous."

About this time, Gretna Green marriages were still possible. A young couple, wishing to elope, took a post-chaise to Gretna Green, the first town accessible within Scotch territory. Here a marriage

could be performed—under the old Scotch law—
merely by a recognition before witnesses, on the
part of the two persons interested, that they considered each other as lawful husband and wife.
One young gentleman ran away with a lady of
some position, and, on his way back from Scotland,
met a relative of the bride, who had started to look
for him.  The bridegroom said to this gentleman,
" I am afraid you look upon me as a sad villain."
The other replied, " Oh no !  Only a d—d fool ! "
There was one celebrated elopement affecting some
of the greatest families in England.  On another
occasion, a gentleman very prominent in politics
went off with a lady ; but it was rumoured that in
this case even a Gretna Green wedding had been
dispensed with, notwithstanding which a slight increase occurred in the population.  These marriages
were celebrated by a blacksmith who knew all the
formalities of the law, and many jokes were made
about forging the chains.  In the last instance to
which I have alluded there were no chains at all,
and great was the scandal that consequently ensued
in what the papers call " the upper circles."  It
ruined the politician's career, and, in spite of the
condonation of old age, the *collaboratrice* never
regained a firm footing in the cream of the cream.

In those days the reaction was nearly complete
from fiction of what was called the Rosa-Matilda
school, and Mrs. Radcliffe's novels.  I well remember
the stories of that class then bought by school-
boys—wonderful mysteries, the adventures of forlorn

and sentimental young ladies travelling with their harps, and turning out to be the heiresses to earldoms. One was called *Fatherless Fanny*, who became Marchioness of Leamington ; another, *The Romance of the Forest*. Soon after Sir Walter Scott had made his appearance, a half-burlesque novel was published, meant to ridicule the school in question. It was entitled *The Heroine*. She was the daughter of a farmer whom she repudiated as a father, and whom she addressed as "Wilkinson" till the Earl was to appear. I remember some lines recited to her :—

> Sweet sensibility! Oh, la!
> I heard a little lamb cry, Baa!
> Says I, "So you have lost Mamma!"
> Ah!
> The little lamb, as I said so,
> Frisking about the field did go,
> And, frisking, trod upon my toe.
> Oh!

The Heroine was delighted.

At this time I made the acquaintance casually of a gentleman to whom, throughout the rest of his life, I was indebted for much kindness—the late Mr. Peter Borthwick. He was then Member for Evesham, and a Protectionist. At the election of 1845-46 he lost his seat, and Protection being then, to all appearance, finally disposed of, he devoted himself to the advocacy in the press of Lord Palmerston's foreign policy. His son, Mr. Algernon Borthwick, now Lord Glenesk, with whom I have been since that date intimately acquainted, was at

Paris, where in 1847-48 he enjoyed the friendship and confidence of Louis Napoleon.

I also saw a good deal of Sir John and Lady Michel, from whom and from whose family I have always received the greatest cordiality. Sir John Michel was afterwards Field-Marshal. His wife, who was a Miss Churchill by birth, was my some-what near cousin. His daughter is Viscountess Frankfort.

The world at that time was very different from what it is now. There were some large fortunes, but nothing equal to those recently accumulated in America and South Africa. Society was on a much smaller scale, bounded, as I believe Sydney Smith said, by Oxford Street on the north and Pall Mall on the south. Kensington and South Kensington were entirely out of the metropolitan limits, and at Brompton, which was considered "off the stones," the post was delivered on Sunday.

Society was very difficult of access to the *nouveaux riches*. One gentleman, Mr. Hudson, known as the Railway King, certainly achieved for himself a considerable position during the railway mania. He had a house in Albert Gate, now in the occupation of the French Embassy ; but the position he attained in Society was due more to his activity in politics as a protectionist than to his large fortune. I recollect his talking of *The Huguenots*, which came out about that time, as *The Hook Nose*.

During the season young men boasted as to how

many balls they had been invited to in one night.
They would go on from one to another.

At that period debtors were liable to imprisonment, and many interesting stories were told of the
manner in which certain well-known debtors evaded
arrest.  On one occasion, the sheriff's officers waited
the whole night in pursuit of a certain gentleman
of good family in London who was constantly in
debt.  They had seen him enter Vauxhall Gardens.
Not wishing for a public exposure, they placed
members of their body at each door so as to arrest
him when leaving.  But they stayed all night.
The Gardens were shut, and he had never appeared.
It turned out that his powers of persuasion were so
great that he had induced the aeronaut to take him
up in the balloon—which was one of the attractions
of Vauxhall—to drop him some miles from London
on the way to Dover, and to lend him sufficient
money to go to the Continent.

Another time this same gentleman, who was the
son of a well-known Member of Parliament, celebrated for his collection of antiquities and old
furniture, was traced by the sheriff's officers into
his father's house.  They knocked at the door, and
found the father just going out.  They told him
their errand.  He said that his son was not in the
house, but that they were quite at liberty to
search it.  This they did, but in vain.  Some
days afterwards they found their prey, with whom
they were always on good terms, and asked him how
he had escaped from his father's house, as they had

traced him in at the door, and waited, and had also searched the house. To this he replied, " Well, I saw you," and he then explained that, in order to escape them, he had dressed himself in an old suit of knight's armour that stood in the hall, and while they were searching the house he had glared at them, holding the sword in his hand.

# CHAPTER IV

Lord Palmerston—Handwriting—Appointed to the Foreign Office—
Comparison between Foreign Office of 1846 and present day—
Clerks in Foreign Office—Mr. Mellish—Mr. Hammond—Other
colleagues.

ONE day I received a letter desiring me to call
upon Lord Palmerston, which I naturally did in
great awe. He was at that time living at the house
of Lady de Clifford in Carlton House Terrace. I
well remember a picture in the dining-room, where
I was shown, representing St. Cecilia playing a
violoncello. My reception by Lord Palmerston
was kindly in the extreme. He asked me several
questions about my education, and, on hearing the
number of different places to which I had been, he
made a remark which was perfectly true—that I
had picked up what I could where I could, instead
of going through a settled course of education. He
desired me, however, to write him a letter giving
him my history, and to allow him to see my handwriting. About handwriting he was very particular,
and there are many stories told by Sir Edward
Hertslet and others of the severe comments he
used to make on agents of the Foreign Office

who wrote indistinctly or in a small hand. At that time a good handwriting was somewhat uncommon, but at the Foreign Office it was considered especially good. That of Mr. Spring-Rice was held up as a model.

Since then, handwriting has made great strides, and the system of telling character from it has been much developed. In France, where it is called *graphiologie*, it is supposed to have led to remarkable incidents. A French gentleman, whose veracity I have no reason to doubt, told me the following story.

A new *préfet* had come to a town where the uncle of my informant was bishop. The bishop requested the *préfet* to employ some one in whom he felt an interest. The young man in question went to the prefecture and told his story, but was asked to make his application in writing.

Some days afterwards the bishop enquired if anything had been done for his protégé. The *préfet* replied, " It is impossible : he is an assassin." This he said he had discovered from the young man's handwriting, and added that the assassination was not of long date. It turned out to be the case.

Of course I cannot vouch for the truth of this story, but I may say that more than one French gentleman to whom I spoke of it cast no doubt on its correctness.

To return to Lord Palmerston. No one, young or old, could resist his charm of manner, which really betokened a very kind heart. When appointed to the Foreign Office in 1845, on the fall of Sir Robert Peel's Government, some of the old employés had intended to resign, as during his last tenure of office he had been somewhat harsh and inconsiderate. On one occasion, he had kept the Office at work for almost the whole night while he was at the Opera, and while they were preparing for a special messenger whose despatches had to be signed by the Secretary of State. On his return to office in 1848 they were most agreeably disappointed. A hint was given them that, having in the interval married Lady Palmerston, his manner had undergone a complete change. Ever afterwards, under the influence of Lady Palmerston, perhaps the most amiable *grande dame* who ever existed, every one dependent upon him was most devoted to his person and his interests. On October 22, 1846, ten days after completing my sixteenth year, I was informed by Mr. Addington of my appointment as Additional Clerk at the Foreign Office, and on the 26th of the same month I entered upon my duties.

The Foreign Office in those days was peculiarly constituted, and had for many years undergone no alteration. On the ordinary staff there was one permanent Under - Secretary of State, and one political. Now, in addition to these two officials, there are three assistant Under-Secretaries. Two Legal Advisers are now appointed to the Foreign Office : in my time there were none. There were

twenty-eight clerks on the diplomatic establishment, of whom seven were Heads of Departments :
at present there are forty-four clerks, of whom eight
are Heads of Departments.   The Financial Department, which in 1847 had only one clerk, has now
five.   There are five also in the Librarian's Department, which formerly had only two clerks.   In
those days there was a Slave Trade Department,
appointed to carry out the provisions of the
various Slave Trade Treaties : that has now disappeared.   A registry has been established, which
did not exist then.   In addition to all this extra
assistance, there are thirty-seven Second Division
clerks, as well as nine lady typists.   The staff of
Foreign Service messengers has been diminished,
but that of the Home Service messengers increased.
Altogether, the force of the Foreign Office has been
augmented to an enormous extent, compared with
former times.   A considerable increase took place
immediately after the Crimean War, when the staff
was very much overworked.   I recollect on one
occasion during that period that, having worked
nearly all Sunday, I went to the Office on Monday
morning at ten, and remained till ten at night.
The next day I went at ten, and remained till four
o'clock the following morning.   On the Wednes-
day I went at ten, and remained till one the next
morning.   In addition to all this, I had cyphers at
my own house for use when necessary at night,
the number of resident clerks being limited to two.
They are now four.

Previously, at the beginning of the century, the numbers were still smaller, and the clerks in the Office worked personally with the Secretary of State. Some of those I knew had worked with Lord Dudley. They said that at a crisis he would walk about their room as though in a fit of absent-mindedness. He would then suddenly pick up some scrap of paper off the floor and write out a despatch. Everything now goes along an official groove, and orders are conveyed through the Under-Secretaries.

The names of those who were in the Office at the time of my joining recall almost the whole history of the French Revolution and the Napoleonic Wars. Mr. John Bidwell, senior, had been appointed in 1798. Mr. Thomas Bidwell resigned in 1841 after fifty years' service. He had been the clerk who opened nearly all the despatches relative to the French Revolution, I believe including the report of the royal executions. Mr. John Bidwell accompanied Sir Robert Adair on his Special Mission to Constantinople in July 1808, and remained in the East till 1811. He was also attached to Sir Charles Stewart on his Mission to the King of Prussia in 1813, and on his visit to the headquarters of the Allied Armies at various places on the Continent.

There had been a clerk in the Office, Mr. Byng, appointed in 1801. I recollect him well. He was known in society for many years, and died only in 1871. He was commonly called "Poodle Byng," but I never knew the origin of the appellation. Lord Torrington was a nephew of his.

In 1824, Mr. Byng had been appointed to attend the King and Queen of the Sandwich Islands on their visit to England, where they both died. Mr. William Bathurst told me that, at the time of their death, a speech supposed to have been made by the king to Mr. Byng was published by Theodore Hook in *John Bull*. It began, "Oh, Poodly Woodly! Me eatee, me drinkee, me die."

The Head of the Department in which I was at first placed was Mr. Lenox-Conyngham. In his youth some accident had deprived him of his leg, and at times he underwent intense pain. This made him a little captious; but he was a man of the kindest instincts. He had married the daughter of Mr. Holmes, an Irish Q.C., who was very much mixed up with what is now called the Nationalist cause. By her he had two children, a son in the Diplomatic Service, and a daughter who married Lord Doneraile and died only recently. Her husband was killed by the bite of a fox. Mr. Conyngham's son was very ill out in Brazil, and his father, wishing to go and see him, underwent an operation from the effects of which he died on November 26, 1866, less than a fortnight after the death of his son.

I fear that, with Sir Spencer Ponsonby-Fane and Mr. Wylde, I am now the only survivor of the Foreign Office as it was in 1846-47. Amongst others who were there at the time of my joining was Mr. Oom, a man of great humour, who belonged to the Canterbury Theatrical Company, which I will allude to hereafter : he was designated the "Apologist." He was known in the Canterbury Bills as Adolphus K. On the occasion of an election at Canterbury, during the Cricket Week, the town was placarded thus : "Oom shall we elect ? Adolphus K."

There were also Mr. Staveley, who had been employed at Paris in 1814, and was secretary to a Commission appointed under the Articles of the Treaty of Peace with France ; and Mr. Thomas Lawrence Ward, a cousin of Lord Bangor, and whose brother was a Secretary of Legation. He had joined the Foreign Office in 1817, and had accompanied Lord Castlereagh to the Conference at Aix-la-Chapelle in 1818. He also was with Sir Robert Adair's Special Mission to Brussels in 1831. Mr. Louis Hertslet, the librarian, so well known for his works on Treaties, had been appointed to the Foreign Office in 1801. I very well recollect meeting Sir Robert Adair at Holland House, where, when I first married, I often spent some days. He came in leaning on the arm of Lord Granville.

It was to Lord Holland that Prince Talleyrand addressed one of his best-known *mots*. Lord Holland, then Mr. Fox, had just been attached to Sir Robert Adair's Mission to Brussels. At a dinner at Holland House, on the eve of their departure, Prince Talleyrand made an address to Sir

Robert Adair, and a separate one to Lord Holland, treating the latter as if he were the Minister and Sir Robert, the attaché.  In laying down several maxims of diplomacy for Lord Holland, he ended by saying, "*Et surtout, point de zèle*," a maxim which has been recognised as a fundamental rule of diplomatic action.

One very marked member of the Foreign Office was Mr. Mellish, who had been attached to the Embassy at Constantinople in 1828 and 1830. Formerly a Gentleman Usher to Queen Adelaide, he had been sent by King William IV. to accompany his sons, the FitzClarences, to the different Courts of Germany.  His father was one of the old chargés d'affaires at the Hanse towns, and his mother was German, so that he really was more of a German than an Englishman.  He was a great admirer of Mr. Canning, who had done much for him, and of whom he had a store of anecdotes.

Mr. Mellish kept the correspondence relative to the quaint and well-known cypher instructions sent by Mr. Canning to Sir Charles Bagot, Ambassador at the Hague.  They ran as follows :—

> In matters of commerce, the fault of the Dutch
> Is giving too little, and asking too much.
> The French are with equal advantage content,
> So we'll clap on Dutch bottoms just twenty per cent.
>> Twenty per cent, twenty per cent,
> Chorus of French *douaniers* :
>> Vous frapperez Falcke just twenty per cent !

This was put into cypher by Mr. Mellish and sent to the Hague.  Some days afterwards a reply came from Sir Charles Bagot, saying that his Embassy did not possess the cypher in which this despatch had been forwarded. The cypher was therefore sent by the next messenger, together with a despatch from Mr. Canning saying that the former one had only contained remarks on the recent commercial negotiations. There was a very amusing answer from Sir Charles Bagot, to the effect that the Secretary of Embassy, Mr. Snape Douglas —who, by the way, was very much in the world during my recollection—when reading the despatch, had observed that he was almost certain the cypher alluded to the commercial negotiations. The lines in question are pretty well known, and I only mention these circumstances as coming from what may be considered the fountain-head.

Mr. Mellish was constantly repeating acts of great good-nature on the part of Mr. Canning. On one occasion a special messenger was sent to the Continent, and, after he had gone, Mr. Mellish found that he had omitted to put in the bag the principal despatch. He at once went in to Mr. Canning to tell him of the mishap, in fear and trembling. Mr. Canning, without saying a word of reproach, replied, "Ring for another messenger." His kindness ensured the devotion of Mr. Mellish, who was a most warm-hearted man.

At one time Mr. Mellish had applied to Lord Aberdeen for an appointment in South America as chargé d'affaires. This had been refused him. Shortly afterwards Mr. Mellish met the lady he subsequently married.   No sooner had she accepted him than he asked for an interview of Lord Aberdeen, and thanked him for not having given him the appointment for which he had applied, as he had been so amply compensated.

Mr. Mellish was deeply versed in . German politics.   Some one once asked Lord Palmerston to explain to him the question of the Danish Duchies.   Lord Palmerston replied, "There are only two people who understand the question— myself and Mellish of the Foreign Office."   The other said that he thought Mr. Mellish was dead. Lord Palmerston rejoined, "In that case, I am the only person who understands the question."

After Mr. Mellish, who at that time was the only decorated member of the Office, having received the Order of the Guelph, came Mr. Hammond, who played a considerable part in the history of the Department.   He was the son of a gentleman who had also been Under-Secretary of State for Foreign Affairs.   When I was first in the Foreign Office, he was almost the junior of the senior clerks.   He had been attached to Sir Stratford Canning's Special Mission to Turkey in 1831, and to Spain in 1832, and was the Head of the Turkish Department, which dealt with matters concerning Russia, Turkey, Persia, Tunisia, Morocco, Egypt, and Siam.   Mr. Hammond was a man of great perseverance, and had made himself completely master of affairs dealing with those countries, and, indirectly, with the world in general.   At that time,

despatches of importance were circulated to the
Ambassadors in all important places. Consequently,
all Heads of Departments knew not only what
belonged to their particular branch, but indirectly
all that was going on elsewhere.

When the Crimean War broke out, Mr.
Addington, the Permanent Under-Secretary of
State, resigned his place after a most distinguished
career. It was felt that no one could succeed him
except Mr. Hammond. He, therefore, was practically charged with the continuity of the business of
the whole Office. In those days that business was
divided into two principal departments—one under
the Permanent, the other under the Parliamentary
Under-Secretary ; but all information of importance
was equally open to both those functionaries. It
would, therefore, scarcely have been possible to
overlook Mr. Hammond's claims to the succession
of Mr. Addington.

Mr. Hammond was a very curious mixture.
He might be designated, in the present day, as
bureaucratic, and certainly the interests of his
office were his first care ; but this did not prevent
great enlightenment, and his advice was constantly
followed by the Ministers of the day. While a
great stickler for discipline, and resenting errors
on the part of his subordinates, he was excessively
kind-hearted and just. No doubt, he had his likes
and dislikes, but these were never unnecessarily or
offensively put forward. He had great eccentricities. When going with Lord John Russell

on his Special Mission to Vienna in 1855, the
other members were much amused at Mr. Hammond's peculiarities.  He insisted on passing the
whole night in his tall hat, and only assumed his
travelling-cap when he got out of the train for
refreshments.  He retired in 1873, and was made
a peer some months later, this being the first
occasion, I believe, on which a Permanent Under-
Secretary had been raised to that dignity.

My closest friend was Mr. Bridges Taylor, a
universal favourite and the confidant of many
juniors.  He was the nephew of two men who
had been very well known in their time—one,
Sir Herbert Taylor, Private Secretary to King
William IV., and the other, Sir Brook Taylor,
formerly of the Diplomatic Service.  I believe he
had been appointed Minister at a small Court in
Germany when he was only twenty-three or twenty-
four years old.

Mr. Bridges Taylor, besides being in the Foreign
Office, had been allowed to hold the post—almost
a sinecure—of Deputy Clerk to the Signet for his
uncle, Sir Brook Taylor, who was Clerk to the
Signet, an office now abolished.  Mr. Bridges
Taylor was at one time attached to the Legation
at Hanover, where he married the daughter of
Sir Hugh Halkett, the generalissimo of the
Hanoverian army.  He had thus come into contact with the Royal Family, by whom Mrs. Taylor
was affectionately treated, and he was also much
favoured by all of them.  Owing to an impediment

in his handwriting from scrivener's palsy, he was unable to work very hard, and he ended his days—or, at all events, his official career—as Consul at Elsinore, where he and Mrs. Bridges Taylor were much beloved.

Mr. Huskisson was also a distinguished member of the Office. He was the nephew of Mr. Huskisson, the President of the Board of Trade, and Colonial Secretary, whose sad end is well known, having been killed at the opening of the Manchester Railway.

Later on the list followed Mr. George Canning Backhouse, son of the Mr. Backhouse who had been Under-Secretary of State. Then we come to Mr. Wylde, son of the general so well known in connection with Spanish politics, who had been sent to Spain on missions connected, I think, with the Carlist war.

Mr. Richard Wellesley was one of the most amiable and popular members of the Office. He was the grandson of Marquis Wellesley, and he had an uncle who was the Principal of New Inn Hall, Oxford.

Mr. Charles Spring-Rice was a son of the celebrated Lord Monteagle, Chancellor of the Exchequer. In the course of a speech in which Lord Brougham was denouncing the Whig Government, he asked whether the country was to be governed entirely by Lord John This or Mr. Spring That. Mr. Charles Spring-Rice, who was among my great friends, was one of the most useful members of the Foreign Office. Before the end of his service he was made an Assistant Under-Secretary of State. He certainly was one of the ablest men I ever came across, and I have always been astonished that he did not make a more brilliant career. He was gifted with great humour, and the story was told of him that, when at the University, some one with rooms above him insisted on practising the piano nearly all day. Mr. Spring-Rice was musical, and this was enough to drive him wild. After remonstrating several times uselessly with his neighbour, he proceeded to purchase a very loud dinner-bell, and whenever the gentleman upstairs began his scales, he used to go to the bottom of the staircase and ring the bell as loudly as he could. This brought his adversary to reason.

Mr. Alston—subsequently Sir Francis Alston—was an exemplary public servant. He was the son of Mr. Rowland Alston, a long time M.P. for Hertfordshire. Before he left the Foreign Office he became Chief Clerk and Head of the Financial Department. He was a man of extraordinary official ability, and many small reforms are due to his orders and sagacity. He was also high up in Freemasonry, in which he was an expert.

Then followed Mr. Spencer Ponsonby—now Sir Spencer Ponsonby-Fane—who certainly deserved better of his colleagues than any one else. Always sympathetic and encouraging in his office of private secretary, first to Lord Palmerston and then to Lord Clarendon, he was ever ready to do what he properly could for the sake of a colleague. Every one had confidence in him and liked him. He accompanied Lord Clarendon to the Congress of Paris, and subsequently accepted the office of Comptroller of the Lord Chamberlain's Household, a place which suited him, I suppose, but which, to my mind, was far below his claims. His wife, whom he married early in life, showed kindness to all, and enjoyed the same popularity as her husband.

# CHAPTER V

Colleagues in the Foreign Office—Under-Secretaries of State—Life at
the Foreign Office—Hours of work—Private theatricals—Holiday
at Spa—Marriage of Lady Dorothy Nevill.

MR. JOHN BIDWELL, junior, was the son of the Head
of the Consular Department. He was a man of
great wit, dramatic power, and physical agility, and
at an amateur pantomime given during the Crimean
War for the Patriotic Fund, at which the Queen
and the Prince Consort were present, he acted the
part of Harlequin in the most perfect manner.
Shortly after the performance he asked Lady
Waldegrave, who was a friend of his, to obtain
an invitation for him to a party at Lansdowne
House. Lord Lansdowne replied that he must
necessarily invite Mr. Bidwell, for, if he did not
come in at the door, he would probably come
through the window, or down the chimney. He
wrote light poetry, full of fun and brilliancy. I
recollect some lines that occurred in one of his
poems :—

> With equal ale and equal stout
> Fill high the pewter amphora !
> If fickle Fortune frown or flout,
> We will not care a d— for her !

On one occasion Mr. Bidwell was having a discussion with a colleague, whom he accused of putting too much work upon his—Mr. Bidwell's—shoulders, and thus escaping the proper share. He ended by saying, "I'll tell you what it is. You're what the Latin grammar calls an *injusta noverca*."

After him came Mr. Greville Morier, the son of Mr. Henry Morier, who had for a long time been Minister in Persia, but whose reputation principally depends on the book that he wrote, called *Hajji Baba*. Mr. Morier had much of his father's wit. His mother, *née* Greville, was still alive, and most hospitable at her house in Charles Street to her son's colleagues. Mr. Croker Pennell was a nephew of the celebrated John Wilson Croker, Theodore Hook's friend, and he certainly was the best-tempered man I ever came across. Mr. Woodford, the son of Sir Alexander Woodford, was the *valseur* of the Office, and no ball in London was complete without his presence. Lord Gifford's son, Mr. Scott Gifford, was very popular for his great good-temper, which almost equalled that of Mr. Wellesley. Mr. Vivian, afterwards Lord Vivian, was well known, having ended his days as Ambassador at Rome.

Mr. Forster was one of the resident clerks, and used to give dinners in his rooms. He was a man very much respected and liked, having been many years in the Office, and an old member of the Travellers'. He was the brother of General Forster, who for some time had held a permanent military post in Dublin, but who more lately became Military Secretary to the Commander-in-Chief. Mr. Forster was very fond of fishing, and constantly used to take a fishing at Christchurch, near Lord Malmesbury's house, Heron Court. I recollect a letter to Lord Malmesbury, in which he signed himself "Your humble Clerk."

Mr. Blackburn was also a very well-known member of the Office, rather celebrated for his wit and repartees. I did not know him very well, as for a great portion of the time I was in the Office he was absent from ill-health.

On one occasion we were talking of a foreign statesman who had married an Englishwoman named Miss Birch. Mr. Blackburn said that he understood she was the daughter of Birch, the City pastry-cook of turtle fame. I replied that such was not the case; that she was of considerable birth, rather highly connected, and no relation whatever to the pastry-cook. Thereupon Mr. Blackburn said, "I had a *soup*çon that she was."

Working in the Foreign Office as an attaché was Mr. Ralph Anstruther Earle. He had distinguished himself at Harrow, especially in English composition, and Lord Clarendon had in consequence offered him an appointment in the Diplomatic Service. Foreign affairs and Parliamentary life formed his great preoccupation. I saw a great deal of him and liked him very much, though he was not generally popular on account of a reserved

manner.   Mr. and Mrs. Disraeli made his acquaintance in Paris, and were much struck by him, and
when the Conservative party came into power
in 1858 Mr. Earle was appointed Mr. Disraeli's
private secretary.   In this capacity he lived very
much at his chief's house, and made himself useful
in Parliamentary matters, which he thoroughly
understood.

In 1866 Mr. Earle became a Member of
Parliament, and Mr. Disraeli, on acceding to office,
gave him the Secretaryship to the Poor Law Board,
a post no longer existing.   Thinking that this
appointment, which entailed no great labour, was
given him so that he might combine his Secretarial
with his Parliamentary work, Mr. Earle used to go
daily to see his chief.   Mr. Disraeli, however, having
appointed another private secretary—Lord Rowton
—wished to dispense with Mr. Earle's services, and
did not welcome these continual visits.   The result
was that Mr. Earle resigned his post, and in Parliament showed his resentment by voting and sometimes speaking against Mr. Disraeli.   At length
he made an especially violent attack on the Prime
Minister, and this put an end to his career.

Mr. James Murray was also in the Foreign
Office, at the head of the Consular Department for
some time, and then Head of the German Department.   He subsequently became Assistant Under-
Secretary of State.   Though born abroad, he was
of Scotch origin, and this he was fond of proclaiming on every possible occasion.   It was currently

reported in the Office that at a country place he possessed somewhere near Uxbridge, he was to be seen in the very early morning digging in his garden, and dressed in a kilt.

During the time I was in the Foreign Office, I naturally served under several Political Under-Secretaries of State, all of them men of great eminence. The first was Lord Stanley of Alderley, at that time Mr. Stanley, and generally known in the world—for what reason I do not know—as Ben Stanley. Lord Kimberley I knew privately, and he certainly, during the tenure of his office as Under-Secretary, was most popular and made for himself a great name. On this account he was chosen by the Government to occupy the post of Minister at St. Petersburg at the time of the reconciliation after the Russian War. He was followed, I think, by Lord Shelburne, who had never taken a very active part in politics, for which, however, he was highly qualified.

Mr. Layard was a man whose reputation is too well known to need any tribute or discussion. Mr. Seymour FitzGerald, who had for a long time been a Member of Parliament, was the Conservative Under-Secretary under Lord Malmesbury. He was a man of great Parliamentary tact and knowledge. Later on he was made Governor of Bombay, and on his return to England again entered Parliament, which he finally quitted on being appointed a principal Charity Commissioner.

At that time the Foreign Office was more like

a convent of Benedictines—men of intelligence, but separated from the world by the nature of their employment. The work they had to do was essentially confidential, and therefore did not bring them much into contact with other offices. In fact, the humblest clerk in the Office was necessarily entrusted with information to which scarcely any-one could have access except a Cabinet Minister.

On one occasion the original of a Treaty had been published in a morning paper, together with the English translation. This produced great agitation, for it seemed as though blame would be laid on the Foreign Office. Lord Palmerston, however, discovered the secret of its publication. When a treaty is drawn up between several nations, each is mentioned first in its own copy, and the others are placed alphabetically. When Lord Palmerston saw the published copy, he at once detected the quarter whence it came by the name that came first, the others being, as usual, in alphabetical order. I believe that Lord Palmerston mentioned this circumstance in the House of Commons, in proof of the rigid secrecy kept by the Foreign Office.

The hours of the Office were different from ordinary official attendance. As the clerks had to remain very late, in order to catch the last mail which left about eight o'clock, they went late in the morning, not much before one o'clock, and this dis-organisation of the ordinary times of employment threw them very much into each other's society.

They all lived together, especially in the old office in Downing Street, which consisted of two houses, 15 and 16, the latter having been the Foreign Office, and 15 the residence of the Foreign Secretary. Mr. Canning had lived there, and one room at the top of the house—used as a smoking-room— was called "the nursery," having belonged to Mr. Canning's children. It possessed a piano, Mr. Wellesley, Mr. Woodford, and others being good musicians.

When I was first at the Foreign Office, smoking was tabooed, as it was distasteful to Lord Palmerston. Subsequently, however, on the accession to office of Lord Clarendon, who was himself a great smoker, the prohibition of tobacco was relaxed, and smoking became universal. It is said that one day, by mistake, a despatch-box, addressed to very high quarters, was found to contain some of Lord Clarendon's cigarettes.

Many of the members of the Office belonged to the Travellers' Club, where they used to dine together, members of other clubs doing the same; but during the dead season, when most clubs were under repair, they used to dine in small parties, often at the "Blue Posts" in Cork Street, well known for its beef-steaks and port-wine, and in later years at the "Wellington" in St. James's Street. In those days there were few restaurants, and none, except Verrey's in Regent Street, where a lady could dine. The St. James's Club, of which I am an original member, was only founded, I think, in

1859, and this provided a resort for all members of the Foreign Office and the Diplomatic Service.

The work at the Foreign Office, as already mentioned, was really hard ; but since the numbers have been increased, and typists have been employed, I scarcely think that such great pressure can still exist.

Shortly before I joined the Office, it had been the habit of some of the clerks, during the dead season, to hire a cottage in the country, where they lived, coming up for their work and going down in the evening. But this I do not recollect. At one time Mr. Spencer Ponsonby undertook the management of the cottage. He showed me a bill addressed to "Sponsonberry, Esq."

The principal amusement of the members of the Foreign Office was private theatricals. A society had been got up called the Canterbury Old Stagers. An interesting history of this society is to be found in a book called *Amateur Clubs and Actors*, edited by W. G. Elliot. It was founded in 1841, I believe, by Mr. Frederick Ponsonby, and Mr. Spencer Ponsonby was always a foremost member. The book to which I allude contains an illustration representing Sir Spencer Ponsonby-Fane, Sir Henry de Bathe, and Mr. Quintin Twiss as they acted in *Cox and Box*.

Among the gentlemen who rather frequented Foreign Office society was a young Guardsman, whose principal quality was that of greediness. One day at the Tower he was president of the mess, and ordered some small cutlets of which he was particularly fond. They were handed first to the gentleman on his left. There were only three cutlets left in the dish by the time it came round to the president's right-hand neighbour, and that gentleman took all three.

Two large tears were seen rolling down the Guardsman's cheeks.

I generally used to spend my two months' holiday on a trip abroad. My first was taken in 1847, when I accompanied Lord and Lady Pollington. We had intended to go farther, but we found Spa so pleasant that we remained there four or five weeks. Our great amusement was riding out in the day on little Spa ponies, while at night there was a theatre, a dance, or the *roulette*. There I made the acquaintance of Sir Henry and Lady Bedingfeld, and of the Marquis and Marquise de Belmont, who afterwards were attached to the Emperor Napoleon's household, besides various persons whose names I do not remember. There were two or three English gentlemen : one of them, who was very popular, underwent the somewhat painful experience of being arrested for debt. He was taken to the prison at Verviers, and for the rest of our stay at Spa we used generally to breakfast at the hotel at Verviers, and pay a visit to our friend.

In 1847, Lady Dorothy Walpole was married at Wolterton to Mr. Reginald Nevill, who was already a distant cousin. There was a great gathering, and the wedding-feast included, as is usual in

Norfolk, a pea-hen and a gosling. The ceremony was performed by the Reverend Thomas Walpole, Rector of Alverstoke, the head of the family next in succession after the present line. He was assisted by the Reverend Algernon Peyton, who had married a cousin of the family and who held the living of Doddington, then the richest in England, being worth about £7000 a year. As the Crown has the right of nomination to any living vacated by the incumbent being made a bishop, the Rector of Doddington, on accepting the living, was bound to sign an undertaking that he would never accept a bishopric. The living has since been divided.

# CHAPTER VI

AMONGST other persons with whom I was acquainted,
and who was very much in the world, was Mr. Jesse,
the author of the *History of England under the
House of Hanover.* He was high up in the
Admiralty, and was the son of the author of a
natural history book called *Jesse's Gleanings.* A
great friend of his was Mr. John Wilson Croker,
the well-known Conservative statesman, about this
time engaged in an animated controversy with Lord
John Russell concerning the poet Moore. Mr.
Jesse had been well acquainted with Theodore
Hook, who was an habitual frequenter of Mr.
Croker's house, where, on one occasion, having indulged a little freely at dinner, Mrs. Croker said to
him, while playing at whist, "We have known each
other so long that I am sure you will forgive me
for asking you to read this little pamphlet." It
was a tract.

Theodore Hook, stopping in his deal, took the

pamphlet, and answered, "Oh yes! I know this. I've read it. I've reviewed it. 'Three words to one who drinks.' It's 'Pass the bottle'!"

This anecdote was related to me by Mr. Jesse, who had actually heard it. The story may be well known, but I should never hesitate to relate anecdotes if told me by those who had learned them first-hand.

I was very dull during my first winter in London until my friends came up for the following season; but I constantly went to the house of the Chevalier de Bunsen, in Carlton Terrace, not far from the Foreign Office. He and his wife were always very hospitable and good to me. She was the aunt of M. Waddington, with whom I had been at Rugby, and at her house I met other members of the family —Lady Llanover, and many whose names I forget. There I used very often to meet the family of Baron Alderson, especially the eldest of his daughters, afterwards Lady Salisbury. One of her sisters married a friend of mine, Mr. Walter Cocks.

Another house that I constantly visited was that of Lady Tankerville, with whose relative, Mr. George Wrottesley—now General Wrottesley— I was intimate. He was an officer in the Engineers, and, as we lived very much together, he introduced me to the house of Sir John Burgoyne, then Inspector-General of Fortifications, son of General Burgoyne of Saratoga. This brings us back to October 1777, the date of the surrender of General Burgoyne and his army. Wrottesley subsequently went as A.D.C. to Sir John in the Crimea, and married his eldest daughter.

Mrs. Wrottesley had most remarkable gifts as an actress, and, at her father's house in Fulham, theatricals were frequently performed. She also used to act sometimes at the house of Mr. Wolley, at Campden Hill, where a regular theatre had been built. It was a charming old house, which I recollected as a young ladies' school where some cousins of mine were educated. It was ultimately burnt down, and the fire formed the subject of an action at law with the insurance companies.

Sir John and Lady Burgoyne kept the most hospitable house I recollect. Every one who was a friend of the family had a general invitation to dinner, and the society was most agreeable. I met there Mr. Ashe, certainly one of the wittiest men and cleverest actors I ever came across. He had been employed in some civil capacity under Sir John in Ireland, and was brought by him to London. He had wonderful powers of comic improvisation.

Sir John Burgoyne, as Inspector-General of Fortifications, was Chief of the Royal Engineers. In this capacity, he encouraged all the young men of the corps to frequent his house. On one occasion, the study of foreign languages was being discussed, and the conversation fell into French. A lady present made some very acute remark on the value of the language, so a young man, bursting with ambition, replied, "*Vous êtes une sage femme!*"

The difficulty for those not familiar with French to avoid literal translation is often ludicrous. I knew an official of considerable rank who, when writing to a foreigner, always subscribed himself " *Votre très vraiment.*"

Unfortunately, a coolness had sprung up between Sir John Burgoyne and the Duke of Wellington. The latter had written to Sir John commenting on the want of preparation for war. This letter, through some unfortunate circumstance, had fallen into the hands of a lady who lived near Sir John Burgoyne at Fulham, and it came into the possession of the press. The letter made a great sensation at the time, and was the basis of a long discussion. Notwithstanding Sir John's explanations, the breach between the Duke and himself was never repaired.

One of the daughters of the house married a gentleman named Gretton, who received a consular appointment in Hayti. On their arrival, they both died of yellow fever, leaving one little baby quite unprotected. Sir John Burgoyne had seven daughters, I think, and one son, a promising naval officer, who went down when the *Captain* foundered.

At that time I also made the acquaintance of Mr. and Mrs. Disraeli, who were great friends of my uncle and aunt, Lord and Lady Orford, and of their daughters, Lady Pollington and Lady Dorothy Walpole—now Lady Dorothy Nevill. Lord Pollington, who had been returned to

Parliament before he was of age, was a very strong Conservative.

Mr. Disraeli used generally to walk home from the House of Commons, usually in the society of Lord Henry Lennox. One night, rather late, I was in the neighbourhood of Whitehall, as the House was breaking up, and I met Mr. Disraeli alone. He asked me to accompany him, and we canvassed the prospects of the Government. I said to him, as there was some talk of the Government resigning, "I suppose that some day, in the ordinary course of things, you will be Prime Minister." He answered, "In the extraordinary course of things."

Between 1847 and 1852 I generally used to call upon Mr. and Mrs. Disraeli every Sunday, and sometimes had luncheon with them. On one occasion I met M. and Mme. Adolphe Barrot. He was a brother of M. Odillon Barrot, and at that time, I think, French Agent in Egypt. I met him frequently afterwards, first at Naples where he was Minister, and then at Brussels. Madame Barrot was English by birth.

At Mr. Disraeli's house, I also made the acquaintance of Mr. James Disraeli and Mr. Ralph Disraeli. Mr. James Disraeli was not married, though the elder of the two; but Mr. Ralph Disraeli had a son by his marriage with Miss Trevor—Mr. Coningsby Disraeli, who was until lately in Parliament.

About that time I became acquainted with the celebrated Mr. Alfred Montgomery, remarkable for his popularity in all good society, and for his wit. I used to dine with him and his sister at their house in Chesterfield Street. His conversation was most amusing, as he always gave some quaint turn to everything he said. Once we were discussing a murder which had attracted a great deal of attention, the murderer having assassinated his victim when dining with him at his house. Mr. Montgomery said to me, with the little stutter which gave point to his observations, "I wonder how you would begin murdering a man at his own table. I should not know how to do so. It would appear to me to be taking such a liberty."

I also knew very well Mr. Baillie Cochrane. He had been one of the prominent members of what was called the Young England Party, in which he was associated with Lord John Manners, Mr. George Smythe, Mr. Hope, and others. Members of this party were distinguished by wearing white neckcloths at a time when they were not in fashion. I saw a great deal later on of Mr. Baillie Cochrane. He was raised to the peerage as Lord Lamington, and was the father of the present peer, a distinguished Colonial Governor.

Another acquaintance of mine was Mr. Stirling of Keir, afterwards Sir John Stirling-Maxwell of Keir, principally known for his books on Spanish history. Many years later, when I was Ambassador in Spain, his son came to present copies of his works to the Historical Society at Madrid, of which his father had been a member. He was received with great cordiality by Señor Canovas del Castillo, the President of the Society, who was assassinated not long afterwards.

Among my particular friends was Mr. Hayward, a man who just missed greatness. He was trusted by many statesmen, and, in the palmy days of the *Morning Chronicle*, had been made editor by the Peelites who purchased it, among whom were Mr. Sydney Herbert, Mr. Hope, and, I believe, Mr. Gladstone. I may be excused for mentioning Mr. Hayward more than once, and perhaps somewhat irrelevantly, as his conversation is constantly recurring to my memory. It was always excessively entertaining, being full of anecdote.

He used to tell very characteristic stories of Martin Farquhar Tupper, the author of *Proverbial Philosophy*. Once, in America, he went to call at a house where the servant made some mistake about his name. Thereupon he said, "Announce the author of *Proverbial Philosophy*!"

On another occasion he was staying with the owner of a Scotch island. In order to catch his boat one morning, he had to walk for some miles, and the young lady of the house offered to act as his guide. He was carrying a small bag with him, and asked the young lady if she would like to carry it. She mildly replied that he had better do so himself. He rejoined, "I thought you would like to be able to say that you had carried Martin Farquhar Tupper's bag for him!"

Mr. Hayward and I had many friends in

common, and after his death Mr. Kinglake and I
wrote a joint article about him in the *Fortnightly
Review*.   His one weakness was his love of alluding
to persons of great rank.

To anticipate a little.   At a time when I was frequenting the Athenæum a good deal, a Cingalese
gentleman, who had come to England to read
for the Bar, was recommended by Sir Roderick
Murchison to all his acquaintances.   One day, finding him dining alone, Mr. Hayward and I invited
him to our table.   Mr. Hayward wished to instruct
him as to the constitution of English society, and
said, "You will find in England that men of distinction, who belong neither to the aristocracy nor
to the richer classes, but have made a mark, either
in literature or by their conversational powers, are
always received in great houses on a footing of perfect equality.   You never go to a great house but
you will see some distinguished literary man received
as one of the most highly honoured guests."

The Cingalese said, very naïvely, " But are these
not called sycophants ? "

There was complete silence.

Amongst Mr. Hayward's anecdotes was one
concerning the Queen of Holland, who had come to
England with the view of making the acquaintance
of the most distinguished persons in the country.
She had therefore sent for Sir Henry Rawlinson,
the well-known Eastern archæological discoverer.
She asked him to assist her in solving a question
which had always been to her a great stumbling-

block.   Did he believe, or not, in the Tower of
Babel ?   She had never been able to bring herself
to believe in it.   A foreign lady, who had married
an Englishman of great distinction, on hearing this,
thought to improve the occasion, and said, with that
absence of the aspirate which often distinguishes
foreigners in their pronunciation of English, " 'E
ought to 'ave told 'er that it is for our comfort
and 'appiness to believe it."

Mr. Hayward was also very fond of telling the
following anecdote of Mr. Montgomery, a popular
preacher, familiarly known as " Satan Montgomery" from a poem he had written on that
subject.   When in Edinburgh, he had been invited
to dinner by Bishop Terrot, who introduced him
to his friends.   One lady, after the introduction,
asked the Bishop, " Is it Mr. Montgomery, the
poet ?" to which the Bishop replied, " No ;  Mr.
Montgomery, *a* poet."

Mr. Montgomery, both as poet and preacher,
was rather dramatic in his methods.   It was said
that, in the manuscript of his sermons, he used to
introduce what in a play would be called "stage
directions."   In one sermon of pathetic character
was inserted, every now and then, as a direction,
[*tears*].

One of the interesting anniversaries celebrated
every year was the day of the Battle of Waterloo,
when the Duke of Wellington gave a banquet.
There was a very quaint old gentleman, whom I
knew well—Mr. Bramley Moore—who made a bet

that he would attend one of these dinners. He
did so, for he was acquainted with the confectioner
who contracted for the Waterloo banquet, and
obtained permission to personate one of the head-
waiters.

An anecdote connected with the Foreign Office
occurs to me, which I give as amusing, though not
perhaps relevant.

A Secretary of the Austrian Legation, Count
Potocki, was on very intimate terms with the Duke
of Devonshire of the day, who, by the way, was
rather deaf. The hospitalities at Devonshire House
formed what is now called a record. On one
occasion Count Potocki asked the Duke rather
earnestly to invite some lady of doubtful antecedents to one of his parties. The Duke made
no reply. Count Potocki therefore renewed his
request, whereupon the Duke of Devonshire
answered, "My dear Potocki, it's a pity that I
am not a diplomatist and that you are not
deaf."

In those days I heard many diplomatic stories.
There was one of an Ambassador and his wife who
were known to be constantly quarrelling. One day
the Ambassador had to take his wife away from
some racecourse before she wished to go, as they
were engaged to dine with the Queen. During the
homeward drive the Ambassador sat on the box of
the barouche, turning round from time to time in
the endeavour to conjure away his wife's ill-temper
by pointing out objects of interest along the road.

He said to her, "*Vois-tu, ma chère, ces jolies vaches?*"

"*Non,*" she replied, "*je ne vois rien que ton vilain dos.*"

On arriving at home, the Ambassador at once went to Buckingham Palace, and explained to the Queen the reason for his wife's delay. Her Majesty was much amused, and gave orders for dinner to be postponed so as to give time for the Ambassadress to appear.

On another occasion a lady was late for dinner at the Palace, but hoped to escape observation, as she was placed behind an épergne which she thought would conceal her from the view of the Queen. Her Majesty perceived her, however, and said, "I suppose some accident occurred on the road?"

The lady replied, "Yes, madam. The carriage."

Thereupon the Duke of Cambridge—father of the late Duke—not letting the question drop, asked what the accident had been.

The guest floundered, and said, "One of the horses fell."

This did not satisfy the Duke, who said, "Where was that?"

The lady replied, "In Holles Street."

The Duke said, "And what did you do?"

The lady said, "I went into a shop."

"What shop?" he asked.

"A chemist's shop," said the guest.

"But there is no chemist's shop in Holles Street," replied the Duke.

At this point, the Queen, who was much entertained, took pity on the lady and said to her uncle, "You should not ask ladies questions. It confuses them."

An anecdote used to be told of Lord Stratford and the diplomatist whom he succeeded in the United States. Every effort was made to prevent their meeting, as both were known to possess very violent tempers. It was, however, impossible to avoid their being together for one evening, and Lord Stratford dined with his predecessor. After dinner, the host offered Lord Stratford a cup of tea. Lord Stratford, beaming with conciliation, said, "This tea is very good." Thereupon his host rose up in fury and said, "I understand the taunt, sir! My father was a tea-merchant!"

There used to be a diplomatist who had the reputation of never speaking the truth. It was said of him, "*X—— est si menteur qu'on ne peut pas même croire le contraire de ce qu'il dit.*"

That reminds me of the story of a gentleman in the Mediterranean, who was also known to romance. On one occasion, he invited an American naval officer to dine with him, and indulged in one or two rather extraordinary flights. After dinner they went into the next room to smoke, and the host began a new story. The American captain fixed his eye upon him steadily, so much that the host rather boggled in his narrative. Hereon the naval officer said, "Go on, sir, go on. I've been a liar myself all my life!"

The person who told me this also related another anecdote of a gentleman describing his journey to England from America. He declared that when they were nearing the English coast they saw a small row-boat, with only one man, some hundred miles from the shore. They offered to take him in tow, but he replied that he had come alone in the row-boat all the way from America, and that he wished to complete the journey in the same manner. An American present said to him, " Give me your hand, my friend. You're my witness. I was the man in the row-boat."

Amongst other reminiscences are those of places of amusement frequented at that time by young men. One was called the " Cider Cellars," in Maiden Lane. Here men used to go in to supper, and songs were sung, not always of the choicest character, till a late hour at night. A similar place was the " Coal Hole," where the same amusements were offered ; but there was another night resort, which was certainly most clever, even if not improving—namely, what was called the " Judge and Jury," where every night a comic trial was given. It took place at an inn called the " Garrick's Head," in Bow Street, and the trials were conducted under the presidency of a man who, I fancy, was the proprietor of the inn. He represented the Lord Chief Baron, and was generally known as Lord Chief Baron Nicholson. He took his seat with great pomp, dressed in appropriate costume, and a table in front of him was surrounded by young men dressed as barristers, most of them being, I believe, attorneys' clerks. A great laugh was always raised, when the Lord Chief Baron took his seat, by his calling out " Waiter! A cigar and some brandy and water ! " But this was the only occasion when he derogated from his great dignity. The trials were, of course, of a farcical description, and were conducted by the barristers on either side in the usual manner, but with great wit. Occasionally the Lord Chief Baron interfered with some pointed remark ; but the most amusing feature of the representation was that of the witnesses, who were dressed according to the parts they represented. I never could find out whether the wit we heard was spontaneous or not, but certainly the questions of the counsel and the answers of the witnesses were very humorous. Five members of the audience were selected as the jury, to return a verdict according to the evidence.

Another place to which I only went once or twice at most was called " Bob Croft's." It was in the Haymarket, and very rough. It was not licensed, and refreshments had to be ordered under assumed appellations. For instance, brandy and water was called " pale white." There were some very uncouth customers who frequented this place, and I am told that occasionally great violence was shown. It did not require a license, I fancy, as it did not sell liquors, which were bought from neighbouring public-houses. At that time a

public-house could be open from twelve o'clock on
Sunday night till twelve o'clock the next Saturday
night, there being some special regulations about
Sunday itself; but a new Licensing Act regulating
public-houses brought to an end these subsidiary
establishments.

One amusement of which I never partook was
that of obtaining an escort from the police to visit
the haunts of criminals. I knew several people
who did this, and were much struck by the nature
of the scenes they visited. One clergyman, who
had a City living, used annually to give a dinner
to thieves, collected for him by some members
of the police force. He said they behaved very
well, and he was especially cautioned by the police
that all his guests expected to be treated as
gentlemen.

# CHAPTER VII

I WAS elected a member of the Alfred Club.
It was excessively comfortable, with beautiful
plate and an excellent library; but it had been
neglected for many years because of a curious
story. Some endeavours were made to revive it
by allowing people to come in with a diminished
entrance-fee, and at the time of my election most
young men coming to London were made members
of the Alfred, so that they might have a club to
frequent until they were elected to one of the
superior ones. There were the two Seymours,
Henry and Alfred; Mr. Chichester Fortescue—
afterwards Lord Carlingford; Charles and Henry
Grenfell; Mr. Baring, who became Lord North-
brook; Mr. George Glyn — afterwards Lord
Wolverton; Mr. Melville Portal, Mr. Henry
Erskine, Mr. Jacob, and Mr. Delaval Astley, together with many others, elected on that account.
The revival, however, did not last very long, and

86

at last the Alfred was amalgamated with the Oriental Club in Hanover Square.

Amongst other people I met at the Alfred was Mr. Tichborne, the original from whom the " Claimant " was copied. He was a nephew of my friends, Mr. Henry and Mr. Alfred Seymour, and, having been abroad a good deal, was somewhat foreign in his ways. These two gentlemen introduced him to their friends, and I must have seen him frequently, the more so as I was asked to support his election to the Club. I had no minute recollection of him, however, and I was therefore unable to give evidence at the trial, though asked to do so. The Claimant had a peculiar way in Court of raising first one eyebrow and then another. Allusion was often made to this trick. Some said that it was a characteristic of his family, and Sir Hamilton Seymour declared that their name originally was " Twitchborne," and taken on this account. Mr. Alfred Seymour had the same habit.

This, somewhat irrelevantly, reminds me of an incident in the life of Sir Hamilton Seymour. When Lord Hertford had left to Sir Richard Wallace the bulk of his property, Sir Hamilton Seymour contested the will, although Sir Richard offered what were considered very handsome terms of compromise. After passing through the inferior courts, the action finally was brought before the House of Lords. About this time, Sir Hamilton Seymour, going to a Queen's ball, met Lord

Chelmsford, a member of the supreme tribunal. Some allusion was made to the action then proceeding, and Lord Chelmsford remarked, " I am always thinking of the text, ' Agree with thine adversary quickly, whiles thou art in the way with him.' " This struck Sir Hamilton Seymour so forcibly that the next day he instructed his legal representatives to accept the terms offered by Sir Richard Wallace.

The story to which I alluded above, as having ruined the Alfred, was as follows :—

At one time, what are called coffee-room dinners at clubs did not exist ; but there was a house dinner at a certain hour every day, to which a limited number of members were admitted, on writing down their names beforehand. I believe at some clubs the dinners were given gratuitously, but on the understanding that a good deal of wine was drunk. At the Alfred there was a house dinner for twelve. On one occasion, as the company were sitting down to dinner, a member came to the Club and sent in a waiter, with the request to be allowed to join the party though he was not in evening dress, as he was going immediately into the country. His request was admitted. During the dinner he proved to be more agreeable to all the members than any one they recollected meeting before. On his leaving for the country, they inquired of each other who he was, and none of them knew. They then sent for the steward, and he informed them that it was Mr. Canning. Nearly all the members of the Alfred were so much afraid of being taken for one of a party of twelve or fourteen who did not know the Prime Minister by sight, that they took their names off the Club.

I was told by the late Sir Fleetwood Pellew, who had been a member for many years, that at one time the Club was so much sought after that persons used to leave cards on their friends, marking them "Candidate for the Alfred," in the hopes of getting support. But the incident I have related practically proved its ruin.

————

As I do not aspire to accuracy in dates, I may as well here mention one or two anecdotes of Archbishop M'Gee, whom I recollect very well. Though they have perhaps been told before, yet I know them to be authentic, and on this account I repeat them.

The Archbishop used to relate a story that once, finding many society people travelling first and second class, and wishing to avoid them, he entered a third-class carriage. There was no one in it except a farmer, who said to the Bishop, "I suppose you'd be something in the clergy line?" to which he assented. The farmer then said, "Is your curacy in this neighbourhood?" The Bishop replied, "No, no. I am sorry to say I have no curacy. I was a curate once, but am one no longer." To which the farmer rejoined, "I suppose it was the drink?"

On another occasion, he was staying with a gentleman in his diocese, and was invited by his host and hostess to go to a picnic. The luncheon-basket had been badly packed, and everything was mixed. The gentleman of the house made use of some very strong phrases, and his wife was anxious as to the effect this would produce on the Bishop. The latter said, "It was fortunate that we had a layman here to make use of the appropriate language."

Bishop M'Gee was once asked to marry a gentleman who was a great whisky-manufacturer in Dublin. The Bishop felt disinclined to do this, being very much opposed to the trade; but, as the gentleman in question had a great reputation, and was known to be very charitable, the Bishop did not like to refuse.

After the ceremony, the bridegroom said, "I do not know how to thank your Lordship. I wish I could do something that might be pleasing to you. All I can say is, 'The Lord be with you!'"

The Bishop replied, "And with thy spirit!"

A Bishop who was about to celebrate his golden wedding once discoursed on the subject at a dinner-party to a French lady next to him. She said, "I do not understand all this about your golden wedding." The Bishop replied, "You see, we have lived together for fifty years." The French lady interrupted, "Oh, I see. You have lived together fifty years, and now you are going to be married!"

I have always found that bishops, like other

men of distinction, have a great sense of humour.
I knew one who composed what is now called a
Limerick.    It ran as follows :—

> There was a young lady of Cheadle,
> Who one day sat down on a needle ;
>     But as from its head
>     There depended a thread,
> It was promptly pulled out by the beadle.

The following seems also to have an ecclesiastical
touch :—

> A learned young innocent curate
> Vainly courted a damsel obdurate ;
>     Till he said with a sigh,
>     "Perhaps by and by
> Your response will be more commensurate."

A gentleman who used to be quoted as a great
wit was Mr. Brookfield, who had the chapel of
John Street, Berkeley Square.    He was said to
be the original of one of Thackeray's characters.
It was related that, in Mr. Brookfield's time at
Oxford, there was a very unpopular don whose
name was Thorpe, and some of the young men
were stimulated to write epitaphs on him.    One
had been composed that consisted of twenty lines.
"No," said Mr. Brookfield, "that's too long."
Somebody else wrote one of twelve lines, to which
Mr. Brookfield made the same objection.    At last
a two-line epitaph was composed, but Mr. Brookfield said, "That is still too long.    Two words are
enough for him—'Thorpe's corpse.'"

In early life, I made the acquaintance of Sir

John McNeill, who had been Minister in Persia for many years. He had begun life in the Indian Medical Service, and was appointed Physician to the Legation at Tehran. Owing to his great ability, he was named Minister in 1836. Subsequently, he acted as Commissioner in the enquiry concerning military deficiencies in the Crimea during the war, and his report, I believe, entailed a great deal of unpopularity for him.

Amongst others of whom I saw a great deal at the time were Mr. and Lady Elizabeth Stanhope; she was the daughter of the well-known Coke of Holkham, for so many years the popular Member for Norfolk, who was afterwards created Lord Leicester. I also frequented the house of Mr. and Mrs. Spencer Walpole. Another friend was Captain Waldegrave, an old naval officer, whom I had known for many years, and who afterwards became Lord Waldegrave.

I knew Laurence Oliphant well, too, in those days. He was charmingly accomplished and bright. Whatever he undertook was well done. He had many friends, and achieved great success as a writer. Subsequently he took to spiritualism, and ended his days as a devout professor of that cult. I recollect his telling me, half in joke, what had first attracted his attention to spiritualism.

When crossing to America, one night there arose a very serious storm at which every one was much alarmed, except one American gentleman who remained perfectly calm. The next day, Mr.

Oliphant said to him, "You appeared not to be at all alarmed by the storm last night." The American replied, "No, I guess I shall have a good time of it t'other side Jordan."

This somewhat frivolous observation remained in Mr. Oliphant's brain, and ended by bringing him over to that peculiar profession of faith.

Mr. and Mrs. Richard Ford were very kind to me in those days. Mr. Ford contributed constantly to the *Quarterly Review*, and had written the *Spanish Handbook*, being a celebrated writer on Spain, and the great authority on that country. His method of bringing his mind to bear on what he intended writing was a curious one. He kept a squirrel in his room, and making the animal turn round in its cage had the effect of bringing his mind into focus for writing. Their son, whom I also knew very well, was afterwards Sir Clare Ford. He had been in the army for a short time, but left it for diplomacy. He was a man of remarkable geniality and intelligence. I met him some years later at Naples, where he was attached to Sir William Temple's Legation, and where he married a very beautiful Neapolitan lady, Miss Garofalo, who died comparatively young. I succeeded him as Ambassador at Madrid.

Mr. Ford's daughter married Mr. Oswald Crawfurd, the novelist, whose father was the great authority at the Geographical Society, and once Governor of Singapore. His mother was the daughter of the well-known proprietor of the

*Morning Chronicle,* and sister to Sir Erskine Perry.

Another acquaintance of mine was Mr. Monckton Milnes, afterwards raised to the peerage as Lord Houghton.   He was a man of great literary power and ready wit, but, though a strong personal friend and zealous supporter of Lord Palmerston, he did not succeed in active politics.

On one occasion, at dinner, a young lady was seated between two elderly gentlemen.    Mr. Monckton Milnes' neighbour said to him, "Do you know the name of that young lady opposite?"

He replied, "Yes, her name is Susanna."

Sir Charles Trevelyan, whom I also knew, though not well, was at that time Secretary of the Treasury, where, with the best and most conscientious intentions, he made himself rather unpopular by the rigour of his decisions.   His first wife had been the sister of Macaulay, the historian, and his son is Sir George Trevelyan.

Early in my life in London, Lady Palmerston was good enough to take notice of me, and from then till the end of her active career, whenever I was in London, she never missed asking me to whatever parties she gave.   She had great charm of manner, and, as I have mentioned before, she exercised a very useful influence over Lord Palmerston.

In those days there lived near me, in Mayfair, Miss Mary and Miss Agnes Berry.   They were constantly inviting me to their house, and I now

regret bitterly not having availed myself more often
of their kindness. In summer, Lord Lansdowne
often lent them his villa at Richmond.

Miss Mary Berry was supposed to have been
engaged to marry Horace Walpole. He died in
1797, being the son of Sir Robert Walpole by
Miss Shorter, the daughter of the Lord Mayor.
This Lord Mayor had not been elected in the
usual manner, but was appointed by order of
James II. Between myself, therefore, and the
age of James II. there are only two links, namely,
Miss Berry and Horace Walpole.

A lady who used to give a good many dinners
was also very kind to me—Lady Robert Seymour.
I think she was by birth Miss Chetwynd, and a
near relative of Miss Chetwynd-Stapleton, who
formed part of a wonderful group of unmarried
ladies with whom I was somewhat intimate. The
others were the Misses Lemon, who lived in a
small house in Upper Brook Street; they were
sisters of Sir Charles Lemon, Member, I think,
for Cornwall, and also of an old lady—Lady de
Dunstanville. One peculiarity in this family was
that they never addressed each other by their
Christian names, but always spoke to each other as
" Brother " or " Sister."

The two Miss Sothebys—daughters of the celebrated poet—were friends of mine, as were also the
Misses Finch, whom I knew very well, and who
lived in Charles Street and gave dinners. There
I met Mr. Godley, so distinguished in Colonial

matters; and at the house of Mrs. Butt—a lady who lived very much in literary circles—I made the acquaintance of Mrs. Marsh, author of *Amelia Wyndham*, and of Miss Agnes Strickland, the historian.

At Mrs. Butt's I also saw more than once Mr. Samuel Rogers, the poet. I never, however, had the opportunity of speaking to him. He had a reputation for making caustic and unpleasant remarks, which were commonly quoted. Those which I heard, however, were not, as I thought, marked with any particular wit or humour. The person, I am told, who, more than any other, could excite him to wrath was the late Mr. Henry Grenfell.

I knew well a lady called Miss Smyth, who was a relative of the Duchess of Grafton, and sister of a well-known man named Smyth of Heath Hall, Wakefield, near which town lived another friend of mine, Mrs. Gaskell—the mother of Mr. Milnes-Gaskell—and Mrs. Daniel Gaskell, his aunt. I also knew Dr. and Lady Louisa Marsh—no relation to the lady lately mentioned. His son, by a former marriage, was a clergyman of considerable celebrity. He also had a daughter who wrote with great success on religious matters, and was the authoress of the *Life of Hedley Vicars*. I believe she is still living.

Two other friends of mine were the Misses Walpole, daughters of Colonel Lambert Walpole, who was killed at the time of the Union of Ireland.

Their mother had been the daughter of Lord
Clive.   I also saw much of an aunt of theirs,
Miss Elizabeth Walpole, who had a house at
Twickenham, and was known by her relatives as
"Cousin Betsy."   She retained all her faculties
to an advanced age, and her letters are full of
interest.

At the houses of some of these ladies, I frequently
met Miss Caldwell.   She had been a great beauty
during the Regency, so much so that, when she
was going away from the Opera, crowds used to
draw up on either side of her path to admire her.
Notwithstanding her beauty, she remained Miss
Caldwell.

Above all was a dear and kind friend named
Miss Leigh, whose father had been well known
during the Regency as a writer of plays, and a
friend of the wits of the day.   I had known her
since my early childhood, and looked upon her in
the light of a relative.   Amongst her other
acquaintances in early life had been Professor
Smyth, who accompanied Mr. Tom Sheridan as
tutor to the University.   He had given Miss Leigh
a very small book, privately printed, describing
his experiences with the Sheridans in general.   I
recollect one or two of these anecdotes which
amused me a good deal.

As is generally known, Mr. Sheridan was very
unpunctual in his payments.   It so happened that
he had not, for some time, made any remittances
to Mr. Smyth for his expenses as tutor.   After

writing more than once to Mr. Sheridan, Mr. Smyth addressed him a letter written in very strong language. Almost immediately afterwards, Mr. Smyth received an invitation to come with Mr. Tom Sheridan and pay the father a visit. Mr. Smyth, by this time, was rather ashamed of the force of his language, and, after being very courteously received by Mr. Sheridan, he said to his host, "I am very sorry I wrote you that letter the other day. I hope you will forgive me if it was too strong."

Mr. Sheridan replied, "Don't say a word more about it."

The next morning Mr. Smyth had occasion to go into Mr. Sheridan's library. On the table were lying many unopened letters, and he saw that none of his own had ever had their seals broken.

This anecdote, which I found in Miss Leigh's book, was also repeated to me by the late Lord Holland.

About that time Mr. Tom Sheridan had been reading the works of some German philosopher, which impressed him a good deal. The philosopher's theory was that nothing, however insignificant, could be done with indifference; for instance, a man touching a table, or his head, though apparently involuntarily, did not really do it with indifference. This theory Mr. Tom Sheridan developed to his father, who, however, did not seem to agree.

The son then asked, "Is there anything you

can do with absolute, complete, and entire indifference ? "

Mr. Sheridan replied, " Yes, certainly."

His son rejoined, " What is it, then, that you
can do with utter, complete, absolute indifference?"

" Listen to you, Tom," was the reply.

# CHAPTER VIII

THERE was a very agreeable little winter society
in London at that time. Small whist-parties were
constantly given, amongst others by Lady Tankerville and Mr. and Mrs. Prideaux Brune. My
cousin, Sir William Hoste, with whom I lived
habitually when he was in London, subsequently
married one of the daughters of that house.

There were a good many others who were
generally in London in winter and joined this little
coterie—Lord John Fitzroy; also Lady Isabella
Blachford, his sister, whose husband had been the
owner of Osborne, which was sold to Queen
Victoria; Captain Gallwey, Sir Arthur Otway,
Sir Richard King, Lady Champagné, Colonel
Ferguson of Pitfour, Lady Poulett, and Mr.
Munro of Novar, the brother-in-law of Mr. Butler
Johnstone, senior, to whom the bulk of his pro-
perty went, while Novar passed to Mr. Munro-
Ferguson, who is known by the same territorial
appellation. There were also Mr. Williamson

Ramsay, Mr. Belward Ray, who had a very pretty place at Edmonton, where he occasionally gave great morning parties, and Mr. Hook, a brother, I think, of the Dean of Chichester. He was married to Lady Cooke, the widow of Sir Edward Cooke, who, early in the century, had been Under-Secretary of State for Foreign Affairs, and was generally known by the nickname of "Kangaroo Cooke."

One lady, who was almost certain to be found in town, was Mrs. Lane-Fox, a very remarkable character, and the sister of General Buckley, a much-trusted servant of the Court. Society was constantly assembled at her house, either to call on her in the morning, or to dine with her later. One of her great friends was Mr. Charles Villiers, a brother of Lord Clarendon, who had more than once been in the Government, and who was singularly gifted with a ready and joyous wit. One instance of it I recollect.

A foreign lady came to London, and went very much into society. She was of enormous size, though quite young. Talking of her one day, some one said, "Do you know Madame —— is only eight-and-twenty?"

Mr. Charles Villiers replied, "I suppose you mean eight-and-twenty stone!"

I saw a great deal of Lady Dormer and Miss Dormer. Lady Dormer was by birth Miss Tichborne, nearly connected with the family affected by the well-known Claimant. Miss Dormer was afterwards known as the Countess Dormer, having been made a *chanoinesse*. Both were intimate friends of Lady Poulett's, and very popular in society. I also knew Mr. and Mrs. Seymour. He was the father of Lady Tichborne, whose son, Roger, was impersonated by the Claimant in the great trial. He had been a *détenu* at Verdun.

Among my intimate friends, whom I have also mentioned elsewhere, were Mr. Henry and Mr. Alfred Seymour, both of them half-brothers of Lady Tichborne. Mr. Henry Seymour had been Under-Secretary of State for India, and both he and his brother were in Parliament. They were grandsons of the Mr. Seymour who was in his youth, I believe, heir-presumptive to the Duke of Somerset, and for many years lived almost habitually in France. Hence their French connections. I travelled with them more than once on the Continent, and I recollect staying with Mr. Alfred Seymour at Knoyle in Wiltshire, a comfortable and quaint old house, built, I believe, by Sir Christopher Wren, who was born in the village. A portion of Mr. Seymour's property has been sold to Mr. Percy Wyndham, who was also in Parliament for a long time, and who erected on a well-chosen site a house called Clouds, which I have never seen.

I was acquainted, too, with Sir James and Lady Hogg, who lived next door to the Seymours in Upper Grosvenor Street. Their eldest son was Colonel Hogg of the Life Guards, who was in

Parliament, and for some time Chairman of the Metropolitan Board of Works. On one occasion, when the Board had to undertake some joint operation with the London municipality, it was said in *Punch* that the three deities of the City were Hogg, Gog, and Magog. Colonel Hogg was afterwards Lord Magheramorne. Another acquaintance of mine was Mr. Fleming, so well known in society. He had been a great ally of Mr. Charles Buller, and ended his days as Secretary of the Poor Law Board. His brother, Sir Valentine Fleming, was a Judge in Australia.

Mrs. Gore, the well-known authoress, and her daughter—afterwards Lady Edward Thynne—were notabilities of society in those days. Miss Gore had a most beautiful figure, while her mother's was rather inclined to be over-opulent. They were consequently known in the world as " Plenty and No Waste."

Amongst my early habitual associates were General Wrottesley, as already mentioned, Sir Arthur Otway, and Mr.—later Sir Charles—Wyke His mother had been a lady in attendance on the Duchess of Cumberland, and he himself had been chosen by the King of Hanover, at the instance of Dr. Jelf, to be the companion of Prince George in his studies. He had originally been an officer in the Royal Fusiliers. On the accession of the Duke of Cumberland to the throne of Hanover, Mr. Wyke had been appointed A.D.C. to the King, and accompanied him to Hanover. Here

he did not find his position comfortable, as there
seemed to be a kind of jealousy of Englishmen.
He therefore begged the King to obtain for him a
post in the English Consular Service. This was
given to him by Lord Aberdeen, who wrote to the
King of Hanover to say that, as he was about to
leave office, this was the last post in his gift. The
appointment was that of Vice-Consul at Hayti.
Shortly after Mr. Wyke's arrival at his post, the
Consul-General went away, leaving Mr. Wyke to
act for him. At that time the revolution broke
out, which ended in the proclamation of Faustin
Soulouque as Emperor of Hayti. The new
sovereign desired to arrange his household on the
model of old European courts. Hearing that Mr.
Wyke had been in the household of the King of
Hanover, he applied to him for advice and assistance in details, which Mr. Wyke was able to give
him, thereby acquiring a great influence with the
Emperor. This he used to a good purpose, principally for obtaining the pardon of some opponents
of the Emperor, whom the latter wished to execute,
as was the habit in that country. Among other
rewards that he received was the Order of St.
Faustin, which the Emperor had founded.

Mr. Wyke's accounts of the rise of the Empire
of Hayti were most interesting, as the Haytians
did everything in their power to form themselves
on European models. They had been well
educated. Their language is French, and the
principal youths of the country are often sent to

study in Paris. The result is that they have acquired great ease in French conversation, and, except for their colour, would be taken for Europeans. I have known several in different parts of the world. When at Madrid, Mademoiselle Judic came to act, and one night at the theatre the French Ambassador invited me to go with him behind the scenes and make her acquaintance. To our great disappointment, we were entirely eclipsed by a junior member of the Haytian Embassy, perfectly black, but paying compliments in the most choice French phraseology.

It is narrated of an American missionary that he visited Hayti, and was taken in some town to be introduced to the Mayor. This functionary, who was deep black, was dressed like a Parisian, and spoke English as well as French. He asked his visitor what he thought of the country. The missionary replied : "It is a most beautiful country. The vegetation is magnificent, the scenery attractive, and the climate good. It is a pity that you should all be so much set one against the other, and constantly fighting instead of working for the good of your nation."

The Mayor replied : "It is all very well for you to speak in this way, as a cold-blooded Anglo-Saxon ; but it is very different with us of the Latin race."

The American gentleman, from whom I heard this story, had many others about negroes. He was a great writer and historian. He told me that, after the Civil War, Congress endeavoured to reconcile the Southerners to their fate by giving them more privileges than their numerical proportion in the States really entitled them to enjoy. This created some anger among the Northerners, especially the negroes. One black clergyman preached a sermon on the subject. He said it was painful to see how Congress encouraged men who had imbrued their hands in the blood of their brethren. He recalled the story of the Prodigal Son; how, first, he lived with the swine, and ate the husks; but in the end, at any rate, he was contrite, repented, went home and apologised to his father. The father accepted the apology, and killed the fatted calf in honour of the prodigal's return. These Southerners, however, showed no contrition, no repentance; they made no apology. They went to their father's house, knocked loudly, and said, when the servant came to the door, "Bring out that veal!"

Mr. Wyke brought himself so favourably before the notice of the Foreign Office that he was shortly afterwards appointed Consul-General to the Central States of America. Here again he acted with great tact and discretion. He was made Minister in Mexico at the time of the unfortunate expedition of the Emperor Maximilian, and very cleverly prevented England from being involved in the hostilities undertaken by the French against the Mexicans. Afterwards he was appointed Minister at Hanover with his old schoolmate, the blind

King. Here he remained till Hanover had disappeared from the list of States, and then he was appointed, first to Copenhagen, and afterwards to Lisbon, at which place he retired from the service.

Amongst other persons whose acquaintance I made when I was very young was Lord John Manners, later Duke of Rutland, father to the present Duke. From him, through life, I received undeviating kindness. I do not think that I ever met with so noble and high-minded a character. He displayed it in the smallest matters. One night there was a very urgent division, and, though Lord John had been in bed for some days, and his temperature was 104°, he came down to the House, and was drawn through the division-lobby in a bath-chair.

At one time a movement was set on foot to publish, for some charity, a volume by distinguished writers, to which Lord John Manners was asked to make a literary contribution. As the book was never published, I think I shall not be indiscreet in reproducing this composition, of which I have the manuscript.

### WORDS WRITTEN FOR "REMEMBER ME"

When 'mid the gay and thoughtless throng
    That fills your Castle-hall,
You search for one to whom belong
    Thoughts you would fain recall;
When your bright eye has glanced all round,
    And failed that one to see,
When all by thee are worthless found,
    Then you'll remember me.

When sympathy in vain you strive
   In worldly hearts to find,
And vainly bid pure Honor live
   In pleasure's sordid mind;
When 'mid those vanities you sigh
   For Love unbought and free,
And Glory's guerdon, bright and high,
   Oh, then remember me!

Wealth, and the power that wealth bestows,
   Its luxuries and state,
I cannot give; its pomps and shows
   On others' brides may wait.
But should you scorn such low desires,
   And loyal-hearted be,
Return these too long slighted fires,
   And, love, remember me!

He enclosed it in a letter to the editor :—

DEAR SIR—The above twaddle is all I have to offer you; if you think it worth printing, pray do so; but I own it seems to me on a par with the original.—Yours truly,

JOHN MANNERS.

BELVOIR CASTLE, *January* 12, 1850.

Lord John Manners' great devotion in coming to the House, under such untoward circumstances, reminds me of an anecdote of skilful whipping, told me by General Forester, one of the oldest Members of the House—if not the oldest—who was generally liked and esteemed.

At the time of an important division, a Member happened to be confined in a lunatic asylum. Every vote was necessary. Arrangements were therefore made to deliver him at the House at the moment required, and he was received by the Whip of his party, who induced him to walk

through the lobby by preceding him with a stick
of barley-sugar in his hand.   This I believe to be
a perfectly true story.

About this time—though I cannot bind myself
to minute chronological accuracy — I made the
acquaintance of Mr. Thackeray.   I used to dine
with him at his house in Young Street, Kensington,
his two daughters being then quite children.   I
first met him at the house of Mr. Kinglake, the
author of *Eothen*, who asked me to stay with him
at his house in Taunton.   Mr. Thackeray was
a great friend of Mr. Charles Buller's.   Both
had had the bridge of their nose broken.   Mr.
Thackeray wished to introduce a gentleman to
Mr. Buller, and, after expatiating on his virtues,
said, touching his nose, " He is one of us."

I recollect a very interesting conversation that
Mr. Thackeray and I had with a farmer, who was a
follower of what is now called the Agapemone.
In those days, individuals of that creed were called
Princeites, after Mr. Prince who had founded them.
They did not seem to have any fixed tenets, except
belief in Mr. Prince, and their chief form of worship
consisted in perpetual games of hockey.   I believe
they still exist, their residence being somewhere
near Bridgewater, where I think Mr. Kinglake had
some property.   Mr. Kinglake I had known in the
country.   He was a great friend of Lord Pollington, later Lord Mexborough, with whom he had
travelled, and who was the " Methley " frequently
mentioned in *Eothen* as Mr. Kinglake's travelling

companion.    Methley is the name of the Yorkshire
residence of Lord Mexborough.

Mr. Kinglake was a man of great humour, with
which he was very ready.    This may be seen from
*Eothen,* one of the most charming books of travels
ever written.

On one occasion, a young man, who was a friend
of both of us, came to the Athenæum, in a very
perturbed state, asking us to get him out of a
scrape.    He told us that he had been sitting with
a good-looking widow, of about middle age, whom
we both knew, and that some genius had tempted
him to kiss her.    She, he told us, had worked herself
up into a great rage, said she had never been so much
insulted in her life, and desired him to leave the
house.    He said to us, " What do you think she will
do ? "    Kinglake replied, " Beware ! she will pursue
you through life with her unrelenting gratitude ! "

Mr. Kinglake and I had a friend, an old lady of
considerable rank, who, however, was constantly
deserted by her husband.    She consulted Mr.
Kinglake on the subject.    Her principal grievance
was that, when absent, her husband, who used to
travel with another lady to whom he gave her
name, would direct his letters to herself, " The
Dowager Marchioness of ——"

All Mr. Kinglake's relatives were persons of
great intellect and charming manner.    He had
one brother, a banker at Taunton, and another,
Dr. Hamilton Kinglake, a celebrated physician in
Somersetshire.    I knew both of them in my youth.

About this time, I also formed an acquaintance with another Eastern traveller, a great friend of Mr. Kinglake's, but rather a contrast to him. This was Mr. Eliot Warburton, the author of a book of Eastern travels, called *The Crescent and the Cross.* Poor man, he was lost afterwards in the destruction of the steamer *Amazon,* in which he was going to Panama on some expedition. He was very agreeable, and somewhat sentimental; while Mr. Kinglake was also agreeable, but a little bit cynical.

Together with these two travellers, I was also well acquainted with Mr. Layard. In later life, I had occasion to see a great deal of him, and to do business with him on Oriental politics.

The occupation I liked best in those days was attending debates in the House of Commons, and this, owing to the good-nature of some Members of Parliament who also belonged to the Alfred Club, I was enabled to do very frequently, and thus witnessed some interesting episodes.

On one occasion, I recollect Lord Dudley Stuart, the great advocate of the Poles, made a complaint against Lord Palmerston. He said:

During the last session, I asked the noble Lord to give me some papers relative to Hungary, and he agreed to my unopposed motion. Later in the session, I asked him why the papers had not been delivered, and he explained that he had been too busy to go through them. Again I called on him at the Foreign Office, and he expressed his great regret at the delay, and pointed out two or three large boxes which he said contained the papers, adding that, as soon as he

possibly could, he would go through them and have them
circulated.  Now nearly a year has passed.  I called upon
him again the other day, and he said to me, "I quite sym-
pathise with you, and if I were in your case I should be very
angry."  I now ask the noble Lord if he intends shortly to
give me the papers.

Every one thought Lord Palmerston was placed
in a dilemma by this address from one of his
supporters, and he rose to answer.  He said:

My noble friend is perfectly right in his narrative of
what has passed.  I did promise him the papers, but I was
unfortunately unable to go through them.  I did tell him I
thought he was very badly treated, and that, if I had been
treated in the same manner, I should feel very much aggrieved.
I did show him the boxes which contain the papers.  All I
can do now is to repeat what I said before—that I think he
has been very badly treated; that I should be very much
aggrieved if I were treated in such a manner myself; that,
unfortunately, the papers are still in those boxes, but I really
will go through them as soon as I can.

The House laughed, and the matter ended, poor
Lord Dudley Stuart having gained very little by
his motion.

One of Lord Palmerston's colleagues in the
Cabinet—well known for his love of dining out—
asked him why a certain Ambassador was constantly asking him to dinner.  Lord Palmerston
replied, "Don't you know?  His Government
always pays for the dinner if a Cabinet Minister
is present.  The Ambassador knows that in you
there is a sure find.  In fact, you pay for nearly
half his dinners.  The rest are distributed amongst
our other colleagues."

There is an old saying that men reach distinction as much by the heart as by the head, and this was certainly the case with Lord Palmerston.  It was pleasant to see the geniality with which he elbowed his way through the crowd of Members who were going into the House of Lords at the opening or closing of Parliament.

About this time, the beginning of my career, a set attack was made upon him by Mr. David Urquhart, who had been in the Diplomatic Service, and had left it on account of a quarrel, I believe with Lord Palmerston, whom he accused of receiving money from the Russian Government.  It was declared that £20,000 had been lent to him by a lady known to be a great friend of his, the Princess Lieven, wife of the Russian Minister, and that, in consideration of this, Lord Palmerston had yielded unnecessarily to some demand of the Russian Government.  Mr. Urquhart was supported in his attack by Mr. Chisholm Anstey, a barrister of enormous learning and research, though sometimes rather prolix in his speeches.  Of course, Lord Palmerston easily disposed of these charges, and made a long speech, going into all the circumstances.  Subsequently Mr. Chisholm Anstey became reconciled with Lord Palmerston, and was invited to one of Lady Palmerston's parties.  Mr. Urquhart, complaining of his conduct, said, " He sold me for a lemon ice ! "

Mr. Urquhart had many peculiarities.  He considered that a Turkish bath was a panacea for all

ills.   Once, I believe, he prescribed one for a child,
which made him very unpopular in his neighbourhood.   He also had a mania that children should
be brought up without clothing of any kind.   A
close disciple of his is said to have taken one of
his sons—no longer very young—entirely destitute
of clothing, into a train.   The other passengers
objected to this absence of costume, whereupon
the father, declaring that it was only an absurd
prejudice, bought an uncut *Times*, and folded it
round the boy.

One day I happened to be dining in the coffee-
room of the House of Commons, which was then
only a temporary building, with very rough accommodation, and Mr. Chisholm Anstey was there.
At other tables were sitting Lord Palmerston and
Sir James Graham.   Mr. Anstey went in a shy
way to Sir James Graham, who was reading a
newspaper, and said, "How do you do, Sir James
Graham?"   The latter looked up at him, and
saying, "How do you do, Mr. Anstey?" resumed
his reading.   Mr. Anstey then went to Lord
Palmerston, and said, "How do you do, Lord
Palmerston?"   Lord Palmerston looked at him
and said, "Oh, Anstey, how d'ye do?   Now sit
down.   You have heard what this man has been
saying in the House.   You know something about
it.   Just sit down and let me know what you think
of his argument."   Mr. Anstey was delighted with
his reception, and the contrast of the two manners
easily showed why Lord Palmerston was so popular,

and Sir James Graham so much the reverse. As
Lord Carlingford used to say, the secret of Lord
Palmerston's popularity lay in the fact that he was
" understanded of the people."

I am not attempting to relate any of these
circumstances in chronological order, but merely
to group them together as well as I can, before
dismissing them.

Amongst other Members of Parliament who had
a great reputation for wit was Mr. Bernal Osborne.
He never rose in the House but to create a laugh.
I was told that at one time he was A.D.C. to
Lord Normanby, then Viceroy of Ireland, and
among others of the Viceregal staff was Mr. Frank
Sheridan, a brother of Lady Dufferin, the Duchess
of Somerset, and Mrs. Norton. Mr. Sheridan was
asked to stand for some constituency, but, though
a great wit, he was a poor speaker, and he did not
know how to address a meeting. The following
arrangement was therefore made between him and
Mr. Osborne. They went together to the town
where the meeting was to be held, Mr. Sheridan
going on the platform, while Mr. Osborne, dressed
in a smock-frock, stood in the crowd as one of the
electors. Mr. Sheridan then made a very short
speech, ending it by saying that he thought the
arrangement most satisfactory to the electors would
be that they should ask any questions they liked.
Thereupon Mr. Bernal Osborne, in his smock-frock,
asked him a pre-arranged series of questions, and,
having received answers, declared himself perfectly

satisfied, and moved a vote of confidence in the candidate.

On another occasion, an elector in the hall contradicted Mr. Osborne, in a manner rather convincing to the audience. Mr. Osborne said : " If the gentleman will only come on to the platform, I can give him a satisfactory explanation." Room being made, the interrupter moved with difficulty to the platform, where Mr. Osborne was seen speaking earnestly to him for a few minutes. Then he came forward, saying, " The gentleman has apologised." Tremendous cheering followed, notwithstanding violent gesticulations of denial by the elector, and the resolution—the last one—was carried in Mr. Osborne's favour.

Once, when the Burials Bill was being discussed, Mr. Lowe rather shocked public taste by saying that he could not make out why so much fuss was made about a lot of musty old bones. This was taken up by Members who were offended at the expression ; but Mr. Bernal Osborne, rising to defend his friend, said that the House must recollect the old adage, " De mortuis nil nisi *bonum*."

Mr. Bernal Osborne was very quick of repartee. Once, at a party, a young lady whom he knew well was passing near him, and he called her to come to sit by him. She remonstrated, saying, " You call me as you would a cab." He replied, " At any rate, a Hansom cab."

There used to be more than one notable wit in the Viceregal Court at Dublin. A gentleman

named Corry Connellan was renowned for his
brilliant sayings.  He was a very bad sailor.  On
one occasion, when crossing the Channel, he made
use of a hatbox he found near him on deck, in
connection with his illness.  The owner of the hatbox came up roughly, and said, " I say, sir, that's
not your hatbox."  Mr. Connellan faintly replied,
" Obviously not."

The following anecdote, though irrelevant to
the general course of this book, is brought to my
mind by the story I have just told.  A French
gentleman once said to my colleague, Mr. Thomas
Bruce, in allusion to sea-sickness : " *Quant à moi,
quand je me sens sur le point de succomber, je pense
à une jolie femme—à Marie Stuart !* "

Another amusing little passage that I remember
took place in the House of Commons.  Mr. Wyld,
the map-maker, when attacking the Government,
made use of the expression, " During the recent
debate, some *party* observed . . ."  Mr. Disraeli,
in his reply, said : " The honourable Member for
Bodmin has stated that during the recent debate
some ' party ' made certain observations.  Sir, *I*
am the party."

Another original in the House of Commons in
those days was Mr. Grantley Berkeley.  He was
a very powerful man in appearance, a great
sportsman, with much humour, and a strong
Gloucestershire accent.  In Parliament at the
same time were Mr. Spooner, who represented the
Protestant party, and Mr. Hume, the economist.

Mr. Hume had said something outside the House which Mr. Spooner disliked. He consequently invited Mr. Hume to come to the House at a certain time for an explanation. I forget what the subject was; but both gentlemen, being very elderly and evidently physically frail, seemed much moved by the incident. After a mutual explanation, Mr. Grantley Berkeley rose, and, appealing to the Speaker, asked him to exact from these two gentlemen an assurance that they would not commit a breach of the peace.

On another occasion, Mr. Grantley Berkeley, who was never on good terms with Mr. Bright, had some difference with him. Mr. Bright quoted some friend of his as observing that if Mr. Berkeley had not been born a gentleman, he would have been a gamekeeper. To this Mr. Berkeley replied that if Mr. Bright had not been born a Quaker, he would have been a prize-fighter.

I recollect a debate in the House of Commons in 1850, when Mr. Roebuck brought in a motion on the foreign policy of the Government concerning Greece. Lord Palmerston made a long and successful speech in reply. I am much pleased still to possess a copy. He gave one to every clerk in the Foreign Office, and in it were many points that helped to render me familiar with the various subjects that I came across when, years afterwards, I was stationed in the Ionian Islands myself, and took some part in the administration.

Amongst others connected with the House of

Commons was an eminent barrister, who, unfortunately, was not very particular about the letter
H.   In one speech he more than once repeated
his astonishment that the gentleman to whom he
was replying "should harrogate to himself" certain
qualities.   The Member, in his answer, described the
distinguished lawyer as "the honourable Member
for Harrogate."

# CHAPTER IX

ON the 10th of April, 1848, I remember seeing a detachment of special constables, among whom, I was told, was Prince Louis Napoleon. Towards the close of the same year, I was present at a party given, I think, by Mrs. Mountjoy Martin, where he was also a guest. Shortly afterwards he left England for France.

In 1846-47 the incident known as the Spanish Marriages had produced the greatest excitement in France. M. Guizot acceded to office on the resignation of Maréchal Soult. The French people fancied that they saw a determination on the part of Louis Philippe to cultivate the goodwill of Austria and other despotic powers, so as to aggrandise his own family, with the prospect of securing the Spanish Crown for one of his grandchildren. The unpopularity of Louis Philippe became more marked in 1848, and the anger of the people culminated at the prohibition of a

Reform banquet by the Ministers. When M. Odillon Barrot, on the 22nd of February, laid on the table of the House of Deputies an Act of Impeachment, great excitement was aroused, which ended in the Revolution. The feeling extended to other countries, even to England. The Chartists made great demonstrations. I recollect on one occasion, when driving down to the Foreign Office in a cab, I was stopped by crowds in Charing Cross, shouting seditious cries. They had got hold of a phrase, much used in Paris at the time, *A bas Guizot!* thinking it applicable to English politics. I give extracts from a few letters I wrote at the time, and which I only recently found among the correspondence of a relative.

FOREIGN OFFICE,
*February 26, 1848.*

I suppose you have heard of the deposition of Louis Philippe, the sack of the Tuileries and the Palais Royal, and the proclamation of the Provisional Government, all of whom, except Odillon Barrot, insist on having a Republic. There was a report last night that Louis Philippe was at Mivart's and was coming. I, however, with a friend, waited till half-past one this morning in the hopes of seeing him; but he has not yet arrived. He was obliged to escape in a brougham.

*April 5.*

I have just been sworn in as special constable, and have been given my badge, staff, and warrant, and am consequently empowered to do anything I like to anybody. Admiral Bowles is my captain.

*April 10.*

Tremendous consternation is now prevailing. Every office in London is armed except ours, and I believe that is to be. Somerset House has a *chevaux-de-frise*, arms, hand-grenades,

a commissariat, and a hospital.  All we have is our staves
as constables.  We were ordered to be here at ten o'clock
this morning, and here we came.  No work is done.  A
dinner is laid out for us, and the windows are being barri-
caded.  I am in charge of my room.  There is a tremendous
row expected.  The Post Office clerks are armed, provisioned,
and organised in bodies of ten.  Colonel Maberley drills
them all.  Every one in London is, I believe, a "special."
Really it is shocking the state London is in. —— in a
tremendous temper, swearing at everybody and everything,
and everybody and everything swearing at him.  The row
will not begin, I fancy, till the afternoon, when it will be
tremendous.

*April* 11.

I continue this to-day.  We had muskets sent here, but
Feargus O'Connor having dispersed the crowd, we had our
dinner at four o'clock, at which everybody attended.  Afterwards about thirty of us went into the nursery and smoked,
singing "God save the Queen."  With trumpets also and
shawms we celebrated our victory.  Some slept here.  At
seven I went away and joined my own division at Half Moon
Street.  Had command of two men.  Patrolled till ten.
Took up a drunken man.  As he would not walk, I commanded all Her Majesty's lieges, constables or not, to assist
me.  We carried him up Bolton and Curzon Streets among
the hoots of the assembled crowd to our rendezvous in
Shepherd's Market, where we left him to sleep off his
drunkenness.  So we had very good fun on the whole.

A circumstance which about this time occupied
the Foreign Office very much was the dismissal of
Sir Henry Bulwer by the Spanish Government.

Lord Palmerston on March 16, 1848, had
written a despatch to Sir Henry Bulwer, criticising
the state of politics in Spain.  In this despatch he
counselled the Queen of Spain to strengthen her
executive government—having regard to the recent
downfall of the King of the French—and to call

to her counsels some of the men in whom the
Liberal party placed its confidence.   This was
communicated by Sir Henry Bulwer to the Duke
of Sotomayor, and an answer was sent protesting
against Lord Palmerston's despatch.   One or two
passages in the reply were singularly strong for a
diplomatic document.   One was :

Your conduct in the execution of your important
mission has been reprobated by public opinion in England,
censured in the British press, and condemned in the British
Parliament.   Her Catholic Majesty's Government cannot
defend it, and that of Her Britannic Majesty has not done so.

The conduct of the Spanish Government
was attributed to an allegation that Sir Henry
Bulwer, at the instigation of Lord Palmerston,
had been engaged in plots against the Government.   This, though never proved, obtained
unsubstantiated confirmation from the fact that
in some military disturbances at different points
in Spain, personal friends of Sir Henry Bulwer's
were said to have taken part.   On the 19th
of March, 1848, therefore, Sir Henry Bulwer
received his passports, accompanied by a peremp-
tory notice to quit the kingdom within forty-
eight hours.   He left Madrid, as was necessary
in those days, in a postchaise, having with him
one of his attachés, Mr. FitzPatrick Vernon, son
of the gentleman who was subsequently named
Lord Lyveden.   Mr. Vernon declared that Sir
Henry Bulwer was writing incessantly during the
whole of the journey, giving him—Mr. Vernon—

his inkstand to hold. At last fatigue overtook him, and he dropped the inkstand over Sir Henry Bulwer, who, being very particular about his dress, was excessively annoyed.

Towards the end of that December, accompanied by Mr.—now Sir Arthur—Otway, I paid a visit to Paris, then abandoned by nearly all visitors on account of the disordered state of politics. The journey to Paris was not so easy then as it is now. I recollect at a much later period than this when it was a novelty for the journey to take only twelve hours.

On this occasion we found it necessary to take our places on a steamer at Dover, which enabled us to reach Amiens the same night. There we slept, and the next day we arrived in Paris. On my journey I received a blow. An English lady and gentleman were travelling in the same carriage. I happened to fall asleep, and, when half awake, I heard the lady say to her husband, pointing at me, " Isn't he like Mr. Toots ?"

Paris, which, as already stated, was very little frequented that winter, was exceptionally cheap. Carriages could be hired for very little. Theatres were only half full. There was a celebrated play, or *revue*, called *La Propriété c'est le Vol*, in which the authors had sarcastically reviewed the events of the year. The representation was supposed to begin with the Creation, and the first scene represented Adam and Eve. The serpent then appeared, with the face and spectacles of

Proudhon, the celebrated Socialist writer who had been a leader in the Revolution, and had published in 1840 a famous work entitled *What is Property?* He re-appeared through every section of the play, always with the same face, until the time arrived when Socialist principles entirely triumphed. Money was abolished, and bargains could only be established by barter. One great joke in the play was a market to which a man came with a stuffed crocodile on his shoulders, asking who would give change for a stuffed crocodile. The change was a small piece of furniture.

Among the few people who remained in Paris was Lady Elgin, who had a house, I think, in the Faubourg St. Honoré, and who gave a party for charity, at which were present the Duke and Duchess of Calabritto, Mr. and Mrs. Butler (he was a brother of Lord Dunboyne), Mr. and Mrs. Montmorency, Sir William Massey Stanley, and many others. I was very hospitably entertained by Mr. Lyon, to whom I had letters, and who lived in the Place Vendôme. He was a relative of Lord Kilmaine's, and well known in Paris for his dinners. By him I was introduced to another gentleman, also well known in Paris—Mr. Wallace Greaves.

Lord Normanby was the Ambassador. The "paid attachés," as they were then called, were Mr. Edwardes—later Minister in Frankfort; Sir Augustus Paget, afterwards Ambassador at Rome and Vienna, and Mr.—later Sir William—Stuart, a brother of Lord Blantyre, who, after a very successful diplomatic career, died comparatively young.

Mr. Windsor Heneage was private secretary to the Ambassador. He was very agreeable and popular in society, to which he was much devoted. It is alleged that on one occasion, late in the morning, the Ambassador wished for the services of his private secretary, and that the servant found Mr. Heneage, on the staircase, returning from a fancy ball in the costume of a devil.

Shortly before that time a lady created a great sensation as an authoress. Her name was Madame Blaze de Bury. Her husband was a well-known writer in the *Revue des Deux Mondes*—if not the editor. Before the rising against Louis Philippe, Madame Blaze de Bury had written a novel called *Mildred Vernon*, in which she was supposed to have been assisted by Lord Brougham. It described the excesses of Parisian society, particularly at a ball given at the Opera, where a well-known lady appeared masked, and attracted universal attention by the skill with which she performed a popular dance of a very free description.

At length came the day when Louis Napoleon was proclaimed President. Sir Arthur Otway, Colonel Gordon-Cumming and I went to the review, piloted by an old soldier, then a celebrated bootmaker, who was a sergeant-major of the National Guard, named Mausse or Mause, who obtained places for us in the ranks of his

Lith.d'après nature par E. Desmaisons

# LOUIS NAPOLÉON BONAPARTE

né à Paris, le 20 Avril 1808

*Président de la République Française.*

Elu le 20 X$^{bre}$ 1848

*Louis Napoléon Bonaparte*

corps. We were provided with muskets, and there was nothing extraordinary in our plain clothes, as many of the National Guard themselves were without uniform.

It was a bright frosty morning, and all Paris seemed in high spirits. Bands were playing gay tunes, and, while waiting for the march past, many of the National Guard danced fantastic quadrilles, all evidently exhilarated by the termination of the struggle. At length the signal was given, and the Prince-President approached with his staff. My friends and I, who were in the front rank, presented arms when he passed. Thus I witnessed his official entry into France.

A foreign gentleman, who was in some business and knew Sir Arthur Otway, afterwards described the difficulty he had when meeting the excited crowds that moved about the streets. He said they were divided into two factions, one the Tricolor and the other the Red. He had therefore a double-breasted coat, on one side of which was the red cockade, on the other the tricolor, and when he had ascertained to which party any crowd that approached him belonged, he buttoned his coat so as to show the proper cockade. Thus he used to be cheered by the crowds on both sides.

An odd thing occurred at that time which I remember being related to me. A French gentleman, married to a very good-looking Englishwoman —he himself not being a man of very strong intellect—was met by a friend walking a long distance outside one of the gates of Paris. This friend asked him what he was doing in so out-of-the-way a place. He replied that he had come to buy some stamps at a little post-office there. His friend said, "Postage-stamps are the same all over the place. Why don't you buy them at an office near your own house?" The gentleman replied, "My wife says there are no stamps like these, and she will not use any others."

Later on I was presented to Napoleon III., when Emperor, at a ball at the Tuileries, and years later again I had an audience of him concerning a proposal for improving the communication between Dover and Calais. The audience was given me at the request of his early friend, Lord Malmesbury, to whom I had been private secretary when at the Foreign Office, and of Mr. Algernon Borthwick, both of whom supported the project. The Emperor was much interested, and invited me to return later to discuss the plan; but meanwhile other circumstances intervened. It was not long before the final catastrophe, and I never saw him again until 1870, immediately after Sedan. It was therefore my lot to see Napoleon III. first in exile; then on his official entry into France as President; next, in the height of his fortunes as Emperor; and last, at his final departure from France and his return as a prisoner into exile. Scarcely any one else, except those attached to him personally, can have witnessed all these events in his life.

# CHAPTER X

Holiday in Spain—Journey to Madrid—Bull-fight—Queen Isabella—
Spanish acquaintances—English friends in Spain—Spanish titles—
Funeral of the Prince of Asturias—Connection of Spain with the
East—Journey to England.

In 1850 I took my holiday by a journey to Spain.
I had heard so much of the charms of that country
from my friend Captain Wrottesley, and from the
family of Sir John Burgoyne, that I longed to go
and see it.

Certainly, it then possessed much of the romance
of the Spain of Gil Blas. My holiday was taken
during the month of May, and I travelled in company with a gentleman of both French and English
origin. Though the weather was occasionally hot,
it gave us the best part of Southern life.

We travelled on the *banquette* of a diligence,
there being no railway farther than Tours. The
diligence, which we mounted at the Rue Notre
Dame des Victoires, was driven to the railway
station. There the whole body in its three
compartments, and with all its passengers and
luggage, was swung by a crane from its wheels and
placed on a truck. On arriving at Tours, it was

again swung off and placed on wheels, on which it
remained as far as San Sebastian.

We stopped at about ten o'clock in the morning
at Chatelhérault, celebrated for its cutlery, and an
hour later the long line of poplars began that
led into Poitiers.   It is an avenue of a mile in
length, along a road cut out of the solid rock,
which, rugged and quarried, is seen overhanging
it.   Below the beautiful river Ain completes the
picture.   I long possessed a hat I bought there,
called in the slang of the day *démoc-soc*, as being
the favourite headwear of the Democratic and
Socialist party.   This was white, and later on I
found in Italy a hat of the same kind, but brown
in colour.   This also had a revolutionary name.
Brown, being the colour of the dress of the
religious orders, was called *color pazienza*.   It was
affected by the revolutionaries, as meaning that
they waited their time.

Bordeaux surprised me very much.   For some
reason I had always expected it to be a somewhat dirty seaside town.   I found it, though
not so large, superior to Paris, with wide streets,
splendid buildings, and lofty apartments.   The
friend who was travelling with me—he was a connection of Admiral Sir Harry Neill—here found
a friend or relative with whom we explored the
tower of St. Michel.   Under it is a vault, having,
as Théophile Gautier expresses it, "the property
of mummifying the corpses placed there."   My
friend was rather fond of good living, and had

spoken of the wonderful Bordeaux cookery, which he had not exaggerated. At Bordeaux, Spain begins to make its appearance. The signs of the shops are both Spanish and French, while the Basque costume and the dark brunettes seem more of the former than the latter nation. Certainly the old diligence-travelling made you better acquainted with the countries you visited than do the present railways.

Having crossed the frontier, we passed the Bay of Pasages, near San Sebastian, a beautiful piece of scenery, no longer to be seen from the train. At San Sebastian we made acquaintance with the Royal Alameda and public walk, and got down at the Parador Real, having seen—for we counted them—thirteen ladies in mantillas. Passing the *fonda*, through a stable, we ascended a fine though somewhat dirty staircase to the first floor of the house, where we found dark lofty rooms and long narrow passages. Though since then I have often been at San Sebastian, I never found this hotel again. It was very interesting—servants, gentlemen, priests and heretics sat at the same board, chaffing the pretty girl who waited. Dolores, the maid of the inn, was very brilliant in this respect : she laughed at my Spanish, boxed the young priest's ears, and gave several proofs of a lively disposition. Alas ! these days are gone. Everything was thoroughly Spanish, and now that seems to have nearly passed away.

The road from San Sebastian to Tolosa was very

beautiful. It is a pity that modern travel is so little picturesque. At Medina del Ebro our luggage was again examined, for, while free trade reigned in the Basque Provinces, strict protective duties were prevalent in Castile. Even at the present day there is a different system in the frontier provinces.

The inn at Madrid, to which we drove, has fallen from its position as the best hotel, though giving up some of its old peculiarities. It was called the Fonda Peninsulares, and still exists in the Calle de Alcala, near the Puerta del Sol. There we had our first view of the Calle de Alcala and an experience of a Madrid *café*. The Fonda Peninsulares was so built that the diligences drove under a high arch into an enclosed yard. A large staircase led up to the first floor, where the bedroom doors opened on a square gallery running round an open yard. The perfume of stables was redolent throughout the building.

One of our first visits was to a bull-fight, but, except on this holiday, when I saw several, I have never attended one. It was very gay and amusing, but has been so often described that little need be said about it. We saw two of the most famous bull-fighters of Spain. One was the celebrated Montes; the other, his nephew, José Redondo—known as the *chiclanero*, being a native of the city of Chiclana. Queen Isabella was rather fond of bull-fights, and this, no doubt, contributed to her great personal popularity. Some time before

our arrival, Montes had performed a feat unparalleled
even in his palmiest days, and Queen Isabella was
so delighted that she offered him whatever he might
require. Kneeling before the Royal canopy, he
begged Her Majesty to pardon one, more sinned
against than sinning, who was condemned to
execution. The prayer was granted, and the
rumour spread like wildfire among the spectators.
As in former years, they showered gold on the
generous bull-fighter. His cap was heavy with
these gifts, and, giving the whole amount to a
friend of the criminal, he said, " Give this to ——.
Tell him he will no longer want, and let him sin
no more."

On returning home, we saw in a large
open barouche, drawn by eight cream-coloured
Andalusian horses, Queen Isabella herself, accompanied by her *camarera mayor*. Behind them, in
another carriage, were the King Consort and his
father. Queen Isabella was always popular. She
had great charm of manner—geniality blended with
dignity. She was thoroughly adapted to the tastes
of the Spanish people, being generous and fond of
amusement, and many of the churches throughout
Spain still possess the diamond necklaces which
she bestowed on the pictures of the Virgin in the
Cathedral.

I made the acquaintance of Don Pascual de
Gayangos, one of the most celebrated literary men
of Spain. He was a great Arabic scholar, and, I
think, Professor of the University of Alcala. He

invited me to stay with him at his country-house, at a village called Pozuelo. Though the place was only six miles from Madrid, in those days the post only came to it twice a week. Here I enjoyed real Spanish life. Don Pascual had married an Englishwoman, and had one son and a daughter. The latter married Señor Riaño, a well-known writer and Director-General of Public Instruction. I met them later when in Spain; but Madame Riaño, I regret to say, died recently. Not far from Pozuelo was the *château* of Boadilla, which then belonged to the Countess of Chinchon, the daughter of Godoy. It was beautifully situated and well wooded. Later, at Florence, I made the acquaintance of the Marquis of Boadilla, Duke of Sueca, who married Miss Martellini, daughter of the lady who had long been confidential Lady of Honour to the Grand Duchess.

We used to make picnics to various places in the neighbourhood. The equivalent of "picnic" in Spanish seems to be *borricada*, which means to donkeys what a cavalcade means to horses.

At this time there was no British Legation at Madrid, no Minister having been sent after the expulsion of Sir Henry Bulwer. The Consulate was occupied by Mr. Brackenbury, of the well-known consular family, who was excessively amiable and serviceable. I also happened to know M. de Montherot, the first French Secretary, a nephew of M. de Lamartine, who had given me a letter for him. At his house I met the Baron de

Bourgoing, the French Ambassador. I was kept at Madrid, as I had undertaken to make some inquiries for Lord Howden, who had just been appointed Minister, and these took rather more time than I had anticipated. As I was going back to Paris, his carriage passed the *malle-poste* in which I was travelling. I had time, however, to see Aranjuez and the Escorial. There I made the acquaintance of one of the most celebrated writers and politicians of the day—Señor Alcala de Galiano. He had been Minister abroad as well as in Spain itself, and was a relative of that distinguished diplomatist, not long ago Ambassador in London, Count Casa Valencia. He showed us all that was worth seeing in the place, and gave us historical descriptions which were most interesting and full of information.

At Madrid, I met Mrs. Stopford, whose husband, Colonel Stopford, had held some office in Spain, and who kept an open and hospitable house. She was the mother of Lady Charles Beauclerk. There were also a few English gentlemen who had fought in the Carlist wars and selected their domicile in Spain. I made the acquaintance of Mr. O'Shea the banker, who had become almost a Spaniard. One of his daughters married the late Colonel Fane, and the other the late Mr. George Vaughan, who was so well known in London. His nephew, Mr. Robert Owen, commonly known as " Don Roberto," was exceedingly kind to us during our stay. Mr. O'Shea's son had married a lady possessing the title of Duchess of San Lucar, and he became, in consequence, the Duke of San Lucar.

In Spain, husbands and wives confer on each other their titles, that is to say, the Duchess of A. marries Count B., and on her cards she inscribes " Duchess of A., Countess B." The husband does the converse. Spanish titles go in direct descent, whether to sons or daughters, and many of the great names of Spain have descended through females, among others those of Alba and Medina Sidonia. Most Spanish grandees have several titles, and these they can confer on their sons and daughters, with the exception of the principal title. The result is that new great families are constantly created, as the wives confer their titles on their husbands, whether or not born noble. If the wife dies, the title goes to her son, and her husband is called the *Duque Biudo*, or the widowed Duke. Thus titles exist in great numbers in Spain. There are more than one hundred dukes, twelve hundred marquises, and twelve hundred counts. The titles which are less numerous are those of viscount and baron.

Some of the grandees have great plurality of titles and several grandeeships. The Duke of Alba's principal title is Duke of Berwick. The names of the late Duke combined, in an interesting manner, his two nationalities. His Christian names were Carlos Maria Stuart FitzJames Portocarrero Palafox Vintimiglia. To these he added, as titles inherited through women, the duchies of Alba di Tormes, of Liria, of Conde-Duque Olivarez and of Peñaranda. He had eleven marquisates, one of them with a grandeeship; fifteen countships, to three of which a grandeeship was annexed, one being the title of Count de Montijo, which he inherited from his mother, sister of the Empress of the French. His residence in Madrid is the Palacio Liria. The late Duchess made an interesting collection of archives and autograph MSS. of distinguished people. She was remarkably intelligent, and daughter of the Duke of Fernan-Nuñez.

The Dukes of Medina Coeli, who were Counts up to 1368, and have been Dukes since 1479, enjoy eight dukedoms, sixteen marquisates, two of them with grandeeships; twelve countships, to one of which a grandeeship is annexed; and three viscountcies.

The grandeeship has very peculiar qualities. An ordinary gentleman or a person with any minor title having a grandeeship takes precedence of dukes whose grandeeship is junior. The only exception is in the case of Court functionaries.

One event occurred during my stay at Madrid which was excessively interesting, namely, the funeral of the Prince of Asturias. Although he had been born dead, there he lay in the palace, on a four-post bed, embalmed and enclosed in a glass coffin. The guards of the palace lined the apartment, and priests in magnificent costumes stood near the body of the Royal infant. The child was a remarkably fine one and resembled his Royal mother.

It was with great regret that I left Madrid. which to me had been quite a new world, full of Oriental notions, where Arabic and Persian art seems to have been the foundation of decoration. In Persia, where I went subsequently, no wine is manufactured for sale except at Shiraz. When Persia was invaded by the Arabs, they took back with them to Morocco the grapes of that district. In Spain they wished to naturalise the new fruit, and this they did at a place they called Xeres, intended for Shiraz, there being no sound equivalent to "sh" in Spanish. There they cultivated the grape and made wine, which now returns to Europe as "sherry," that word being a paraphrase of Shiraz. Shiraz wine is very similar in taste to sherry.

I took leave of my friends one afternoon at the Café Suizo. Amongst others was a young Spanish gentleman who had been excessively amiable, and who spoke English with a certain fluency, having, however, only studied it from books. He said he would come to England. I asked him whether he intended to live at a hotel or to take lodgings. He replied, "It is my intention to take apartments in the most fashionable quarter of London — in Holl-born." I am sorry to say I have never seen him since.

At Bayonne I met Mr. William Eliot, an old friend of mine. He had been appointed attaché to the Legation, and was about to proceed to Madrid. I knew him very well in different parts of the world. The last time I saw him he came

to stay with me at Corfu.   In 1877, by the death
of his father and brother, he became Lord St.
Germans.

I have always regretted not going to see
Biarritz.   In those days it contained only one or
two small houses in a wild fishing village, and
was much frequented by the Countess Eugenie
de Montijo—subsequently Empress of the French
—and her mother.   Before I left Madrid, she was
expected from Andalusia, and among her party
was Major Andrew Cathcart, who, besides his
other good qualities, was much admired in Spain
for his riding.   From Madrid they rode on to
Biarritz.   I met Major Cathcart at Bayonne, and
subsequently in Paris.

# CHAPTER XI

I VERY well recollect the Exhibition of 1851. It was the most beautiful thing I ever saw, both from its delicacy and vastness. A large piece of Hyde Park had been put under glass, including some of the trees; and the glass and galleries were beautifully coloured by Mr. Owen Jones, whose acquaintance I made subsequently. There were naturally great crowds at the Exhibition, and foreigners came in large numbers, who gave their representatives a good deal of trouble. Questions used to arise as to the costume which should be worn on different occasions. One lady, not quite knowing how to dress for a Court function, wrote to her Ambassador, "*Comment doit-on s'habiller ce soir? Petite exposition, ou grande exposition?*"

That year I paid another visit to Lord and Lady Pollington, who were at Baden. There I renewed my acquaintance with Lord Augustus Loftus, who was Secretary to the Legation at Stuttgart, but was then detached to Baden, where he resided as chargé d'affaires. I also met Mr.

140

Douglas Irvine, who was in the Diplomatic Service, from which he retired in 1862. He died a few years afterwards.

At the end of 1851, Napoleon III. made his *coup d'état*, and the discussion between Lord Palmerston and Lord Normanby is well described in Mr. Evelyn Ashley's attractive *Life of Lord Palmerston*. The removal of the latter from office by Lord John Russell, his old friend, created great excitement throughout the country, and much sympathy was felt for him by all classes of society. This was manifested in a remarkable way socially. On February 9, 1852, a party was given by Lady Palmerston at her house in Carlton Gardens (now Mr. Balfour's). It was crowded. The *Times* headed the account with the words, "The Expelled Minister." The Duke of Wellington arrived early and stayed upwards of an hour. The Liberals naturally attended, and the Duchess of Bedford represented the Russell faction; but there was also a strong contingent of Conservatives, among others Lord Salisbury, the father of the late Prime Minister, Lord Douro, Lord Malmesbury, Lord and Lady Mahon, Lady Lyndhurst, and Mr. and Mrs. Disraeli. Mr. Gladstone and Mr. Sidney Herbert were also present.

During this period I used to see a great deal of Mrs. Gurwood and her daughters. She was the widow of Colonel Gurwood, the friend and confidant of the Duke of Wellington, whose despatches he had edited. Mrs. Gurwood was

French by birth, and had a daughter by a former husband, Miss Eugenie Meyer, who afterwards married Lord Esher.

My most remarkable acquaintance was Lola Montes, whose adventures were then universally discussed.  She had had a *liaison* with the old King of Bavaria, and had been created a Bavarian Countess by the title of Countess de Lansfeldt. The King's infatuation for this lady was the cause of a revolution, and actually of his abdication. He ordered her to leave the capital; but she only went a few miles out of Munich, and returned dressed as a man.  She was arrested, placed in a postchaise, and sent to Switzerland.  Thence she came to England.

The Countess was a very handsome woman, and being, I believe, English by birth, spoke the language perfectly.  At all events, her mother was English, and she herself had married an English officer, from whom she was divorced.  She took a house not far from my lodging in Half Moon Street, where she used to receive of an evening.  The society was very mixed.  There were several old friends of hers — prominent men of the world — and also some queer foreigners, evidently of a very Bohemian order.  She professed ultra-republican opinions, and was always quoting the language of a Mr. Hobbes, whom I never saw, but whose name was well known in all revolutionary circles, and who, I fancy, had been her adviser when in Munich.  The Countess's own opinions were those

of Mr. Hobbes, but she had little power of expressing them, and did so in a very superficial manner.
She had with her a very pretty little girl, whom
everybody believed to be her daughter, from the
great likeness between them. A short time ago
I saw in the papers the case of a *clairvoyante*,
who was brought before the police-courts, and
said to be the daughter of Lola Montes; but I
never had an opportunity of ascertaining whether
or not it was the same person. If it is the
little girl I used to know, she must now be about
sixty-five.

The cause of Lola Montes' leaving London was
also singular. She was very fond of dogs, and
had been struck by the beauty of one she had seen
in the Park, driving in the phaeton of Mr. Heald,
an officer of the Life Guards. She sent to the
owner a message by another officer, Captain
Edwin Burnaby, asking him to bring the dog
to see her. This he did, and within a week she
was married to him. His family then routed up
some story of her divorce not having been legal,
and she was therefore accused of bigamy. I do
not recollect the issue of the case, but not long
afterwards she left England, and I fancy she never
returned. Indeed, I have heard that she died in
America.

Many years later, I made the acquaintance of
another celebrated dancer, who was best known
as Mademoiselle Taglioni. I recollect seeing her
in my youth in the celebrated *pas de quatre*, which

consisted, I think, of herself, Cerito, Carlotta Grisi, and Fanny Elssler. This latter lady was well known at the time for her relations with the Duc de Reichstadt, the son and heir of Napoleon I., who had begun life with the title of King of Rome. Madame Taglioni, as she was called late in life, had married Comte Gilbert des Voisins ; but afterwards she fell into poorer circumstances, and gave dancing-lessons to young ladies in London.

In 1852, Lord John Russell's Government was defeated on a motion of Lord Palmerston's, and Lord Derby succeeded him, making Lord Malmesbury Secretary of State for Foreign Affairs. In that year, while I was sitting at my desk in the Foreign Office, a message came to me to go upstairs and see Lord Malmesbury. He informed me that I had been appointed attaché to Sir Henry Bulwer, recently named Minister at Florence.

At that time the English Government was very unpopular on the Continent. Rightly or wrongly, Lord Palmerston had been accused of undue interference in the affairs of other countries, and of stimulating revolutionary movements against constituted Governments, and these were especially annoyed at his having circulated, to the different British Missions abroad, Mr. Gladstone's pamphlet on the state of things in Naples. For these reasons, all despotic Governments seemed to have leagued against him. Tuscany was in the occupation of Austrian troops, under the command of Prince Friedrich Liechtenstein, a general officer of great distinction. The Tuscan Government in one case sheltered itself under Austrian protection, but Lord Palmerston refused to admit the interference of Austria in Tuscan affairs, and therefore on both sides there was a great deal of irritation.

Mr. Erskine Mather, an English gentleman, nineteen years of age—while listening to a regimental band, with a brother about three years younger—was struck by an Austrian officer with the flat side of his sword. On turning round to see who had thus assaulted him, he was cut down. Such was the substance of a communication made by Mr. Wawn, Member for South Shields, to Lord Granville. Complaint was made to Mr. Scarlett, chargé d'affaires. Mr. Charles Lever, who at that time lived at Florence, called on Mr. Mather in hospital and acted towards him in a very friendly manner. Lord Granville, then Secretary of State for Foreign Affairs, wrote urgently to Mr. Scarlett, and in one of his despatches the following passage occurs :—

I have to instruct you to state to the Tuscan Minister that Her Majesty's Government deeply regret the necessity of making repeated remonstrances to the Tuscan Government on the subject of the outrages and vexations to which British subjects in Tuscany are now exposed ; and you will point out to his Excellency that more complaints reach Her Majesty's Government of the misconduct of persons in authority towards British subjects from Tuscany than from all the other States in Europe.

It appears that Prince Liechtenstein received Mr. Scarlett's remonstrances in a most conciliatory spirit, yet he justified the act of his officer.

Lord Granville authorised the employment of a well-known advocate, Signor Salvagnoli, on behalf of Mr. Mather, as the Tuscan Government agreed to institute an enquiry. Lord Granville also wrote on the subject to Lord Westmorland, then Minister at Vienna. A long time elapsed, however, without any reparation being made to Mr. Mather. Meanwhile Marshal Radetsky, who commanded in Lombardy, approved the institution of an official enquiry, and this perpetual reference to Austrian authority aggravated the irritation in England. In fact, Prince Schwarzenberg, while expressing his regret, generally declined to enter into details such as compensation. The matter attracted the attention of Parliament, and meanwhile the British Government changed. Sir Henry Bulwer, who had been in America, was appointed Minister at Florence.

In his instructions to Sir Henry Bulwer, Lord Malmesbury desired him to make use of "firm but temperate language, carefully avoiding an irritating tone, but still not disguising that there is a limit beyond which forbearance on the part of Her Majesty's Government cannot be pushed; and least of all admitting in the case of Tuscany that the presence of an Austrian military force can justify or excuse the commission in Tuscany of wrong towards a British subject, or can exempt the Tuscan Government from the obligation to make redress.

For all acts done in Tuscany to the prejudice of British subjects the British Government must hold the Tuscan Government to be solely responsible."

Pending Sir Henry Bulwer's arrival, Mr. Barron, a Secretary of the Legation, became chargé d'affaires owing to the serious illness of Mr. Scarlett. Mr. Barron accepted the offer of the Tuscan Foreign Office to give compensation—not of £5000, as had been asked, but of 1000 francesconi (about £222)—and allowed the case to be mixed up with another which had nothing to do with the question. It appears from Mr. Scarlett's despatches that this sum was given as an act of generosity, and not as admitting the responsibility of the Tuscan Government. The Tuscan Foreign Office had, in fact, said that it was necessary " to repeat in the name of the Grand Ducal Government that the latter can in no case admit its responsibility for the acts of individuals who are not subject to its jurisdiction."

Sir Henry Bulwer was instructed on the 29th of May to insist on the principle of Tuscan responsibility being admitted, and he was told that, in case the Tuscan Government refused to accede to his demands, nothing would remain but for him to make arrangements for quitting the Grand Ducal Court.

Mr. Mather refused to receive any money compensation, and the Tuscan Government finally recognised its obligations to protect British subjects " in all those cases in which the ordinary tribunals cannot be applied to, including such as may arise during the present arrangement with Austria respecting the auxiliary troops of that Government stationed in the Tuscan territory."

Sir Henry Bulwer thus brought to a satisfactory conclusion his first negotiations with the Tuscan Government. There were others of a much more delicate character which he conducted to a successful close, as will be related hereafter, the settlement of which was due to the quality mentioned in a letter to him from the Duke of Casigliano :—

Votre lettre est empreinte de ce tact exquis des convenances qui vous caractérise.

# CHAPTER XII

AT Florence I found Sir Henry Bulwer residing at the Villa Salviati, out of the Porta San Gallo, afterwards the residence of Mario and Grisi, and I stayed at a hotel. I left this for a lodging in the Borgo SS. Apostoli, a house with enormous rooms, but very gloomy, where I established the Chancery. One day I heard, at a great distance in the building, cries in a man's voice, "*Sautez, mademoiselle, sautez!*" Asking the people of the house what this meant, I was told that a French professor of gymnastics resided there, and that he undertook to turn young ladies into young gentlemen. This was all I ever heard of the matter.

While at this lodging, I was afterwards told that I had viséd a passport which appeared in order, but which belonged to Mazzini under an assumed name.

On the arrival in Florence of Mr. Robert Lytton, later Earl of Lytton, I left these rooms, and together we took a small house in the Via Larga, now, I believe, called the Via Cavour.

149

My other colleague was Mr. Fenton, who had been both in Spain and America with Sir Henry Bulwer. He was a man of great but unostentatious merit, who refused considerable promotion, and continued to reside privately at the Hague, which had been his last post as Secretary of Legation. He has died quite recently.

There were many English and Russian ladies in Florence, who formed the principal part of society. Amongst the former were Lady Walpole and Lady Catherine Fleming. Lady Walpole was possessed of much humour as well as great learning. She was very fond of animals, and maintained a kind of hospital for invalid dogs. She herself possessed two Mexican greyhounds which appeared to have no hair. Her two daughters inherited her attractive qualities. One married the Duca del Balzo, of Naples, and the other Prince Palagonia, a Sicilian who lived at Naples also, having a considerable property there. She died young. Both Lady Walpole and Lady Catherine Fleming lived habitually in Florence, and one, if not both, died there.

Among the principal Russians was the Countess Bobrinska, a lady of great family, one of whose daughters married the Marchese Pucci. She used frequently to hold receptions. I also made the acquaintance of two very interesting sisters—Russian ladies from Odessa, named Kolontaiev. The elder was a Maid of Honour to one of the Grand Duchesses, and the other had great gifts as an artist in pastels. They had been sent to Italy at

Florence.

By Edward Lear.

the expense of the Imperial family, to enable this
lady to pursue her studies.    She afterwards married
Admiral Makouhine.    Years later I met her with
her husband at Sevastopol, where I stayed for a
few hours on my way from Batoum to Odessa.
The other married Count de Balmain, whose uncle
had been Russian Commissioner at St. Helena to
watch over Napoleon in his exile.    Strange to say,
this family is of Scotch origin, and their name is
Ramsay of Balmain.    I met this lady and her
husband again at Florence some years afterwards.
Later she devoted herself to religious and charitable pilgrimages to Jerusalem.

There are many Scotch names in the Russian
service.    I    recollect    meeting,    at    Philippopolis,
officers named Hamilton and Leslie.

The Italian lady at Florence who held the largest
receptions was the Countess Nencini.    She had
been a great friend of Napoleon I.    Her palace, the
Casa Nencini, had been designed by Raphael himself, and was beautifully proportioned.    Amongst
other ladies of very prominent position was the
Marchesa Ricci.    She was born Poniatowski, sister
to Prince Charles and Prince Joseph Poniatowski,
both very popular members of Florentine society.
They were great musicians.    Prince Charles sang,
and    his    brother    had    composed    some    operas.
Prince    Joseph    Poniatowski    was    Minister    for
Tuscany in Paris ; but during the Empire he was
naturalised a Frenchman, and became a member
of the Senate.    Madame Ricci was twice married.

Her first husband was Count Bentivoglio; they had one daughter, who married Count Walewski, and a son who was in French diplomacy, and much assisted in his career by his relationship to his sister. By Madame Ricci's second marriage she only had one daughter, who married the Marchese Tolomei, a member of the family of Pia de' Tolomei, mentioned by Dante.

The Marchesa Oldoini was a lady very much beloved. She had been, and still was, strikingly handsome. The most salient feature of her household was a beautiful daughter, then quite young, afterwards the celebrated Countess Castiglione, one of the great ladies of the Court of Napoleon III. I think she was the most beautiful woman I ever saw. A lady rather older, but who really rivalled the Countess Castiglione, was Countess Ferrari. Hers was not, however, a specimen of Italian beauty, for she was the daughter of Count Moltke, who had been Danish Minister at Florence. Her loveliness was entirely of the northern cast, and at entertainments and assemblies she used to look like a Scandinavian dream.

There were also Count and Countess Orsini, who occupied a very high place in Florentine society. She was *née* Orloff. The Duc de Talleyrand kept a very hospitable house. He was the nephew of Prince Talleyrand, and, I believe, the head of the family. He had been known in early life as the Duc de Dino. One of his great friends, who was also very hospitable, was Count Melianewsky.

As a proof of the sympathetic intimacy that existed in Florentine society, I will extract a short passage from a letter written to me by Mr. Lytton on the 18th of February, 1853, when I was away :—

Poor Melianewsky is dead. Died yesterday. He had been for some time, I believe, suffering great pain, the bone of the leg splintering in various places. Mortification ensued, and he died, I hear, quite quietly, leaving a large sum of money for the repose of his soul. Lady Cath [Lady Catherine Fleming] sat up with him all night, which, as his room, they say, was sickening from the smell of putrefaction, was really the part of a *sœur de charité*.

Among distinguished professional Italians, I knew very well Salvagnoli, an advocate and lawyer of extraordinary power. His career, though a great one, was checked by his strong Liberal views. The same may be said of Professor Zanetti, a remarkable surgeon and physician. Though taking no active part in politics, he had been identified with the Liberal cause, which impeded his professional advancement, owing to the prejudice of the retrograde party. He was afterwards sent for to attend Garibaldi.

Two of the most engaging persons in Florence were Gordigiani and his daughter. He was a celebrated composer of songs called *stornelli*, and was also of a peculiarly ready wit. His daughter, who afterwards married Count Fantoni, the head of an illustrious family, partook of many of her father's joyous characteristics.

A gentleman whom I knew well was the Marquis Gualterio. He was an author of great merit, a moderate and constitutional Liberal, who had recently written a book on the later political movements in Italy, entitled *Gli Ultimi Rivolgimenti*. His wife was a member of an old Piedmontese family, and his house was frequented by persons of all political colours, while he was looked upon as the representative of the moderate Liberals in Italy. In October 1853, after I had left Florence, M. Gualterio sent me a most interesting memorandum, which I still possess. In this he sketched out what he thought should be the ultimate organisation of Italy. The document was submitted to Lord Palmerston, who, I believe, paid a great deal of attention to it, though he merely acknowledged the receipt of the paper.

There were two or three especially interesting figures in Florentine society at that time. One was a gentleman commonly known as Piero Dini, then in an advanced stage of life, but universally popular. He was one of the most obliging men I ever came across, and had no enemies. The next was a very singular man called the Chevalier d'Arlens, by birth a Swiss of some property, who had been, I think, in the French army, and, after having lost his fortune, lived at Florence. He was a man of a most gloomy, mournful appearance, which I am told he had worn even at the height of his wealth and worldliness. The Duc de Talleyrand was a great friend of his; they pretty nearly lived together. It was very much the fashion to invite the Chevalier, though the world laughed at his enormous appetite.  One of his accomplishments was a little singing, and he occasionally composed a piece of music of mournful character.  Once I had not seen him for a long time, and asked him what he had been doing.  He replied that he had composed a song which had obtained some circulation.  The name, he told me with a strangely cavernous intonation, was "La Tombe."  This was most characteristic.

There was an Italian gentleman—whose name I will not mention, as it would be ill-natured to do so—who was of advanced age, and whose one desire was always to appear young.  For this purpose he had many wigs.  He would tell his friends one day that he intended to have his hair cut, and then put on a short wig which lengthened every day until the end of the month, when he again would say that he must have his hair cut.  Another trick of his was to ask his friends to an early breakfast, and receive them in his bedroom, saying that he had overslept himself.  This was to give authenticity to the wig.

A remarkable type found in those days at Florence was Mr. Kirkup.  He was much sought after, especially by English travellers, on account of his thorough knowledge of Italian art, being himself an artist.  He was very shrewd, and sometimes cutting in his observations.  Among other studies he had endeavoured to master the secret of the philosopher's stone.  He declared that one gentleman, who had been very poor and to whom he explained the process, had died rich, and he was convinced that this wealth had come from his knowledge of the secret. I recollect an English gentleman who was very intimate with Mr. Kirkup, and who had separated from his wife, writing to ask him, half in earnest and half in joke, to make a wax figure of the lady into which he might stick pins.

Mrs. Macdonnell lived in a beautiful house called the Casa Annalena. She had a large family, most of whom became very distinguished. One of her sons was the late Sir Hugh Macdonnell, Minister at different places. Late in life she married the Duc de Talleyrand. One of her daughters became Madame de las Marismas, a great lady of the Empress Eugenie's Court. I believe another married General Sir George Brown.

All the noble Florentine names still figured in society—the Strozzi, Frescobaldi, Antinori, Torrigiani, and Palagi. Amongst others who occasionally visited Florence were the Marquis and Marquise de Boissy. She had been a famous beauty when Countess Guiccioli, Lord Byron's great love.

Mrs. Somerville—so well known as a mathematician and astronomer—and her daughters lived in Florence, and were much in request. There was also Mr. T. Adolphus Trollope, whose daughter, though very young, was a universal favourite from her manners and intelligence. A very remarkable Englishman, who lived in a villa in the neighbourhood, but whom I did not know, was Walter Savage Landor.

Mr. and Mrs. Browning were also living at Florence, and there, I believe, their son was born. To Lady Normanby was attributed the saying, " Now there are not two incomprehensibles, but three incomprehensibles."

# CHAPTER XIII

ON my journey to Florence I had fallen in with
the Vicomte de Gabriac, who was going there as
chargé d'affaires of France, in the absence of the
Minister. The Minister came shortly afterwards;
I and my family were long intimate with him and
his wife — the Comte and Comtesse de Mont-
tessuy. She was a daughter of Prince Paul of
Würtemberg.

The German chargé d'affaires was Monsieur de
Reumont, a well-known historian. The Minister,
who lived at Rome, was Baron Usedom; his wife
was an English lady by birth, Miss Malcolm. Count
Villa Marina was Sardinian Minister; he afterwards
attended the Congress of Paris as Plenipotentiary.
The Spanish Minister, who only came rarely to
Florence, was Monsieur Curtois, one of whose
secretaries, Monsieur Conti, married a daughter
of Mrs. Macdonnell. Count Riario-Sforza was the

Neapolitan Minister; during his absence the Duke of Santo Paolo was in charge.

One of the most prominent diplomatists at Florence was Baron Hügel, the Austrian representative. His wife was a beautiful English lady, whose maiden name had been Farquharson. The Baron's position was very powerful, owing to the connection of the Grand Duke with the Austrian Imperial family, and still more so on account of the Austrian occupation. He had been, I believe, Secretary to Prince Metternich, and had travelled extensively in the East.

Near Florence, at the Villa San Donato, lived Prince Demidoff, a well-known Russian magnate, the husband of Princess Mathilde Bonaparte, daughter of King Jerome, and sister of Prince Napoleon, known otherwise as Plon-Plon. His house was filled with every kind of object of art, especially furniture; he had tables, chimney-pieces, and even steps made of slabs of malachite.

The principal Florentine officially was Signor Baldasseroni, the Prime Minister. He went but little into society. Next to him came the Duke of Casigliano, Minister for Foreign Affairs. He was the elder son of Prince Corsini, to whose title he ultimately succeeded, and a man of peculiar appearance, as he dressed oddly. In the evening he wore a light blue coat, called a Chamberlain's coat, covered with gilt buttons and with Grand Crosses so numerous that the ribbons had to be crossed on his breast. His brother, the Marchese de Lajaticho, also occupied a leading place in society, and they had a younger brother.

The Great Chamberlain was, if I recollect aright, the Marchese Ginori, who was also profusely decorated. I do not know whether or not he was actually the owner of the celebrated Ginori porcelain works; but his family, which was a very great one, had by some circumstances, of which I am ignorant, become the proprietors of that factory, which restored to them a portion of the fortune they had lost.

Amongst other Italians whom I knew were Prince and Princess Pio di Savoia, and their daughter, Marchesa Fransoni. Madame Fransoni was a most remarkable pianist, and people came from all quarters to hear her. Her husband was a nephew of Cardinal Fransoni. He was a man of much literary taste, and had written a very remarkable essay, comparing what he called the alphabets of music and of words. Like his father-in-law, he kept a most hospitable house in Florence. Another daughter of Prince and Princess Pio married Marchese Pitti, whose ancestor, the great architect, built the Palazzo Pitti.

I was also acquainted with Mr. and Mrs. Sloane, who had been formerly employed, one as tutor and the other as governess, by the family of Monsieur and Madame Boutourline, Russians of great mark. Having saved a little money, they married and bought some copper mines in a place called La Cava, which brought them enormous wealth.

They purchased Careggi, the well-known villa, where Lorenzo de' Medici was exhorted on his deathbed by Savonarola. The house contained a fine picture of the incident, painted by Watts. Mr. and Mrs. Sloane were fervent Roman Catholics. Both, I believe, were naturalised Tuscans, and there was some talk, at one time, of appointing him Tuscan Minister. Out of gratitude for the past, they left all their property to the family of Boutourline.

Mr. Charles Lever and his family lived at Florence at that time. He was a man of great wit, but was, at the same time, endowed with much deeper knowledge and feeling than would be gathered from his works.

An English lady, well known in Florentine society, astounded her friends by marrying the doctor of the police. On this subject, I recollect Lever saying, " Mrs. —— has made a most illustrious match. She has married the last of the Medici."

Amongst other residents at Florence—though I did not know him well personally—was Mr. Leader. He had been a foremost member of what were called the Philosophical Radicals, of which Sir William Molesworth was a leader, and Member, if I am not wrong, for Westminster. I have since then seen some letters of his relating stories of mistakes made in a foreign language. He told one of Sismondi, when travelling in England. It is here perhaps better to say that trunks in Italian are called *bauli,* pronounced in three syllables. Sismondi, staying with friends in Devonshire, was heard to call out, " Will you bring up my luggage and my small bowels ? " Mr. Leader was the author of a very interesting account of the old Venetian nobility.

Of course a great number of British travellers passed through Florence, amongst them Sir Henry Ponsonby, Private Secretary to Queen Victoria, whom I had known from the time we were children. A good many young Englishmen were travelling with their tutors. One was Sir Courtenay Honywood ; then came Lord Andover, and Mr. Amyas Poulett, whose mother and brother I had known for a long time. Lord Ebury, then Mr. Grosvenor, also arrived with his tutor ; he is the only survivor of these, all of whom I met subsequently at Naples.

Florence was very full, not only of strangers, but of Italians who came from other parts of Italy, and who contributed to the gaiety of the place. It was cheaper than other Italian capitals, and the society was most amusing on account of the large number of foreigners who lived there. About that time, however, its pleasures had been much diminished by the presence of the Austrian troops. All the Italian society was divided into two sections—one, the smallest, which approved of the appeal to Austria and represented the party known as the Codini (pig-tails) or retrogrades ; and the other, exactly the reverse. Some of the

latter were very strong Liberals, but all of them
had Liberal tendencies and resented the occupation. The result was constant friction. Italian
ladies would not dance with Austrian officers, and
quarrels were frequent.

Before this time society at Florence had been
as one large family. On fine nights in summer,
every one used to turn out on the Lung' Arno,
young men taking with them their guitars. Small
dances were suddenly organised, and the Grand
Duke and Duchess walked calmly up and down,
receiving the salutations of their subjects. All
this, however, had changed before my time, and it
was difficult to have a predilection for one person
more than another, for fear of being compromised
politically. Anything like a political discussion
was unknown.

As has been said before, the Commander-in-
Chief of the Austrian army of occupation was
Prince Friedrich Liechtenstein, a member of the
royal family of that principality, and a very high-
minded man, who endeavoured, as far as possible,
to diminish the friction between his army and the
Tuscan people.

At that time Guerrazzi was in prison, and his
trial went on during my stay, which was somewhat
broken by occasional absences. For two months,
however, I was left in sole charge of the Legation,
as Sir Henry Bulwer had been sent to Rome on
two very delicate questions. The principal one
was that of the resumption of diplomatic relations

with the Papal See.  This had been previously
discussed between Lord Minto and the Papal
authorities, and some hopes were entertained of
making it feasible to maintain regular diplomatic
relations with Rome.  This was especially desired
at that moment, as a complete change was looked
for in the whole aspect of Italy, owing to the
supposed Liberal tendencies of Pius IX., who had
just succeeded to the Papacy.  A Bill had been
introduced into Parliament to legitimise these
relations, and it was passed ; but a strong feeling
existed against the presence of a Roman ecclesiastic
as Papal Nuncio in England, and Lord Eglinton
had introduced into the Bill a clause prohibiting
any such appointment.   On this account, the Pope
refused to send any Minister, and also declined to
receive an envoy from England on a unilateral
footing.  This may be gathered from Mr. Evelyn
Ashley's *Life of Lord Palmerston*, in which the
following passage occurs:—

> The truth was that representations made to the Pope
> from Ireland induced him to imagine that we were in such
> a state in Ireland that we should be compelled to yield.
> When Lord Minto asked whether he would on his part
> receive as an English Minister one of our Archbishops, or
> the Moderator of the Church of Scotland, in full canonicals,
> he frankly owned that he would not.

Lord Palmerston was in favour of the Eglinton
clause, thinking that great embarrassments and
inconveniences would arise from a Roman priest,
invested with diplomatic privileges, holding his

court in London, surrounded by English and Irish
Catholics; but this clause proved fatal to the
success of the measure.

Up to that time, our business with the Papal
Government had been carried on in an informal
manner, a member of the Florence Legation, residing at Rome, having been received unofficially
by the statesmen of the Pope. This was Mr.
Petre, a Roman Catholic.

In October 1852 I received a letter from Mr.
Lytton, who was then at Rome with his uncle, in
which he said :—

I hear Florence is filling. Rome still very dull. Nobody
here, and the ruins quite a take-in. I spend the greater
part of my time in the studios, and am making a head of
Antinous which is to adorn our Florentine mansion.

I think it still very uncertain how much longer we may
remain here, but I hope to get away by the end of the
month. They are difficult people to deal with, and the
Government here is just like the household of the Great
Lama. One never gets to the Great Lama himself—such
an atmosphere of mystification—the difficulty of all negotiation being further increased by the fact that both Petre and
O——,[1] the only ostensible mediums of communication
with the Pontifical Government, are both Roman Catholics,
if not, as I suspect, Jesuits. Petre is an extraordinarily
well-read fellow, with a scholar-like and cultivated mind,
stored with a good deal of solid learning, and improves
on acquaintance. He is more than middle-aged and greyish.
O—— is a younger man, good-looking and clever; as full
of intrigue as an egg is of meat, and well versed in the
smaller arts of antechamber diplomacy. He has been in
Greece and the East, and it was he who got up the Greek

---

[1] A gentleman privately employed by Sir Henry Bulwer.

Question against Palmerston, having been very much *lié* with the Greek king, whom he calls "Otho." He is bold, ambitious, and active, full of plans and schemes—many of them wild, all of them clever. If you have ever read *Devereux*, and remember the Jesuit in that novel, you will be able to picture him when I say he is the type of that cleric. He professes a great fancy for me, and has told the Pope that I am on the eve of conversion!

Two other questions also occupied Sir Henry Bulwer's time—one was that of the Madiai, with which I shall deal later on, and the other the case of Mr. Murray, of which the following account was transcribed in the *Times* from the *Roman Journal*:—

"Edward Murray, born at Cephalonia, was brought by his father to Italy, and, after being engaged for some time in banking operations at Rome, he removed to Ancona where he resided ten years, and married Ursula Gabrieli, a native of Loretto.

"During the catastrophes of 1848 and 1849, he was appointed Inspector of Police at Ancona. The state of the population at that period is well known. According to the correspondence of Mr. Moore, the English Consul, with Sir George Hamilton (our Minister at Florence)—

"The greatest disorder prevails in the town, where an infuriated rabble publicly stab, killing right and left all those who chance to read the newspapers. These murders were perpetrated at the rate of three per day. Many of the assassins were well known; but nobody dared to arrest them, the police and national guards refusing to act.

"In a letter to Lord Palmerston, dated April 22, 1849, Sir George Hamilton calculated at from six to eight the daily number of victims, which on the previous Sunday amounted to ten.

"A few days afterwards, an English ship of war having arrived to protect the English Consul, who appeared to be menaced, the Governor caused several of the murderers to be arrested on the night of the 27th of April. Amongst them was Murray.

"To-day these facts are overlooked. Pity is expressed, not for the victims of terror, but for Murray who abetted it. His case has been brought before one of the Parliaments of Europe, and, accepting as true the assertion of a public newspaper, it was alleged that pontifical tribunals were slow and accessible to corruption."

This case was subsequently satisfactorily settled.

I recollect meeting some of Murray's relatives later in the Ionian Islands, but I forget the nature of their business with me.

About this time, Sir Digby Wyatt and Mr. Owen Jones arrived at Florence on some artistic mission connected with the Exhibition of 1851. They were well received by the Tuscan authorities.

Meanwhile my own labours were very limited. I had a little discussion with the Tuscan Government concerning the duty on English beer, on which I received a note from Sir Henry Bulwer at Rome :—

I have looked into the great Beer case, and enclose you a note which you can address to the Duke of Casigliano in my name. The note will be, in the first instance, semi-official.

Sir Henry Bulwer was, as ever, very busy, not only about the points he had to treat, but in obtaining valuable information from various sources.

# CHAPTER XIV

THE third case with which Sir Henry Bulwer had
to deal was that of the Madiai.

On the 17th of August 1851, an English gentleman named Walker was arrested. I knew him
well. He had retired from the Army. His family
had lived a great deal in Italy, two of his sisters
having married Italians, Count Baldelli and Marquis Incontri. Another sister married Captain
Fleetwood Wilson, and was the mother of Sir
Guy Fleetwood Wilson, now Under-Secretary at
the War Office. I still recollect so well seeing
Mrs. Fleetwood Wilson, a lady of great attractions,
walking down the hill out of Florence, with her
two children in baskets on a pony. She has only
quite recently died in London.

Captain Walker was a man of strongly pronounced religious tendencies, who occupied himself
a great deal with the Protestant movement. He
was arrested while visiting the Madiai, a man and

his wife who had been courier and maid in English families. An Italian Bible and other books were afterwards removed by the police from the table where the party had been sitting, and a small Bible, which Captain Walker always carried with him, was taken from his pocket. The Madiai were also arrested.

The police accused Captain Walker of reading and expounding the Protestant version of the Bible to Tuscan Roman Catholics, and of attempting to proselytise. In spite of his assertion that he was an Englishman, and innocent, he was hurried off to prison. Captain Fleetwood Wilson addressed himself at once to the police authorities, who, however, refused at first to allow him to see Captain Walker; but through the intervention of Mr. Bligh, the attaché, who had been instructed to intervene in the matter by Mr. Scarlett—then at Pisa—Captain Walker was liberated, though not till he had been kept for twenty-one hours in the cell of a common prison.

The two Madiai were convicted under a law of 1786 on the grounds of proselytism. The husband was condemned to fifty-six months' reclusion in the House of Forced Labour at Volterra, and the wife to forty-six months' imprisonment in the Ergastolo. An appeal was, however, made to the Courts of Tuscany.

This case excited a great deal of interest. During the period when I was alone in Florence, a deputation arrived, consisting of Lord Roden,

Lord Cavan and Captain Trotter, accompanied by some leading Swiss Protestants and delegates from France, Holland, Würtemberg and Prussia. On the 27th of October, Lord Malmesbury instructed Sir Henry Bulwer to repair to Florence—all fear of capital punishment being executed on Murray having been removed—in order to give this deputation, unofficially, every assistance, and to use all the means in his power to procure for them an audience of the Grand Duke. This was, however, refused.

At the time of Sir Henry Bulwer's arrival, the Prussian Minister at Rome, Baron Usedom, also accredited to Florence, came there, not avowedly but in reality, to do what could be done in the case of the Madiai. The Baron did not, however, mention the subject in his interview with the Grand Duke, but wrote a letter to the Duke of Casigliano stating the great interest his Sovereign and nation took in the affair. Count Arnim, Grand Seneschal at the Court of Prussia, brought an autograph communication from his Sovereign to the Grand Duke, pleading in favour of the unfortunate persons in confinement; but both the answer of the Duke of Casigliano to Baron Usedom, and that of the Grand Duke to Count Arnim, expressed the same sentiment—namely, that the Tuscan Sovereign requested to be left at liberty to act in a case relative to his own subjects, under the laws of his own nation, according to his own free will and conscience.

On the 12th of November 1851, a letter on the subject had been addressed to Lord Palmerston by General Sir Henry Cumming, the two Madiai having been in the service of his family for a long time. Rosa Madiai had been with them for seventeen years, and had been very attentive to his son - in - law, who was attaché at Florence, during his last illness; she had also been in the service of Lady Caroline Townley, and many others. Lord Palmerston took up the case very warmly, and addressed a despatch on the subject to Mr. Scarlett on the 17th of November 1851, only a few days before his leaving office. Several English Corporations addressed petitions to the Grand Duke; but these the Duke of Casigliano refused to receive, and both he and M. Baldasseroni informed Sir Henry Bulwer that further demonstrations in favour of the Madiai would only frustrate their own endeavours. About that time the Grand Duchess had a child, and many prisoners received the royal clemency, but this was not extended to the Madiai.

In the midst of all these disputes, the following story was told of the Grand Duke of Tuscany. When he was driving through the streets of Lucca, a tradesman threw something out of the window into the Grand Duke's carriage. In a great fright, he ran down to implore for pardon. His Highness replied : "Never mind. It is lucky that it was not an Englishman; otherwise, by this time, I should have had all the British Legation on my back."

In January 1853, Lord John Russell acceded to power. A report was circulated that Francesco Madiai had died, in consequence of the hardships he had undergone, and the *Times* published two indignant leading articles on the subject. The statement proved to be incorrect, though it was true that the unfortunate man had suffered severely both in mind and body. On the 18th of the same month, Lord John Russell sent Sir Henry Bulwer an emphatic despatch on the subject, a part of which I quote :—

According to the last accounts received from you, the Grand Duke of Tuscany still hesitates on the subject of the Madiai. But this is a matter on which hesitation implies capital punishment. It is the same thing, in effect, to condemn a man to trial by fire, like Savonarola, or to put him to death by the slow torture of an unhealthy prison. It seems to be imagined, indeed, by some Governments on the Continent, that, if they avoid the spectacle of an execution on the scaffold, they will escape the odium to themselves, and the sympathy for their victims, which attends upon the punishment of death for offences of a political or religious character. But this is an error. It is now well understood that the wasting of the body, the sinking of the spirits, the weakening of the mind, are but additions to the capital punishment which long and close confinement too often involves.

If therefore, as has been lately reported, one of the Madiai were to die in prison, the Grand Duke must expect that throughout Europe he will be considered as having put a human being to death for being a Protestant.

It will be said, no doubt, that the offence of Francesco Madiai was not that of being a Protestant, but that of endeavouring to seduce others from the Roman Catholic faith ; that the Tuscan Government had the most merciful intentions . . . that such offences cannot be permitted to pass unpunished. But this . . . will avail very little. Throughout the civilised world, the example of religious persecution will excite abhorrence. . . .

You are therefore instructed to speak in the most serious tone to the Minister of Foreign Affairs, and to lay before him all the considerations stated in this despatch. You will do it in the most friendly tone, and take care to assure the Government to which you are accredited, that none are more sincere in their wishes for the independence and happiness of Tuscany than the Queen of Great Britain. . . .

Sir Henry Bulwer, therefore, once more pressed the question, and in so skilful a manner that M. Baldasseroni thought it advisable to submit the matter again to the Grand Duke. At the moment, however, Sir Henry Bulwer was forced to leave Florence on account of his health, and Mr. Erskine, Secretary of Legation at Turin, was named chargé d'affaires. On the 16th of March the Madiai were hurried, with the greatest secrecy, on board a vessel at Leghorn, and at Marseilles they were set free, on condition of their never returning to Tuscany.

During the rather hard work entailed by the Madiai case, Charles Lever frequently called. On one occasion he was left in the waiting-room for some time, and occupied himself in writing a parody on Hood's " Song of the Shirt." It ran like this :—

> Scratch, scratch, scratch,
> Scratch for ever and aye,
> I shall never be done with this d—d despatch
> In the case of the Madiai.

> To think that bread should be so dear
> And flesh and blood so cheap,

was altered by Lever as follows :—

> To think that pen and ink's so cheap
> And brandy and water so dear!

Among the many people who took a great interest in the Madiai case were Mr. and Mrs. Edmund Phipps. He was the brother of Lord Normanby, and a man of very devout views. He came with his wife to spend some little time in Florence, bringing their son, Constantine, who since then has occupied several important posts in the Diplomatic Service, and has now retired.

At Florence I also made the acquaintance of Sir James Hudson, our very distinguished Minister at Turin—a man lovable in every way, of great charm of manner and good-nature. He was a strong Liberal, and to him Italy was largely indebted for her ultimate liberation.

I was told by the late Sir James Lacaita that Sir James Hudson lived on the most intimate terms with Count Cavour, and, in the Italian manner, called him by his Christian name. On one occasion, though unfortunately I cannot remember which, Cavour was hesitating as to the course he should pursue, and Sir James Hudson said to him, "*Dunque hai paura, Camillo?*" This decided the forward course adopted by Cavour, which ended in remarkable success.

After leaving Florence officially, I frequently

went to Italy to visit some relatives, and therefore felt familiar with the whole country. When passing Turin, I constantly saw Sir James Hudson, with whom later on I had considerable correspondence while I resided at Corfu. In fact, the annexation of the Ionian Islands to Greece was closely connected with the liberation of Italy.

My constant private visits to Florence have very much mixed up my personal chronology as to that country.

Subsequent to the time when Mr. Erskine was temporarily in charge, Mr. Scarlett returned; but after some time Lord Normanby, who had been Ambassador at Paris, was appointed Minister. Lord Normanby had resided a great deal at Florence during his youth. A villa which he had formerly occupied was known as the Villa Normanby, or, as it was sometimes called by the peasants, "Lorbambi," and he looked forward with great pleasure to revisiting the favourite resort of his younger days. He and Lady Normanby were much liked in Florentine society; but, after his differences with Lord Palmerston, he seemed rather to veer from his early Liberalism, and gave strong support to the Grand Ducal policy.

A Club had been formed at Florence, of which I was an original member, and Lord Normanby, on his arrival, was made President. A young gentleman of a family with whom Lord Normanby was friendly came to Florence, and passed a great deal of time at the Club, where he lost money at cards.  Lord Normanby, out of good-nature towards him, and out of friendliness to his family, wrote a letter to the relatives advising them to induce the young man to leave the place, "as he was always being robbed at the Club."  This letter was forwarded to the young gentleman, and was fastened by him to the fireplace for every one to read.  The incident, to a certain extent, detracted from Lord Normanby's popularity.  He remained at Florence from December 1854 until March 1858, when he was recalled, on the accession of Lord Derby to power.  I believe it was considered impossible, considering the active part he had taken in English Liberal politics, for him to remain in an inferior capacity under a party to which he had long been hostile.

Mr. Scarlett, who for a long time had been in Tuscany as Secretary of Legation, frequently acting as chargé d'affaires, was appointed Minister to Brazil, and later came back to Florence in that capacity.

# CHAPTER XV

IT may be as well for me to say a few words concerning Sir Henry Bulwer. He was a very kind man, full of *douceur*—an expression of which he was fond. He had a curious mania for having more than one place of residence in the same town, and also for appointing private secretaries. These gentlemen he frequently employed instead of his regular official subordinates, which often gave rise to annoyance. He told me that he really did so from good-nature, not liking to trouble his official secretaries with work, which with him was constant. One reason for this was his untidiness about papers, which were always being lost, and his constant corrections and re-corrections of his manuscript despatches. Odd stories were told of him.

It was said that once, when he had engaged a new secretary, he introduced him privately to some friends, saying to them that he was a most accomplished man and very able, but adding confidentially that it was desirable, when he came to the house, not to leave any small change lying about. I do not believe in the truth of this story, but it used to be cited as an instance of Sir Henry Bulwer's eccentricity. There is no doubt that he was a most remarkable man, very popular with his friends, and unpopular only with people who made no allowance for eccentricity. There was a party for and a party against him everywhere. He passed a most brilliant career, and was much in the confidence of Lord Palmerston, by whom he had been sent to his first important post—that of Minister to the Queen of Spain. Before that he had been to Berlin, Vienna, the Hague, Paris and Brussels, and he was Secretary of Embassy at one time at the Porte. While there, owing to some difference of opinion with the Ambassador, it was said that he refused to reside at the Embassy, and lived in a tent which he pitched in the neighbourhood. In America he was most successful, and concluded the well-known Clayton-Bulwer Treaty. It was currently reported that he signed that Treaty with the American plenipotentiary, smoking a cigar and over a glass of punch. Florence was too small a place for his active abilities. Consequently in 1855 he was pensioned. He did not long remain unemployed, but in 1856 was appointed Commissioner under the 23rd Article of the Treaty of Paris to investigate the state of the Principalities, and to propose a basis for their organisation.

When Sir Henry Bulwer was at Bucarest, an extraordinary political event occurred with regard to Moldavia and Wallachia. The object of the Commission was to create two separate States, for each of which a constitution was laid down. Although the people of the two Principalities wished very much to be united, the tendency of the Congress of Paris had been to keep them apart. It had also been decided that the people were to elect their own Prince. In doing so, they frustrated the views of all Europe, as by some private and secret understanding both principalities elected the same candidate, Colonel Couza, henceforward called Prince Couza. The two Principalities together now take the name of the kingdom of Roumania.

The instructions given to Sir Henry Bulwer as Commissioner by Lord Clarendon are interesting, showing, as they do, the divergences existing between the different Powers that signed the Treaty of Paris. Austria and the Porte were vehemently opposed to the union of the Provinces, which France, on the other hand, as strongly supported; while Russia was known to be favourable, and expressed a desire to defer to the wishes of the inhabitants.

It had been a matter of discussion whether Prussia and Sardinia should be represented on this Commission. The interests of those Powers in the questions to be discussed were remote, and Lord Palmerston's Cabinet considered that advantage would have resulted from their not taking part, as the chances of a divergence of opinion would have proportionately diminished; but the Prussian

The Sweet Waters of Asia.

Government expressed an earnest desire to be represented, and the Sardinian Government did the same.

In 1858, Sir Henry Bulwer was appointed Ambassador at Constantinople. There I paid him a visit in 1864, when I was introduced to Prince Couza, who had come to pay his respects to the Sultan, and was then living in a palace lent to him at the Sweet Waters of Asia. This is rather anticipating matters, but I claim the right of anachronism.

Most of the stories about Sir Henry Bulwer were, no doubt, invented, but I myself, when at Constantinople, was witness to one remarkable choice of a secretary. I found with the Ambassador an old Irishman, considerably over seventy, whom he had known in Paris in opulent circumstances. When this poor man was ruined, Sir Henry Bulwer, as a last resort, offered to make him his secretary, and he came to Constantinople, where he was very much out of water. He consulted me what should be done. "You know," he said, "that Sir Henry Bulwer is kind enough to make me his secretary. I have been here for some time, but I do not recollect that he has ever employed me. Oh yes," he added, "he did once. He asked me to direct some *anvelopes*."

Another incident illustrative of Sir Henry Bulwer's peculiarities was his purchase of an island called Plati, in the Sea of Marmora. He thought it might be developed into an enormous market-garden, and here he also intended to breed those large white donkeys, which are especially used, I think, by Armenians. Some are of great height, standing as high as ponies, and costing often two hundred pounds. This part of his project did not succeed, as one day a special boat was sent to tell him that the donkeys had created the most terrible ravages, pulling down the fences and destroying the shrubs. I believe that he subsequently sold the island to the Khedive.

I merely mention these peculiarities to prove the utter hollowness of the bitter opposition shown to him by some inferior minds. Sir Henry Bulwer, in addition to his great abilities, was a man of the most obliging nature and affectionate disposition, and wished to do well for every one. I have found as regards other distinguished diplomatists that there has always been a clique to run them down. Such was the case with Lord Stratford and Sir James Hudson, as well as Sir Henry Bulwer. I do not believe anything more serious than such eccentricities as I have mentioned could be alleged against him, but I well recollect the bitterness with which he was assailed.

When Sir Henry Bulwer was first appointed Ambassador at Constantinople, it was decided that Lord Stratford, who had so long been Ambassador there, should return on a special mission to deliver his letters of recall. Though outwardly on good terms, it was generally known that great irritation existed between them.

One Sunday the two Ambassadors went to church, and sat in the same pew. The chaplain—not a man of remarkable tact—thought he would reconcile them from the pulpit, and took for his text 2 Cor. v. 10, "We are ambassadors . . ." and proceeded as follows :—

There are heavenly ambassadors and earthly ambassadors, and the earthly ambassadors are divided into classes. There are ambassadors ordinary and ambassadors extra-ordinary. There are ministers and there are chargés d'affaires. If any of you who are now listening to me belong to those categories, let me recommend you earnestly, as a heavenly ambassador, to live at peace one with the other.

No doubt the clergyman's recommendations were fully appreciated by the two earthly Ambassadors.

This reminds me of a story of a former Ambassador at Constantinople, Lord Ponsonby. He was once sent to some distant post on board a ship commanded by a naval officer called Phillimore. On one occasion they entered on some discussion, in which Lord Ponsonby obtained rather the best of the argument. Captain Phillimore thereupon put the Ambassador under arrest.

This Captain Phillimore was well known for the extraordinary nature of his correspondence. In his time it was the custom for Lords of the Admiralty, when writing despatches to commanders of ships at vast distances, to sign themselves "Your affectionate friends." It was considered a kindness to show friendliness towards them, and to show they were not forgotten. When

Captain Phillimore obtained command of a ship, he answered a despatch from the Lords of the Admiralty, signing himself "Your affectionate friend." The Admiralty did not quite appreciate this, and sent a despatch saying that, though the Lords of the Admiralty wrote in this manner to a captain at a distance from home, it was not considered necessary for the captain to answer with the same formula. To this Captain Phillimore replied:

I have received your Lordships' despatch, and can assure you that I will never again sign myself—Your affectionate friend, Phillimore.

Sir Henry Bulwer's conversation was not only agreeable but very instructive. He was continually quoting aphorisms, and once gave me a collection of maxims, written by himself, which I published some years ago as an article in the *Nineteenth Century*. Lamenting his age, he used to say it reminded him of the Duc de Richelieu, who, on being told by a lady that he was not really old, replied, "I know that I am old, for there is one certain sign of it. When I was young, if I paid a compliment to a lady, she took it for a declaration. Now, if I make a declaration, she takes it for a compliment."

In 1870, when travelling abroad, I received at Vienna a message from Sir Henry Bulwer that he was at Trieste, staying with Charles Lever, whom we had both known so well at Florence. I went to see him. He was on his way to Egypt for his health, and died on his journey home, I think at Naples.

Mr. Robert Lytton, who afterwards obtained such distinction as poet under the name of "Owen Meredith," as Ambassador, and as Viceroy of India, was the nephew of Sir Henry Bulwer, and son of Sir Edward Lytton, the well-known novelist, orator and statesman, whose friendship I also enjoyed, thanks to my acquaintance with his brother and son. By the way, I recollect hearing Sir Robert Peel, in the House of Commons, characterise Sir Edward Lytton and Mr. Disraeli as "two fashionable novelists."

Through life, Robert Lytton and I were very intimate. He was best man at my wedding, and I was trustee to his marriage settlement, and had a considerable amount of business in connection with the details of his marriage.

Mr. Lytton proved by his subsequent life that eminent merit and ability which were universally recognised. He had the same affectionate disposition as the rest of his family, and, in addition, an extraordinary plasticity of accomplishment. I have seen him at work on philosophical instruments and on toys. He was equally capable of modelling a piece of sculpture and of constructing a fire-balloon.

He was a great favourite with Lord Beaconsfield, and also with Lord Salisbury. As I shall not return to his Indian career, it will perhaps not be out of place here to introduce an interesting

letter he wrote to me in October 1879, relative to
the Afghan War :—

I am extremely grateful for your very kind and considerate
letter written after your visit to Hughenden.  It is, of course,
an immense comfort and support to me to feel that I have
the continued confidence of the Chief in this new and very
trying phase of our Afghan difficulties.  I feel most keenly
the cruel position in which the Ministry is placed by so
wholly unexpected and unmerited a blow.  And you may
be sure that my utmost endeavours will be directed, as they
have hitherto been, to *strengthen* the hands of the Prime
Minister, and enable him to meet Parliament in the strongest
position on this question that is compatible with due regard
to those paramount national interests which are systematic-
ally ignored by a thoroughly unscrupulous Opposition.  I
am persuaded that a sacrifice of those interests would not
really strengthen the present position or future reputation
of the Government, and the task now before us is full of
difficulties.  I am not yet in a position to indicate any
definite course of action.  Such a course, to be safe and
sound, must be guided by a much fuller knowledge than
we yet possess of the circumstances of the massacres, and
the present condition of the Afghan Provinces ; but, whatever it may ultimately be, I feel confident that the final
result of it will be an accession of strength to the Empire
and of credit to Her Majesty's Government.  " Thy servant
slew the lion and the bear, and who is this uncircumcised
Philistine that he should fear *him* ? "

As soon as I am able to see my way more clearly to a
practical solution of the problem, I will gratefully avail myself
of your friendly offer, and furnish you with a full and early
explanation of all my plans and proposals, and all the facts
in reference to which they are formed.

Nothing that has occurred shakes my faith in the sound-
ness of the policy which resulted in the Gundamak Treaty.
In my mind the aims and principles of that policy remain
not only unchanged but confirmed by all that has happened ;
though I recognise the necessity of a considerable change in

some of its methods. It is no longer possible to leave independent of our supervision and control the internal administration of any Afghan Government whose existence is dependent on our support, and, in the present condition of the country, no stable Afghan Government could exist *without* our support. Abuses must be reformed and grievances redressed with a strong hand. The people will welcome any authority that does this for them. I mean the real people—not the scoundrelism just now collected at Kabul. And to any future arrangement, of a formal or permanent character, the Sirdars must certainly be interested and recognised parties, in accordance with the policy which has answered so well in Beluchistan.

Afghanistan has at all times been a thoroughly artificial political unit. The natural tendency to disintegration is now so strong that I think it cannot be wisely disregarded or opposed; but the control of it is in our hands. I was always persuaded—and this I told the Ameer—that the Treaty of Gundamak was the last chance left for the integrity of the Afghan Kingdom. Meanwhile the value of the new frontier secured by that Treaty has been conspicuously proved by the rapidity with which, I trust, we shall have occupied ¡Kabul before this letter reaches you, notwithstanding the desperate defence of the city which is going on while I write, and also by the ease with which we have already reoccupied Kandahar, where our return is welcomed, as that of a deliverer, by the whole population of Western Afghanistan. The Ameer, his Sirdars and Ministers, the Herati Colonels and the Kabul people, were all convinced that it would be impossible for us to move forward in any force before the spring of next year; and they have been quite bewildered by the failure of this calculation, on which they had made all their plans. But had the crisis found us confined to our old frontier, the calculation would have been perfectly correct.

I will take the earliest practical opportunity of writing to you fully on the whole situation; and meanwhile believe me, my dear Wolff, with renewed thanks for your kind and encouraging letter—Yours very sincerely,     LYTTON.

*P.S.*—I trust you left Lord Beaconsfield in good health. Were he only twenty years younger I should feel much greater confidence than I do now in the destinies not only of the Government but of the country.

A Bengalee paper said of Sir George Campbell, M.P., " He thought himself the Cactus Grandiflora of Bengal, and flouted the native gentlemen with contumelious lip; but the House of Commons soon stripped him to rags and tatters, and exposed his *cui bono* in all its naked hideousness."

Pray remember me to Lady Wolff. L.

In 1891, when on my way to Bucarest where I was Minister for a short time, I stayed in Paris in order to see Lord Lytton. I had been ill for many months, and had been obliged to leave Persia. From a hotel in the Faubourg St. Honoré, where I was staying, I sent to ask when I could see the Ambassador. I was told that he was not well, and I was obliged to go on my journey. The next day I heard that he had died suddenly while writing.

When living in Florence I became engaged, and we were married very quietly at the Consulate at Leghorn. My best man, as I said before, was Mr. Lytton. Sir Henry Bulwer gave away the bride, and her bridesmaids were the two daughters of Lady Walpole, Miss Du Boulay, and an Italian lady. From Leghorn we went to Lucca for a few days, and thence to Carrara. Nothing can be more beautiful than its marble quarries: they are at the top of a mountain. The road leading there is on the border of a clear, rapid stream, and strewn with fragments of white marble dropped

Adeline Walff

from the carts that carry it down to the sea. We ascended this road on donkeys.

There was little to see at Carrara, except an opera-house made of marble, where there was a company of great merit. We stayed there with the British Consul, Mr. Walton, a kind and hospitable gentleman, full of good feeling and intelligence. His one peculiarity was that, though between sixty and seventy, he was always dwelling on the sad fact that he was an orphan. Whenever we said anything in admiration of his attachment to some relatives in England, he used to answer, " We are all orphans."

On returning from Carrara, we stayed for a few days at the villa of Mr. Spence, one of the " lions " of Florence. He was a painter, an excellent companion, and a man of great humour. He had been married to an Italian lady, who had died, and his house and children were governed by his sister-in-law.

After this visit we took boat at Leghorn, and proceeded to Naples, where we remained for some time.

# CHAPTER XVI

AT Naples we found a most agreeable and interesting society.  Sir William Temple, brother of
Lord Palmerston—to whom the latter was much
attached—was Minister, and maintained the credit
of his country with great dignity.  His position
was a very difficult one in consequence of the
differences between Lord Palmerston and the
various absolute Governments, and on account of
the opposition of England to the oppressive policy
of the King of Naples, known as Bomba.  Sir
William Temple was very different from his brother.
With all his *bonhomie,* he had a manner quite the
contrary of Lord Palmerston's.  He was very
quiet—almost shy—and from a long diplomatic
career had learnt to moderate the expression of
his political feeling.  He was, however, much liked
at Naples by the great mass of the people, though
some were afraid to consort with him, knowing
that he was looked upon with disfavour by the
Neapolitan Court.

Besides  the  Minister,  the  British  Legation

consisted of Mr. William Lowther as Secretary, the
father of the present Speaker; Mr. Clare Ford,
whom I had known in London, and who was
subsequently Ambassador at Madrid, Constantinople, and Rome; and Mr. Fagan, who had
long lived in Italy, and whose mother was an
Italian.   In consequence of this, and the fact that
he spoke the language like a native, he was mis-
trusted by the authorities, and the following curious
incident occurred.   I quote from a newspaper of
the day :—

A few evenings since Mr. Fagan, First Attaché to the
British Legation at Naples, was charged by his Minister
with a commission to Prince Satriano, the Superintendent
of Theatres.   To execute it he was obliged to go to the Teatro
del Fondo, the commission being simply to request a benefit
for Signora Paressa, an English lady now singing in Naples.
On his entering the Prince's box, the Director (Minister)
of Police, who was opposite, began to make signs of the
greatest anger and the most menacing gesticulations in that
direction, to the great astonishment of Prince Satriano, who
was unable to divine the reason of it.   On the following day
the Director sent for Signor Attanasio, one of the employés
of the Superintendenza, and, heaping the lowest insults on
Prince Satriano for having received such a man as Signor
Fagan, who was stigmatised as a *birbante assassino,* and an
enemy of the King, ordered him to inform the Prince that
he prohibited him from ever again receiving Mr. Fagan in
his box.

Another attaché to the Legation was Mr.
Fletcher Norton, son of Mrs. Norton, the
authoress, poetess, and beauty, who was a sister
of the Duchess of Somerset and Lady Dufferin.
Mrs. Norton herself was in Naples, during the

greater part of our stay, with her son Brinsley. M. Barrot, whom I have mentioned already, was the French Minister. There also resided at Naples Mr. Augustus Craven, who had been in diplomacy. He had a very pleasant and hospitable house, where he gave not only dinners, but private theatricals. His wife was by birth Mademoiselle de la Ferronaye : she was much liked in all European society.

The Russian Minister was a man well known in the world—Count Chreptovitch. He had married a daughter of Count Nesselrode, a very acute and clever woman. Later on he was accredited to London, but before long gave way to Baron Brünnow, who had been Minister before the war. A curious incident occurred while I was at a ball at their house. The Russians have a sweetmeat made of sugar, manipulated in a certain fashion until it assumes the form of a reed-plant. Guests break pieces off from the points of the leaves to eat. On this particular occasion, there was present a Neapolitan who had the character of possessing *la jettatura,* or the evil eye, so that anything he looked upon underwent some misfortune. As I was standing near the imitation reed, which formed the principal ornament of the table, he came and, like every one else, broke off the end of a leaf. As he touched it, the whole thing came down with a crash. I had met this gentleman at Florence, and knew of his reputation. When this occurred I saw him turn perfectly white : he made some exclamation of annoyance, and left the house.

We also made the acquaintance at Naples of Count and Countess Bernstorff, whom we subsequently knew very well in London, where he succeeded Baron Bunsen. He was here for a long time, and was much liked. I still possess the card inviting us to the great ball given by them at Prussia House, at which the Queen and Prince Albert were present, at the time of the Crimean War.

Amongst the Italians of whom we saw a good deal were the Marchese Caracciolo and his younger brother, the Duke of St. Arpino. Both were sons of the Duke of San Teodoro. Marchese Caracciolo married the widow of Lord Burghersh. He succeeded first to the title of his younger brother, who died, and later on to that of his father. Other Italians who lived very much with the English and spoke our language were the Duke of Forli and Prince Dentice. The young men of Naples who had sympathy with England all bought English bulldogs, whom they used to address in such terms as, "G— d— you, come here, bulldog ! "

The Court lived in great seclusion and gave no entertainments. The only hospitality shown by royalty was the reception of morning visits by the Count and Countess de Trapani. She was a Tuscan princess. There were also some very interesting French plays given from time to time by the

Count of Syracuse, in which members of Neapolitan society took part.   I recollect that on one
occasion the celebrated French song *"La corde
sensible"* was excellently sung by Count Marcello
Gallo, said to be a descendant of Marcellus Gallus.
This brought the old world and the new somewhat
close together.

There were a great many travellers, some of
whom I have already mentioned, having known
them in Florence, amongst others Colonel West, a
son of Lord De La Warr.   In Naples we met
Mr. and Lady Hermione Graham, who were
only just married.   She was a niece of Mrs.
Norton, and we saw them constantly, as Sir
William Temple's friends all lived in a little
clique, dining together almost every day.   But
the great feature of society was the house of
Lord and Lady Holland, the Palazzo Rocella.   In
their home was one continual round of entertainment.   Though Lord Holland was a strong
Liberal, and came of a staunch Liberal family, he
was acceptable to the whole of Neapolitan society.
Lord Holland was a relative of Lady Walpole, and
her trustee—Mr. Spencer Walpole also being a
member of the trust.   Lady Holland was through
life a great friend of my wife's, and we still possess
many letters of hers giving the most interesting
social and political news.

I have many reasons for gratitude to Lord
Holland up to the time when I left England in
1859, the year he died.   He had three houses

besides the one already mentioned : Holland House
in London, St. Anne's Hill, Chertsey, and a house
in Paris, which they visited occasionally.   All four
were made pleasant to the guests admitted to them,
and, wherever Lord and Lady Holland lived, there
was always to be found the cream of social success.

One of their great friends was a gentleman
named Ridgway, an old man with curly hair, who
was related, I believe, to the publishing firm.   He
was very rich, giving constant dinners, and was
always making little presents to ladies.   Two of
Lord Holland's special intimates were M. Masson
and the Comte de Pontois, who had been French
Ambassador at Constantinople.   Like many of
their friends, M. Pontois was an Orleanist, while
M. Masson was also a politician of great moderation.   In a letter written to my wife by Lady
Holland, she says :—

I will transgress your orders and answer your kind line,
for this reason, that as you happen to mention M. Masson
and Count Pontois, I feel an itching to tell you that the
former has just been named *Préfet du Département du
Nord*, and the other has been made happy by the restitution
of that part of his pension of retired Ambassador of which
he had been most iniquitously deprived.

Shortly after Lord Palmerston's death Lady
Holland wrote as follows :—

I am very unhappy about poor Palmerston.   He is the
last of the set I remember at Holland House when I entered
it, and *she* has ever been a kind and true friend to me.   I
have had a long letter from Fanny Jocelyn.   She says her
mother is weak, but bears up and is calm and resigned—

happy that he went first, as she feels she was essential to him, which is perfectly true.

Another time she writes :—

Poor Lord Dalling! It has been a grief—a great grief—to all of us. He had taken a fancy to Mary,[1] and their correspondence was regular and charming. It is a heavy penalty for life, that of losing dear friends.

The following was written when Paris was destroyed, during the Commune :—

You come to me for consolation! Alas! I am in the depths of despondency. I regret to have lived to see such horrors. Vandalism in the nineteenth century! Oh, what a people! Voltaire says — where? I forget—"*singes et tigres.*" I cannot forgive the sinners the faults they have committed. J. Favre and Thiers are cause of all—not to disarm, then going to Versailles, and taking two months to collect an army which now will be one of the great difficulties, leaving time for the perpetration of horrors. A male population of upwards of a million supine while their capital was being prepared for utter destruction! You ask me if any of my political *habitués* know where the country is drifting. My *habitués* are few just now. Poor old Pontois has received the last Sacrament at Boulogne-sur-Mer, but has rallied since. Broglie is gone to look after his wounded son. I have a letter from a friend just fresh from Versailles. He says he can't find a solution for the present difficulties, and adds : "*Monsieur Thiers joue les monarchistes blancs et tricolores. Les républicains jouent M. Thiers. Les d'Orléans jouent les Bourbons, et il se pourrait qu'au lendemain de la chûte de Paris, les deux drapeaux sérieux fussent celui de la république et celui de l'Empire!*" I don't believe in either, but I feel no interest more. Paris destroyed! I care not for the destroyers or those who have allowed the destruction.

Goodbye. I am too wretched. I cannot write.

---

[1] Lady Holland's adopted daughter.

Lord Holland wrote to me from Naples on April 27, 1858, as follows :—

I send you a letter to put in the post, and write in hopes of hearing from you, for I have nothing to tell you interesting from here.

Dizzy's Budget seems to be a success.  I am glad for him.  It always gives me pleasure to see talent successful and triumph over humdrum.

I do not think the state of Europe is at all comfortable. It seems to me that the Emperor at Paris has got into trouble and difficulties foreign and domestic by his violent terror since the crime of Orsini.  He has been blowing hot and cold, and lost his calm impassibility.  I fear that to divert ill-will at home, and to give other interests to foreign nations and people, he will judge (perhaps not unwisely) that war is the only game left to him to play.  He grinds his teeth at us, but I suspect he does not mean to strike at us.  He has no immediate point to gain.  His blows, if he does deal them, will be against others; but, sooner than fall, he will see all Europe up in arms and trust to his " Star," which, though not so bright as it was, does not seem setting yet, to get some material advantage somewhere in the scramble.  All Italy and, I believe, Vienna too are trembling—some of the governed with hope—all that govern, with fear.  Pray write.

In another letter from Naples, he wrote :—

M. Brenier is here.  The King ran away to a distant and fictitious hunt in the country.  The Foreign Minister and several of the courtiers have taken to their beds to avoid even the imputation of having spoken to him.  He has quietly observed that if the King does not fix a day he shall go back and leave with His Majesty the responsibility of having refused to receive him.

On October 3, 1854, Lord Holland wrote me the following letter from Paris :—

Your friend, Mr. Lytton, dined with us yesterday, so we have lost no time in trying to make acquaintance. Odo Russell and —— also came. The latter is to succeed Odo at the Embassy here, which I much regret, as Odo is very agreeable, and ——'s intellect, I am willing to suppose, is far beyond the comprehension of such prosaic beings as myself. . . .

Hübner's felicitations on the victory in the Crimea was not from Austrian Minister to French Minister, but from Emperor to Emperor. A friend of mine saw the original despatch!

Lord Odo Russell was always a most popular man. When at Rome, as unofficial agent, he managed to obtain the good graces of the Pope, Pius IX. One day, after an audience, His Holiness expressed to a Cardinal, who was with him, his liking for the English Agent.

The Cardinal said, "*Forse qualche giorno sarà cattolico.*"

Pio Nono's reply is said to have been, "*Non mai cattolico, ma cattivissimo protestante.*"

I know many other instances of the wit of Popes, and hope the two following anecdotes have not been related before.

Gregory XIV., who was much addicted to taking snuff, offered a pinch to a country priest.

"*No, mille grazie, Santità,*" was the reply. "*Non ho quel vizio.*"

The Pope said, "*Se fosse un vizio, l' avreste.*"

The late Pope, when a Cardinal, went a great deal into society, where his wit and conversational powers were much appreciated. Once, at a dinner-party, he perceived that at one end of the table a snuff-box was being shown by one of the guests to his neighbours, and also that precautions were apparently being used to prevent the Cardinal from seeing it. These were useless, and he requested that the box might be sent up for him to inspect. On the lid was the representation of the nude figure of a woman. When the Cardinal saw it, he said to the owner, "A very handsome woman! You are quite right always to travel with a picture of your wife."

A story was once told me of the Bishop of Agen. He had been married before he became a priest, and his daughters did the honours of the episcopal palace. A very *dévote* French lady called upon him, and was rather astonished when a young man came into the room, whom the Bishop introduced as "*Mon fils.*" A few minutes later another young man came in, whereupon the Bishop said, "*Mon second fils.*" The lady then started up, saying, "*Une fois passe. A tout péché miséricorde. Mais deux fois — ô monseigneur !*" and she left the room.

# CHAPTER XVII

Return to Florence — Journey to England — Prince Louis Lucien
Bonaparte—Chemical and philological studies—Family—Mutual
friends—Meetings with Prince Louis Lucien.

AFTER our stay in Naples, we returned to Florence
and found Mr. Scarlett installed in lieu of Mr.
Erskine, who had returned to Turin.  Mr. Scarlett
did not remain there very long, as he was appointed
Minister at Brussels, and Lord Normanby succeeded to the post he desired.  This change, however, took place after I had returned to the Foreign
Office in London.

On our journey to England, we stayed in Paris
and saw Prince Louis Lucien Bonaparte, whom
we had both known for many years.  With him
was an Italian officer, who had been in the French
army and was known as Commandant Cavagnari :
it was his son who was killed in Afghanistan.

Prince Louis Lucien was a very remarkable
man and a great student ; an eminent chemist,
as well as a great philologist.  One of his special
studies in chemistry was that of poisons, and how
far they could be utilised for the benefit of
humanity.  It was his idea that hydrophobia was

caused by the circulation of the blood being over-
stimulated, and, as an antidote, he considered that
the poison of vipers would be beneficial, its effect
being to diminish rapidity of circulation.    With
this object he used to collect vipers, and, having
put pressure on their throats, he held a watch-
glass, on which they would deposit two drops of
venom.    This remedy was tried on a man in
the last stage of hydrophobia, and, though his life
was not saved, his violence was softened and
tranquillised.

On one occasion Prince Lucien was showing
his vipers to a young lady of sentimental disposition, who professed to wish to terminate her
existence.    She asked him for a viper, so as to
carry out her object, and he, knowing that the
viper had been rendered innocuous some hours
before, gave her one immediately.    The young lady
said, however, that her death would grieve her
mother too much, and so she relinquished the idea.

The Prince's linguistic studies were excessively
minute and careful, and he had begun a dictionary
in, I believe, fifty-two languages.    He had also
erected a monument to the last woman known to
have spoken Cornish.    He paid special attention
to English dialects, and, though not himself able
completely to formulate the pronunciation of
English words, he defined very clearly the rules
by which pronunciation should be guided.    The
Song of Solomon was translated by his orders into
every English dialect.

The following is an instance of his analytic powers :—

> *Chary* is an adjective which signifies not only "careful, cautious," and sometimes even "sad," but also the French adjective *ménager*, so that *chary - woman* means *char-woman*, or, vulgarly, *chare-woman*. *Chary*, in effect, is, as well as *careful*, the adjective of *care*. Spiers' French-English and English - French dictionary gives *ménager* as one of the meanings of the English *chary*, and in the *Ormulum*, i. 1274, one finds : *For turtle ledeth chariz lif*, "For the turtle leads a mournful life." In the sense of "sad," *chary* is rarely used, but in that of *ménager*, *ménagère*, it is the synonym of *char* in *char-woman*, who, after all, is only a *care-woman*.
>
> *Care* and *chare* have also the sense of the French *souci* and of the Italian *cura*.
>
> The Anglo-Saxon root of *care* is *caru*, "sorrow, care," and that of *chary* is *cearig*, "full of care," which is itself derived from *cearu*, the Anglo-Saxon synonym of *caru*.

Prince Louis Lucien was the son of Prince Lucien Bonaparte, the brother of Napoleon I. who refused a crown. He was the younger brother of the Prince of Canino, who was of a far more turbulent nature. Prince Louis Lucien was high in the confidence of the Emperor Napoleon III., and I believe was one of the guardians appointed to the Prince Imperial. He was much depressed by the death of the latter, and, though he had always led a very secluded life, was still more of a recluse afterwards. The downfall of the Empire seriously injured his financial position, though I believe he inherited some money from his nephew, Mr. Stuart, the son of Lord Dudley

Louis-Lucien Bonaparte

Stuart, who had married his sister.    Mr. Gladstone, who had a great respect for him on account
of his literary qualities, conferred on him an
English pension, being enabled to say with truth
that he was a British subject, as he was born at
Thorngrove House, in Herefordshire.

In feature, the Prince presented a striking
resemblance to the Emperor Napoleon I.    He had
discarded the strong Liberal principles professed
by his elder brother, the Prince of Canino, and
his younger brother, Prince Pierre.    When about
sixteen, he had written a poem against the
Papacy, which later in life, however, he upheld
and reverenced.    He was a perfect encyclopædia
of learning, ancient and modern, and wrote English
idiomatically, as a result of much study.    He had
two semi-detached houses in Westbourne Grove,
now called Norfolk Terrace, Bayswater.    In one
of them he lived ; but he devoted the other to
science, forming a magnificent philological library,
and converting the cellars into a chemical labora-
tory.    In his library there was the following
inscription :—

> O beata solitudo,
> O sola beatitudo !

He never interfered in politics.    The early part of
his manhood was passed in a little villa called the
Villino Bonaparte, outside the Porta San Gallo
at Florence, on a rivulet, the Mugnone, not far
from the Villa Palmieri.    Here he sought the
society of professors and philosophers.    He also

possessed a villa at Montughi, left to him by his uncle, the Comte de St. Leu—Louis, ex-King of Holland, brother of Napoleon I., and father of Napoleon III.

In London, where I first knew him, Prince Louis Lucien often went to the house of some relatives of mine, who had lived on terms of great intimacy with him at Florence. In London they kept up the old Italian habit of receiving every evening, and their house was quite cosmopolitan. They were most hospitable and kind-hearted, and had a large acquaintance of a miscellaneous character; but, being advanced Liberals of the Continental type, they at times received the principal revolutionary leaders, and were cognisant of their plans and proceedings. Prince Louis Lucien, who was a faithful friend, did not desist from frequenting the house, though often deploring the political tendencies of those he met there. He made it a point of pride, when his fortunes were prospering, not to abandon his early friends, and, even as a first cousin of the Emperor Napoleon III., he was frequently constrained to meet at this house persons whose political labour and methods were distasteful and even hostile to him.

I recollect on one occasion, in 1856, the lion of the evening was Orsini, who had recently escaped from prison at Mantua. I did not speak with him; but I remember his face, the dominating feature of which was a restless pair of black eyes. Prince Louis Lucien drove me home that evening, and I gathered from his manner how much annoyed he had been at the meeting, and at the conversation he had heard of the Italians present. He scarcely spoke.   His mood was one of sorrow at meeting persons so hostile to the head of his family, from whom he was receiving great benefits. On leaving me at my door, he expressed a wish to see me again soon, but added that thenceforth it had better be at his own house.   He did not entirely abandon his old friends, but never went to see them unless satisfied that there were no strangers.   After the attempt by Orsini, I fancy he discontinued his visits altogether.

At the outset of the French disasters in 1870, he came to me at the Athenæum, of which we were both members, and, curiously enough, took me in his carriage with the Bonaparte liveries to the door of the Prussian Embassy, where I endeavoured to obtain some authentic news. This occurred a few days before my going abroad and visiting the seat of war.   At the fall of the Empire, the Prince naturally lost his allowance as well as his pay as Senator, and, having made some bad investments, he was at one time reduced to considerable pecuniary straits.   He would never, however, at any time part with his library, which contained some thousands of Bibles, or with his collection of chemicals, including some very valuable metals which he intended at one time to leave to the British Museum ; but he found some technical difficulty in carrying out this wish.

# CHAPTER XVIII

W HEN I got back to the Foreign Office, I found
considerable changes. Lord Aberdeen had become
head of the Government, and Lord Palmerston
Home Secretary. Lord Clarendon was at the
Foreign Office, with Lord Wodehouse as Under-
Secretary. Mr. Hammond had been appointed
Permanent Under-Secretary, and Mr. Spencer
Ponsonby was again private secretary to the
Secretary of State.

Since that time, I have been very much struck
by the necessity of the Foreign Office being represented in the House of Commons, either by the
Secretary of State or by the Under-Secretary. A
great deal of harm was done during Lord Palmerston's administration, for neither Lord Clarendon
nor Lord Wodehouse had ever been in the House of
Commons. The result was that the whole burden
of defending our foreign policy fell upon Lord
Palmerston, who naturally could not give the same

attention to details as a younger man less over-
whelmed with business.  The work of representatives of a department in the House of Commons
lies not merely in debating, but in conversing in
the lobbies with other Members, and in ascertaining the real spirit which pervades Parliament.
This clearly could not be done by a man of Lord
Palmerston's calibre.  After all, the talks in the
lobbies, though merely a superior kind of gossip,
are most important as indicating the current of
public opinion.

The result was that, when Lord Palmerston's
Government was turned out, it was on a question
of foreign policy.  He had successfully overcome
the opposition to the Chinese War, and had also
obtained the upper hand in the subsequent dissolution ; but on the Conspiracy Bill, which was the
means taken by the new Parliament to upset him,
he had no notion, it is said, until the division was
taken, that there was such strong feeling in the
House on the subject.  Mr. Clive intended to move
the adjournment just before the division, but this
Lord Palmerston declined, knowing that a much
more disagreeable question, of a personal character,
would shortly be raised.

Lord Wodehouse was succeeded by Lord Shelburne, and thus the Foreign Office was again at
a disadvantage from having no representative in
the popular House.

I found that I had returned to really hard work,
for we were approaching the Crimean War.  It is

difficult now to realise the great labour that fell to our share in the Foreign Office, for several countries were involved, both belligerent and non-belligerent.  Prussia, though non-belligerent, took active steps in favour of Russia.  Austria, though also neutral, sympathised with the Allies, and would have finally joined in the war had Russia shown any reluctance to accept the peace when offered.  At the height of the war, the following nations were concerned : England, France, and Sardinia, as belligerents ; Austria and Prussia as non-belligerents, and many minor countries were similarly affected—Saxony amongst them, whose Minister at Paris was very active in working for peace.  He was Count Seebach, who had married a daughter of Count Nesselrode, Countess Chrepto-vitch's sister.

The result of this was an enormous amount of work.  Of every despatch coming or going, in con-nection with the war, at least seven or eight copies had to be made for the information of the Missions to the different Courts especially involved.  In addition to this, there was the ciphering and deciphering of telegrams, fair records of which had also to be sent whenever a Queen's Messenger started with a bag.

I was placed in the Austrian and Prussian Department, which was more burdened with work than any other.  Telegrams from Constantinople were sent by telegraph to Adrianople, where Queen's Messengers were waiting to carry them to Belgrade, whence they were sent to Vienna, then the nearest telegraph-station. Thus these telegrams came under the Austrian Department. The wonderful journeys of some Queen's Messengers on horseback were common topics of conversation. One of them told me that whenever he had to change horses, it was impossible for him to get off one horse or to mount the other. He used, therefore, to be carried, saddle and all, to the relay horse. The services of one Queen's Messenger, Colonel Townley, were so valuable that Lord Palmerston eulogised them in Parliament.

As for my own part in the business, I often wonder how I got through it. Not only had I to work at the Office in the day-time for many hours, but, as there was no special telegraph service established—it being then quite new—I had to keep the ciphers at my own house, and used to be called up at any hour to decipher despatches. When this was done, I had to make four or five copies : one for the Queen, one for the Secretary of State, one each for the Leaders of the House of Lords and the House of Commons, and one for general circulation in the Cabinet. We all cudgelled our brains to find some means of facilitating this work, and I recollect later going with Lord Shelburne to one or two places to examine inventions with this object. Alas! type-writing was unknown. It would have spared some lives, and the health of many, for the labour was really killing. But work, and hard work, engenders the power of more work,

and while all this was going on I also undertook
some literary employment.

There was a good deal of amusement, too, considering the general pressure. Lady Palmerston
and Lady Clarendon gave their usual receptions,
as did the other Ministers' wives. Two balls in
uniform were given about this time—for I cannot tie myself down to exact dates—one by the
Turkish Ambassador, and one at the Prussian
Legation.

Count Walewski, the French Ambassador, who
married, as has already been stated, the daughter
of Marchesa Ricci, also gave numerous parties and
receptions. At one of these I recollect that Miss
de Rothschild, daughter of Baron Lionel de
Rothschild, made her first appearance, and was
much admired for her marvellous beauty. She
subsequently married her cousin, Baron Alphonse
de Rothschild, who has recently died.

Amongst my friends in the diplomatic corps,
the principal ones were Count Corti and Count
Gropello, of the Sardinian Legation, and Monsieur
Sarmiento, son of Baron Moncorvo, the Portuguese
Minister. Mademoiselle Sarmiento, his sister,
married, I believe, Mr. Sandeman. The whole
family were always very good-natured and cordial.
I also knew, though not so intimately as those
just mentioned, the Marquis d' Azeglio, Sardinian
Minister. He was the nephew of the great
Massimo d' Azeglio, whom I had also met more
than once at Florence, and with whom, on one

occasion, I made the journey from Leghorn to Genoa.

Lady Holland had been good enough to give to my wife letters to her friends, who were very kind ; and when they themselves came to London, we were constantly at Holland House.  Society there was notably international, with a strong element of old Italian.  It was there that Madame Castiglione made more than one appearance.  I recollect that, when going from Holland House to a party at Lansdowne House, she met a lady who had known her well during her childhood and youth in Italy, and who said to her, " *Come siete bella !* "  Madame Castiglione replied, " *Lo dicono, ma io non lo so.* "

Lord and Lady Holland consistently maintained the reputation of the house.  His mother had been a very remarkable and eccentric woman, who kept control of her dinner-table by placing near her chair a page, named Harold, whom she sent with messages to her guests.  Mr. Macaulay was a constant frequenter of her house.  They say that his defect was holding forth at too great length.  He was only checked by a message sent to him by Lady Holland through Harold : "Her Ladyship's compliments, and she hopes Mr. Macaulay will change the conversation ! "

At the head of what may be called the Anglo-Italian society was Sir Antonio Panizzi.  He was, I believe, Modenese by birth, and a man of great literary ability, which led to his being made Chief Librarian at the British Museum.  He was fully trusted by the Whig party, and gave them advice at a time when Italian politics were very much to the fore.    He had one quality of an extraordinary character, namely, the knowledge of the backs of books.    If any one required a list of the authorities on any given subject, Sir Antonio Panizzi would sit down, and, without consulting any book of reference, write a list of works that exhausted the whole subject.    The former librarian at Holland House had been a gentleman who also had most extensive knowledge : he was known as " Lady Holland's Atheist," being an unobtrusive disbeliever in all revealed religion.

In those days I had a very little house in Berkeley Square, just opposite Lansdowne House, where I met with much kindness both from Lord Lansdowne and his son, Lord Shelburne, who after the Peace was raised to the peerage, and became Under-Secretary for Foreign Affairs.

At the time of the renewal of relations with Russia, Lord Wodehouse was appointed Minister at St. Petersburg, having as his First Secretary Mr. Julian Fane, a man of great accomplishments, who was much beloved.    They were both extraordinarily young for the posts to which they were appointed. In conjunction with Mr. Lytton, Mr. Julian Fane later wrote a poem called *Tannhäuser*, which had a great popularity.

Amongst other letters that I brought to London were two from Sir Henry Bulwer and Mr. Lytton to their brother and father, Sir Edward Bulwer

Lytton. From that time, till the day of his death, I was fortunate enough to have his confidence and friendship, and I passed much of my time at Kneb-worth. A short time previously, I had endeavoured to write a novel, which, fortunately for me, is now buried in oblivion; but at Mr. Lytton's suggestion I had sent a copy of it to his father, from whom I received in return the following interesting letter of advice:—

I have read your tale with much interest. It is marked by freshness and originality, and gives great promise, if you will do justice to that promise by deep and careful study of those principles of narrative composition by which alone you can adequately work out the results you would have in view. A first work of this kind is generally struck off without method from vivid impressions that would reproduce themselves spontaneously. But he who desires to become a master in the art of fiction will afterwards learn how to concentre his impressions and experience so as to have one clear and strong conception of the leading ideas he would present, and he will then pass from conception to execution with deliberate forethought as to the most effective and skilful modes of impressing the ideas upon the widest range of human minds. To do this he will consider what scenes in his story he should select for most effect, and consider how they are to be worked up through passion or humour to their fitting grade in the scale of feeling. There are three masterpieces in narration which can never be too much studied—the *Œdipus Tyrannus,** *The Bride of Lammermoor*, and *Tom Jones*.—Yours truly,

E. B. L.

* The Drama differs in its laws from the Novel, but should be carefully studied no less by the Novel-writer. Voltaire's plays instruct much as to the art of telling a story and leading to a catastrophe—in other words, to the sustainment of *interest*.

Although I am anticipating by rather a long

period, I may perhaps couple with Lord Lytton's letter another, on Fiction, written to me many years later by Mr. Kinglake. I had been invited to address a literary institution at Huddersfield. Mr. Kinglake, like myself, was very fond of novel-reading, and at that time a set had been made at novels, which we considered pedantic and unfair. The following is Mr. Kinglake's letter:—

In making a choice of books, I hope you will not overlook the Novel. Of course, a great novel does not lecture or preach, but for that very reason the more it governs the heart of the reader. What the *Iliad*, what the acted drama has been to mankind, the novel is at this day. It tells one of Life—life freed from its humdrum details; life, in short, with the dull parts left out; so that at one and the same moment the happy reader can enjoy the independence of solitude, and the charm of the most delightful society— society caught and seized by the power of genius at its fairest and brightest moments.

It is mainly, I think, by novels that a high ideal of human excellence is maintained; and—as though for the furtherance of that very end—there is always a tacit convention between the author of the novel and its reader. The author is under-stood to engage that the "hero," whatever his faults, shall at least be brave, honourable, generous, and that the "heroine" shall be a true, enchanting woman. With this understand-ing, the readers—before even cutting the pages—vow and promise a kind of allegiance; my lady undertaking to love, honour, and—theoretically—obey the yet unseen "hero," who, because of the accepted "convention," is almost sure to be worthy of her; and the man-reader fondly betrothing himself to one who, because she is the "heroine," must needs be lovely and true. The author, on his part, does not dare forget the "convention"—does not dare make the "hero" a mean fellow, or the "heroine" unwomanly. If he were to do so, the injured readers would fill heaven and earth with their complaints, and this quite justly, because in such case they would be dupes who had been led to promise their affections to unworthy objects. So, from the healthy relations thus established between the teacher and the taught, it follows that a higher and higher ideal is always being offered by the novel, and is always, too, being accepted by the docile, grateful reader.

Hence it is that amongst us novel-readers there obtains a conceptional elevation of the moral character which tends to make us better than our neighbours—much better, for instance, than you busy statesmen who blunt your souls with blue-books.

I am only, of course, speaking of that single, though great step towards excellence which consists in having a high ideal; and we must not forget the real examples afforded us by sacred and profane history; but still I must own that to novels—good novels—I owe what approach towards perfection I have hitherto been able to make.

I hope you will tell your hearers that, whenever they are reading a really good novel, they may be sure that they are holding converse with a mind of the highest order; and the lighter the touch, the greater in all probability is the intellectual strength of the artist. I once read an article in a magazine upon a grave, if not abstruse subject, and it was written with so much power, with such judgment, with such absolute command of the subject, and, besides, in such sterling English, that I was led to ask the name of the writer endowed with so much strength. The answer was, "Mrs. Oliphant"! I had long been under the charm of her delightful novels, and had recognised, of course, the fertility of her invention, her subtle knowledge of character, and her faculty of keeping one interested at every page; but that answer taught me that a part of the spell, after all, was a powerful intellect reinforcing that faculty of swift perception, which is peculiarly the woman's gift.—Always, my dear Wolff, very truly yours,          A. W. KINGLAKE.

*P.S.*—You now ask me to say which of Mrs. Oliphant's novels I like best; but I could not well answer the question without having, as it were, a kind of remorse at the notion of leaving any of them unpreferred. Still, for the sake of one of the most charming characters she has created, I will say that you might well counsel your young friends to read *The Three Brothers.* The more they come to love the "Padrona," the worthier they will be of this heart-stirring, human existence, in which, after all, such a one as the "Padrona" is possible.

# CHAPTER XIX

As I have said before, I took frequent journeys to Italy. I went there for my usual two months' leave shortly after my return to England, and again in 1854, when, in consequence of an attack that affected my eyes, owing to writing late at night, I was ordered complete rest. I therefore went with my family to Elba, a place I had long wished to visit as being one of the few, connected with the history of Napoleon, which had not been ransacked. It certainly contained, within its narrow limits, a great variety of interesting features.

By the Treaty of Fontainebleau, Elba had been allotted to Napoleon as a sovereignty, and it was of his own choice, for Corfu and Corsica had also been proposed to him. At Elba he found, as Lamartine has said, " the horizon, the sky, the air, the waves of his childhood." It was full of historic associations, and it was here he elected to stay with such of his followers as saw fit to remain faithful to him.

On his way to the South, an incident occurred which was an unhappy prelude to this period of practical imprisonment.  A man named Maubreuil, one of the Household of the Queen of West-phalia, was furnished with extraordinary powers for an object suspected but never avowed.  The Minister of Police placed his services at the command of Maubreuil, as did the Minister of War, who gave similar orders to his troops, while Generals Sacken and Brockenhausen gave strict directions that Maubreuil should be obeyed, and in the manner he should require.  There can be little doubt that it was intended to make away with the Emperor; but he was saved by the fidelity of some of the Commissioners attached to him. Strange to say, at the time of the Congress of Paris in 1856, an application was made by a man, who signed himself Maubreuil, for pecuniary assist-ance from the Allied Powers.  He stated that the circumstances of his secret mission in 1814 were known to their respective Governments.  The existence of this application was communicated to the representatives of those Powers; but no notice apparently was outwardly paid to it, though it was generally believed that means were taken to satisfy him.

On April 27, Napoleon arrived at Fréjus with his sister, the Princess Pauline, and embarked on the *Undaunted* for his new dominion.  On leaving

France he observed, " *Il n'y a que les morts qui ne reviennent pas.*" On the morning of the 1st of May, the *Undaunted* fell in with two or three English ships, detached to occupy Bastia and Calvi, and the officers were astonished at the amount of general knowledge which the Emperor displayed.

At Elba I found that many of the interesting relics of Napoleon had been collected in a museum at San Martino, belonging to Prince Demidoff, the husband of the Princess Matilde Bonaparte. By his orders, no strangers were allowed to visit the museum, which had been the favourite residence of the Emperor. It appeared that the Prince had forbidden all access to the collection, on account of some remarks made by the *Indépendance Belge.*

On our visit we came across M. Holard, who had been gardener to the Emperor. He had submitted to Napoleon the sacrifices he had made in his service, and was named gardener to the Emperor's sister, Princess Elise of Piombino, afterwards Grand Duchess of Tuscany. In 1814, circumstances had forced him to leave that employment. The Emperor then appointed him director of the Imperial gardens, both at Porto Ferrajo and on the neighbouring island of Pianosa. He was employed at the palace of Malmaison during the Hundred Days, and he and his wife both endeavoured to follow the Emperor to St. Helena. Unable to do this, they returned to Piombino to live on a small property given them by the Princess. Holard was recommended by the Duke of Wellington to Lord

Burghersh, afterwards Minister at Florence. Unfortunately, he found his property had been confiscated, and for some time was reduced to great straits. Prince Demidoff, however, engaged him as gardener at San Martino, where he would have been happy but for the somewhat oppressive character of Prince Demidoff's agent in the island.

I had some correspondence with Claude Holard after I left Elba, and I now have in my possession four letters from him, which, however, are rather difficult to read. I am happy to say that by the representations I made to Count Walewski—then Ambassador in London—I succeeded in bringing M. Holard's case before the Emperor Napoleon III., who gave him and his wife a pension for life.

I received from Count Walewski the two following letters respecting poor Holard. The first is dated March 2, 1855, from Albert Gate House :—

I thank you for having thought of sending me the portrait of the old gardener in the island of Elba. I shall hasten to take the first opportunity of obtaining for him the kindness of the Emperor. Your account of the island is certainly of a nature to excite the interest of His Majesty in favour of Claude Holard.

Another, of the 18th of June, is written from the Foreign Office at Paris :—

I have just received the letter which you did me the honour to write on the 12th of last month. I have had great pleasure in helping to smooth the lot of Claude Holard, and instructing the Consular Agent of France at Porto Ferrajo to place pecuniary assistance at his disposal.

Elba was full of souvenirs of the Emperor. On the steamer going to Porto Ferrajo, we met M. Larabit, a French senator. Forty years previously, he had passed ten months at Elba as the only officer of Engineers attached to the miniature army of Napoleon. During that period, he had been entrusted with the construction of all the works undertaken in the island, and, having accompanied the Emperor on his return, he had witnessed most of the occurrences of the Hundred Days. Since then he had risen to distinction. As a Deputy under Louis Philippe, he was most active in the preservation of all connected with the First Empire, and under Napoleon III. his services had been rewarded by his nomination to the dignity of Senator. With these recollections, his journey to the island created no slight sensation amongst his fellow - passengers and on the island itself, and I need not say how fortunate I was in finding so valuable a companion.

In order to reach the Governor's house, formerly the only palace of Napoleon, it is necessary to ascend one of the streets of stairs, similar to those for which Malta is celebrated. The resemblance may have been intentional, as Cosmo I., the founder of the city, had destined the island for the residence of the Order of St. Stephen, which existed in modern times as the principal decoration of Tuscany, on the same footing and with the same purposes as the Knights of Malta. The house itself is a small building, the best perhaps in the town, but barely large enough to contain the family of a gentleman of moderate fortune. Here the Emperor resided with his sister, whose bust is almost all that remains to recall the illustrious inhabitants. In a garden at the back of the house is the flagged walk, bordered by a small parapet, where the Emperor used to take exercise, walking rapidly up and down, or looking through the telescope in hopes of some arrival. The room then used as a sitting - room by the Governor had been occupied by the Emperor as a bedroom, and the spot where he was shaved was pointed out. The marks of his horse's hoofs still remained on some bituminous pavement where they were made by a fall down two steps. The place where the Emperor played with his favourite monkey was also to be seen, and the words he used, "*Jénar, mon pauvre Jénar*," were well remembered and frequently quoted to visitors by the inhabitants of Porto Ferrajo.

A small library of about eleven hundred volumes had been left, consisting principally of military and historical works, a set of *Moniteurs* bound up, translations of Latin and Greek classic authors, and occasionally some lighter productions; amongst others, elementary works on botany, mineralogy, and other branches of natural philosophy, procured evidently with a view to becoming acquainted with the products of the island, which seems designed from its extensive and even at times incongruous collection for studies of this nature. Some of the

XIX MARCIANA

volumes bore marginal notes in the Emperor's own handwriting. He had also thought of studying English, and requested Sir Neil Campbell to procure him a grammar. There were two French grammars of English in coarse paper covers, labelled with a rough cipher " N " pasted on the back ; but the leaves were mostly uncut. The only volume that he seems to have perused in this study was a dull moral work, in which the original English was placed side by side with the French translation. The book bore two titles—*The Hundred Thoughts of a Young Lady* and *Cent Pensées d'une Jeune Anglaise*—and purported to have been written by " Mistress Gillet."

One of our excursions was to a place called Marciana, where, as usual, we were entertained by a gentleman resident in a richly furnished apartment, consisting of a sitting-room and bedroom, such as is kept in every house at Marciana for purposes of hospitality. We heard the story, mentioned in all the memoirs, of the visit of a lady with a child, supposed by the islanders to have been the Empress. Our host related the circumstances of the visit, and also the reasons which led him to believe that the lady in question was no other than the Empress Marie-Louise.

In the beginning of August 1814, a Polish or German colonel, whose name does not transpire, arrived at Elba, and was immediately received by the Emperor, then living at Marciana. Marie-Louise was at that time residing at Aix, in Savoy.

The colonel remained only a few days, and then went away. Not long after this a Genoese *felucca*, the interior of which was fitted up in a luxurious manner, arrived at Porto Ferrajo, bringing a lady, a little boy, and the aforesaid colonel. In the course of the day of their arrival, the Emperor, accompanied by General Bertrand, Captain Baillon and my informant, started on horseback as though for San Martino. Arrived at the cross-roads to San Martino and Marciana, the Emperor, continuing his route to the former place with General Bertrand, ordered his two other followers to wait at this spot for a carriage that would soon pass, and to desire the coachman not to proceed farther till His Majesty's return. On his leaving, Captain Baillon said to his companion, " *Voilà, nous avons l'Impératrice à l'île d'Elbe!* "

They had not to wait long for the Emperor, who, on riding up, entered the carriage, while General Bertrand was observed to speak to the lady with marks of extraordinary respect. On arriving at Procchio, the party took boat for Marciana Marina, whence they proceeded to the Madonna of Marciana, a hermitage of celebrity, situated on one of the highest granite peaks, where tents were provided for their accommodation, the Captain being desired by the Emperor to give a bed in his own house to the Polish colonel— a command with which he complied, no doubt delighted at having an opportunity of displaying his cordial hospitality.

The following day, as the child was playing about under the chestnut-trees, the Emperor came up to Doctor Fourreau, who was in conversation with the Captain, and asked him what he thought of the child. The Doctor answered, " He appears to be much grown since I had the honour of seeing him at Fontainebleau." The Captain was not sure whether he heard the words *Sa Majesté* applied to the child; but his answer was evidently displeasing to the Emperor, who answered abruptly, " *Qu'est-ce que vous chantez donc ?* " and turned away, leaving the poor Doctor almost in tears, and in a state only to be understood by those attendants who unfortunately fell under their master's displeasure. Turning round to the Captain, he said, " How could I be expected to know that I was to be secret ? A man has not the power of divination of a God."

These circumstances naturally provoked speculation, and the Captain asserted that the pictures he had seen of the Empress and the King of Rome resembled the lady and her son, and that the age of the latter tallied with that of the King. He was therefore induced to form the conclusion, which nothing could alter. The Emperor, however, seeing that the Captain had observed that the child called him " Papa," asked him what the Elbans thought of his visitors. The Captain answered, " They think that Elba is honoured with the presence of the Empress and of your Majesty's son." The Emperor rejoined, " He may well be my son, and yet not the King of Rome." After this the Captain observed that the suite of the Emperor avoided all conversation on the matter, no doubt having received orders to that effect.

In opposition to this evidence, I must state that a person who saw the child declared to me that he was not the King of Rome, whom she had also seen; and that a gentleman stationed at Malta in 1814-15 informed me that it was from that island that the lady, whoever she may have been, started on her visit to the Emperor at Elba. I subsequently became acquainted with a distinguished diplomatist who avowed to me indirectly that he was the child in question. *Count Walewski*

# CHAPTER XX

ON my return to London I resumed my duties at the Foreign Office. These were rather more difficult, owing to the illness of certain of the elder members who were completely upset by work.

At the beginning of 1855, the amateur pantomime, to which I have previously alluded, took place. It would be interesting to introduce the play-bill, but, unfortunately, I cannot find one. I have in my possession another play-bill, however, of the same performance by the same company, but given on another occasion. It was called "Harlequin Guy Fawkes, or, A Match for a King!" The Prologue promised to introduce "an Original, Esoteric, Æsthetic, Historical, Highly-personal and Personally-dangerous, Intellectually-physical, Musical, Acrobatic, Terpsichorean, Well-meant but Exceedingly rash attempt to perform a pantomime." I believe the Prologue was written by Mr. Tom Taylor.

227

It was announced that the Capillary Attractions were by Mr. Wilson.

The play-bill is too long to be introduced here, but I may perhaps give the plot as summarised at the beginning :—

First, how Catesby wished to save : Monteagle from an airy grave. How, before their coming quarrels : Fawkes and Catesby placed the barrels. (Not of the Lynn or Yarmouth school : but kindly lent by Mr. Rule), because Guy Fawkes declared that century : should see the first *Train Parliamentary*. How, whilst Fawkes sought his evening beer : Monteagle came in feeble fear. And how by Catesby being chidden : was by him 'neath the barrels hidden. How, in a serious long palaver : Fawkes found that Catesby seem'd to waver. How each determined, in a duel : the other should procure his gruel : (A "Desperate Combat" of the age : when Hicks adorn'd the Surrey Stage). How beaten Fawkes essay'd to bolt : but was restrain'd by Catesby's "Colt." How Astaroth claimed Fawkes, and seized him : and how a Fairy good releas'd him. And how, amidst recrimination : they all came to the

### TRANSFORMATION.

Lest they escape from Memory's cells : we name again these active swells :

> *Harlequin*—Signor Giovannini.
> *Columbine*—Miss Rosina Wright.
> *Pantaloon*—Mr. Hayward Heath.
> *Lover*—Mr. Martin le Grand.
> *Clown*—Little Hulme.

There were acrobats called the "Bounding Bricks of Babylon," "engaged from the Arabian Amphitheatre of Aleppo, at an unlimited expense. Money has been no object with the proprietors of

this Exhibition to present an entertainment to
their patrons uniting Classical Beauty of Figure
with that Herculean Muscularity and Flibberti-
gibbet-like Flexibility only known to the Children
of the Desert." Their names were printed in
characters apparently Arabic.

The end of the play was described as a " Chorus
of Congratulation and Dance of Delight that it's
all over (which the Audience will, in all probability, reciprocate ; indeed, it will be unlike every
other Amateur Performance if they do not)."

A note at the foot of the play-bill remarked :
" As these Bills will not be sold until the Audience
is in the house, there is no occasion to state what
time the doors open ; and as all the Tickets are
already paid for, information as to the price of the
places is equally superfluous."

Communications were to be addressed to
Edmund Yates, Arthur Smith, or William Hale,
Esqs., Fielding Club, Maiden Lane, Strand.

The principal characters were :—

> *Harlequin*—John Bidwell.
> *Pantaloon*—Arthur Smith.
> *Clown*—Joe Robins.
> *Columbine*—Rosina Wright.
> *Lover*—Edmund Yates.

In the performance previous to the pantomime,
T. K. Holmes, Albert Smith, Billy Hale, Ibbetson,
Langford, O'Dowd, and Morgan J. O'Connell took
part.

That same year, Lord John Russell was sent on

a Special Mission to Vienna, with the view, if possible, of concerting with the Austrian Government some means of securing peace. He was accompanied by Mr. Hammond, but returned without achieving the object of his mission.

Shortly afterwards the Queen and the Prince Consort paid a visit to the Emperor and the Empress of the French, during which, no doubt, every method of promoting peace was seriously discussed, as Her Majesty was accompanied by Lord Clarendon. Whatever may have been the conversation at the meeting, peace very soon loomed in the near future. Austria stepped in, and it was said that she was prepared to join the Allies, if Russia rejected reasonable terms.

In 1856 the Conference was held at Paris, in which Lord Clarendon took part, and the Treaty of Peace was signed on the 30th of March in that year. The news was made public by the following announcements in the *London Gazette Extraordinary*.

FOREIGN OFFICE, *March* 31, 1856.

A despatch has been this morning received from the Earl of Clarendon, Her Majesty's Principal Secretary of State for Foreign Affairs, dated Paris, March 30, announcing the Signature of Peace, at two o'clock on that day, at the Foreign Office, in Paris.

The Plenipotentiaries of Great Britain, of Austria, of France, of Prussia, of Russia, of Sardinia, and of Turkey, have affixed their signatures to the Treaty which puts an end to the War ; and which, while definitively settling the Eastern question, establishes the tranquillity of Europe on solid and durable bases.

The exchange of the ratifications will take place at Paris in four weeks, or sooner if possible; until that time the stipulations of the Treaty cannot be made public.

Foreign Office, *March* 31, 1856.

The Honourable Spencer Ponsonby arrived at the Foreign Office this morning from Paris, with the Definitive Treaty for the Restoration of Peace, and for the maintenance of the integrity and independence of the Ottoman Empire, which was yesterday signed at Paris by the Plenipotentiaries of Her Majesty, of the Emperor of the French, of the King of Sardinia, and of the Sultan, and also of the Emperor of Austria and of the King of Prussia, on the one part, and of the Emperor of all the Russias on the other.

Shortly after the signature I went to Paris, and stopped at the Louvre, where Mr. Spencer Ponsonby and all the Mission sent to the Congress were also staying.

I dined with Lord and Lady Holland, and there met Count Cavour, the Sardinian Minister and Plenipotentiary. He was a mild man, who wore spectacles, and seemed anxious for information. I also met a lady known as Madame Gould, the wife of a Portuguese merchant, but an Englishwoman. She had been, in early life, a friend of Madame Montijo, and had chaperoned the Empress about Paris before her marriage. It was said that it had been by her advice that Napoleon III. was persuaded to propose to the Empress. The result was that Madame Gould became one of the most influential persons about the Court. She was a very kind and amiable woman, the mother of two or three sons, one of whom entered diplomacy and ended by being Minister, I think, in Servia.

At the same party I met Madame Montijo, the Empress' mother, and with her I had a long conversation about Madrid. Narvaez was also there, and the Duchess of Alba, grandmother of the present Duke, and sister to Madame Montijo. Miss Sneyd was there, too, a great beauty, who had "come out" at Paris under the chaperonage of Madame Gould. She afterwards married Mr. —later Sir George—Petre.

About this time a very curious thing occurred, in the sudden resignation of Mr. Henry Howard, appointed Minister at Florence. He had been married to Miss Mactavish, a well-known American beauty. Both Mr. and Mrs. Howard had long been known favourably in Parisian society.

It appeared in conversation that Lord Clarendon was not satisfied with Count Walewski, the French Plenipotentiary, nor with the Emperor of the French, who was said to have partly opposed and partly supported Count Walewski. Lord Clarendon was supposed to have insisted on some wrong points. When, however, he did insist, the Emperor gave way. Napoleon III. wished to yield on the question of the frontiers; but the British Plenipotentiary carried his point, as he did those of the appointment of consuls, the Aland Islands, and the neutralisation of the Black Sea. No men-of-war of any nation were to be allowed entrance, except those of the riverain powers. As to Nicolaiev, it was not touched: there was only a promise that ships of war should not be built there.

In fact, on looking over old papers regarding the negotiations, I conclude that we had to fight very hard for our position, and that we were chiefly successful when Lord Palmerston himself took questions in hand.

I had to go to Marseilles, and there I met Mr. March, from the Librarian's Department of the Foreign Office. He was a brother of the gentleman so well known on the Continent as the *principino*, a wonderful linguist. Mr. March told me the following story of Sir Edward Bulwer Lytton.

A lady one day remarked to him how odd it was that a dove (*colombe*) should have been sent to find the old world, and that Columbus (*Colombe*) should have found the new. Sir Edward replied, "Yes, and the one came from Noah; the other from Genoa."

The Peace created no great sensation. The *Sun*, however, appeared with black lines between the columns, as a sign of mourning, and made a violent attack on pacific measures.

About that time I saw a good deal of Sir Edward Monson, who was rather my junior. He had taken a First Class in Modern History at Oxford, and had just been appointed attaché at Paris. I also met Mr. Dillon there: he is now Lord Clonbrock. At the same time I saw a good deal of a third young diplomatist, Mr. Wodehouse, a brother of the Under-Secretary of State for Foreign Affairs. Mr. Wodehouse had just been appointed

234 COMPETITIVE EXAMINATIONS CH.

to Vienna, and Mr. Dillon to Washington. Mr. Wodehouse died young.

Lord Palmerston was at that time given the Garter. He was the first member of the House of Commons who had received that honour since Lord Castlereagh. It was said that this order was the one ambition of the great Sir Robert Peel. The simple title of knighthood for the Garter was assumed the last time by Sir Robert Walpole.

During the Crimean War, notice had been called to several administrative failures. A great stir was made about it in Parliament by Mr. Layard, Sir Arthur Otway, and others, and a society was created for the purpose of what was called administrative reform. It was then that examinations for the Civil Service were introduced, limited at first in their requirements, yet the foundation of the system which is now universal. The movement was very general, and gave rise to public meetings all over the country.

Amusing anecdotes were told of the first examinations, which were naturally made easy, as no preparation was possible for so new an institution, and as officers were urgently required for the army.

A gentleman, who was the godson of Lord Adolphus FitzClarence, was examined for one of the regiments of Guards. One question asked him was, " Who was the greatest military commander of modern times?" to which he replied, " The

Duke of Wellington." This was naturally satisfactory.

He was then asked, "Who was the greatest
naval commander of modern times?" To this
he replied, "Opinions differ, but in mine, my
godfather Dolly FitzClarence is as good as any
of them!"

Though not sufficiently precise, the young man
got through.

About this time I met a gentleman who was a
great contractor for coals, and for some reason or
other—I suppose I had been civil to him abroad—
he asked me to dine at his club.

He told me that he was a great student of
prophecy, and that he believed the following would
shortly be fulfilled :—

And I will bring again the captivity of my people of
Israel, and they shall build the waste cities, and inhabit
them ; and they shall plant vineyards, and drink the wine
thereof; they also shall make gardens, and eat the fruit of
them.

He believed that Palestine would be emanci-
pated. "And," he added, "I am told that there
are some very valuable deposits of coal in the
Holy Land."

This reminds me of an incident which shows
how every one is inclined to look at things simply
from his own point of view.

In a town where I was at school a new clergyman had just arrived. The hairdresser came on a
certain day to cut the boys' hair, and was asked

what he thought of the vicar. His only reply was, "Very poor head o' hair, sir."

I remember a very popular gentleman who was in the House of Commons at the same time as myself. His popularity was proved by his always being called by a nickname. This I believe to be an infallible test. A man who is usually called Tom, Dick, or Jack is invariably a favourite. This gentleman — whose name, let us say, was Jack Hillier—was very dangerously ill, and many members of the House constantly enquired after his health at his residence in the north of London. One morning I happened to call upon one of our Whips, who asked, "Do you know how poor Jack Hillier is ?"

I said, "I called last night. They told me he was very bad."

The Whip replied, "Poor Jack! I am very anxious about him. He only got in by seven votes."

During the time I was in the Foreign Office, I naturally made a great many acquaintances, many of whom I have already mentioned; but there were some who became my friends as I went on in experience, and whom I shall always recollect. Mr. John Delane, the editor of the *Times*, was exceedingly kind to me. I was introduced to him by Sir John Burgoyne. He had a homelike, old-fashioned, panelled house—16 Serjeants' Inn. Here he used to give most agreeable dinners, and there came Mr. Bernal Osborne, Mr. Lowe, and the

most amusing people in London.   On one occasion
we were talking of a member of the Government
supposed to be a great failure.   Some one said,
"They want to make him a peer."   Mr. Lowe
retorted, "No, they want to make him disappear."

I had a friend much associated with Mr. Delane—
Mr. Bayley, the protagonist in an episode which is
still undecided.   He was a writer in the *Times*, and
his articles were much appreciated.   He told me
that one night, during the contest about the Repeal
of the Corn Laws, he had attended a meeting in
favour of the Repeal, and had been much struck
with the great enthusiasm shown by the Free
Trade section.   Leaving the theatre where the
meeting was being held, he drove to the *Times*
office where he saw Mr. Delane, who was editor
at that time, the father of Mr. John Delane.   Mr.
Bayley explained the reasons which made him
think it necessary to abandon the cause of Protection, which the *Times* had hitherto advocated,
and Mr. Delane instructed him to write an article
in the sense he pointed out.

There are other stories concerning the reason of
this change.   Some say that a remarkable lady, in
the confidence of a Cabinet Minister, had heard
from him of the intention of Sir Robert Peel at
once to introduce a measure for repealing the
Corn Laws; that she had driven down late to
inform Mr. Delane, and that this information,
immediately acted on, was the cause of the change.
Anyway, I believe Mr. Bayley was the writer

of the article.    Later he became a Colonial Governor.

I also knew Mr. Dasent, a brother-in-law of Mr. Delane, a very able and acute writer, and especially well known for his knowledge of Scandinavian literature.

Another brother - in - law was Mr. Mowbray Morris, the business manager of the paper.    By his judicious selection of writers and correspondents, he had contributed to achieve for the *Times* the vast influence it has since possessed.

I was invited occasionally to the meetings of a society in the Temple, called the Dodeka, at the head of which was a writer of great eminence on the *Times*, Mr. Wingrove Cook, with Mr. Hans Busk, who took a very active part in the promotion of the Rifle Volunteers, and Mr. Bates Richards.    The last had married a beautiful Italian lady, generally known as Mrs. Gaggiotti Richards, who came from Ancona, where I subsequently met her.

A gentleman named Vaux, who was, I think, employed at the British Museum, used also to have regular weekly parties of literary men, and attendance at these various gatherings was both interesting and instructive.

# CHAPTER XXI

In July 1856 I was appointed attaché to a Special Mission to Brussels. It was merely complimentary, and sent to congratulate King Leopold on the twenty-fifth anniversary of his accession to the throne. The Envoy chosen was Lord Westmorland, an old personal friend of the King, having been with him, I believe, at Waterloo.

On the 19th of July, Lord Westmorland was received by the Vicomte Vilain XIIII. The numeral was conferred on the Viscount's family as a perpetual distinction by Louis XIV. His arms are, I believe, fourteen castles, the capture of which also earned him the distinction. Lord Westmorland, together with Lord Howard de Walden, Her Majesty's Permanent Minister at Brussels, called on the Belgian Cabinet Ministers and dined afterwards with Lord Howard. At the dinner were

present : Viscount Vilain XIIII., Baron de Brock-
hausen, the Prussian Envoy, also an old friend of
Lord Westmorland's, Mr. Barron and Mr. Johnston,
attachés to the Legation, and myself.

Preparations were on a very grand scale.  Cars
were constructed for a great historical *cortège*, each
representing a separate province.  They filled a
whole street, which had been covered in as a
coach-house for them.  Triumphal arches were
erected everywhere, with flags, scutcheons, and
ornaments, and the whole town was illuminated.
Never was a king so popular, or a people so ready
to celebrate the virtues of their sovereign.

Lord Westmorland's son, Lord Burghersh, was
also attached to this Mission.  He had only recently returned from the Crimea, where he had
greatly distinguished himself.

On the 20th of July, Lord Westmorland repaired to the Palace in a royal coach to present
to the King his letters of credence.  This he did,
accompanying the letter with a speech expressive of
the attachment and esteem in which the sovereign
and people of Belgium were held by the sovereign
and people of Great Britain.  His Majesty appeared
deeply affected during the delivery of the address,
frequently interrupting Lord Westmorland with
remarks of pleasure and gratification.  In reply,
His Majesty expressed his sense of acknowledg-
ment of the language in which Lord Westmorland
had conveyed the feelings of his sovereign and his
country.  He declared his affection and admiration

for Great Britain, saying that there he had on
every occasion been treated with justice. He
concluded by welcoming Lord Westmorland cor-
dially and affectionately, alluding to the long
period of their acquaintance. Subsequently the
Special Mission dined with Lord Howard de
Walden, meeting M. and Mme. Van de Weyer,
Colonel White, and Mr. Harris. Colonel White
was a distinguished author, and had written a
novel called, if I recollect aright, *Almack's Revisited*.
He was generally known as " Huffy White," for
what reason I cannot tell. Mr. Harris, whom I had
known before, had been abroad for a long time,
and for a certain period had been a Chamberlain to
King Charles Albert. I also had the opportunity
of again seeing M. and Mme. Adolphe Barrot. He
was the brother of the celebrated Odillon Barrot,
and was French Minister at Brussels. I had met
him formerly in London at the house of Mr.
Disraeli, and again renewed my acquaintance with
him when he became French Minister at Naples.

During the whole of Lord Westmorland's stay,
the King treated him with the greatest distinction, not allowing him to join the ordinary *corps
diplomatique*, but giving him a place among the
Royal Princes who had come for the occasion
—amongst others, the Duke of Saxe-Coburg and
Prince George of Saxony. During the week,
Queen Augusta of Prussia—afterwards the German
Empress—paid a visit to the King, and I had the
honour of being presented to her.

The solemnities were magnificent.   Opposite
the entrance to the Place St. Joseph was erected
a canopy for the King and the Royal Family,
reached by many steps, draped with red and
gold, and supported by columns formed of gigantic
figures.   On the right of the Square was a church,
in front of which a large platform contained
hundreds of the clergy in white surplices.   Opposite
was an altar for the celebration of the Mass.   The
King, with his suite, dismounted at the entrance to
the Square and proceeded on foot to the gallery.
Then he advanced to a transverse street for the
purpose of receiving the Duchess of Brabant and
Princess Charlotte.   Their beauty called forth the
most enthusiastic admiration.   The King took his
seat in front of the canopy.   On his right was
the Duchess of Brabant, on the left his daughter ;
near the Duchess, the Duke of Coburg ; near the
Princess, the Prince of Saxony ; at either end the
two Belgian Princes.   The semicircle was completed on the right by Lord Westmorland, Count
Mensdorff, who was related to the King, and the
gentlemen of the foreign suites ; on the left by the
Belgian Household.   Behind the King were the
members of the Diplomatic Body.

The Presidents of the Legislative Chambers
read addresses of congratulation, to which His
Majesty replied ; then followed a *Te Deum*, composed for the occasion by the celebrated musician,
M. Fétis.   After this, a procession defiled before
the throne of deputations from the regiments of

the Belgian army, from the clergy, the univer-
sities, schools, tribunals, and trades, and from all
the towns and villages in Belgium, screaming and
shouting, while the drums were beating and the
bands played the National Anthem.

This over, His Majesty descended, proceeding to
the Palace on foot, accompanied by his Court, and
halting for a few moments to confer with the
Cardinal.

The order was perfect, the public acclamations
spontaneous, and the weather splendid. The King
repaired to the Palace, where he was serenaded and
rapturously applauded when seen from the balcony
by the crowd; but never more so than on one
occasion when seen standing between Lord Westmorland and Lord Burghersh.

In the evening a banquet was given by the
Chambers. The staircase was decorated with a
profusion of flowers, and the temporary saloon
displayed a brilliant appearance. After dinner the
King's health was proposed and received with
lively enthusiasm. The King then repaired to
some public gardens called Waux Hall, where
the crowd and the manner of his reception
were of the same nature as those already ex-
perienced.

During the day the weather was fine. On
Sunday it had been rainy and gloomy, and apprehensions were entertained that the state of the
weather would disturb the splendid and costly
arrangements. But the sun appeared when the

King entered the Place St. Joseph, and the weather was fine, though cold, during the day.

On the 22nd, the festivities were begun by a serenade, followed by a review. Lord Westmorland and his son accompanied the King on horseback. By the kindness of Count Marnix, the Grand Marshal, I was placed in a window of the Palace, together with M. and Mme. Van de Weyer.

While conversing on the spirit of order pervading the Belgian populace and their respect for the law, M. Van de Weyer related an illustrative anecdote of some interest. On one occasion, at the commencement of the Revolution, there was some fighting going on in the Park. The Belgians found themselves running short of powder. Orders were immediately given for supplies, and some barrels were sent round by a road in the rear of the fighting. The Belgians from the town watched earnestly for the arrival of their powder to assist the belligerents, and became alarmed when some time had elapsed without its appearance. At length some of the leading men determined on going round themselves with a party, in case an attack had been made by the Dutch. On their arrival, however, they found the convoy delayed by one man with a white night-cap and the two words "*La barrière*." Thus 280 men were stopping each to pay his two and a half sous before proceeding to engage.

In the evening Lord Westmorland and his

Mission had the honour of dining with the King. They sat at the King's table, there being two other tables presided over by the Princes. The dinner was given to the superior officers of the Army.

As a proof of the great popularity of the King, an officer related that in a detachment of his regiment, garrisoned in Hainault, the men had by their own spontaneous act subscribed 1500 francs towards illuminations.

The Mission afterwards accompanied the King to the gala spectacle at the Opera. A cantata was sung, together with acts selected from several celebrated operas. Later on, the Court drove through the town to see the illuminations. Along the boulevards and the Allée Verte we passed through long avenues of illuminated festoons ; clusters of Turkish lamps hung suspended in the middle, and throughout the town there was an uniformity of decoration that testified to the unanimity of feeling, as well as to the good taste of the Commission to whom was confided the task of arranging the *fêtes*. Some of the public buildings presented a wonderful spectacle, especially the Hôtel de Ville, where the whole of its celebrated architectural design was traced in lamps. In the course of the evening, Viscount Vilain XIIII. informed the Mission that the King had been pleased to decorate them.

The 23rd of July was the last day of the *fêtes*. The sun rose magnificently—a cause of great rejoicing, as the festivities of this morning had for some months occupied the attention and drawn on the energies and generosity of the Belgian people.   At twelve o'clock the King received the *corps diplomatique,* inviting them to stay to witness the historical cavalcade that was to pass by the windows of the Palace.   This cavalcade consisted of fifteen cars representing the different towns and provinces of the kingdom.   They were decorated in a costly and even extravagant manner, but with a taste so perfect that there was no appearance of gewgaw or theatrical expedient.   Some of the cars were of enormous height, towering over the first-floor windows of the Palace.   It is impossible to write a description of them in a rapid summary. Each being distinguished by salient characteristics, no comparison could be drawn.   The cavalcade of Bruges represented the First Chapter of the Golden Fleece, and the industrial car of Liège, followed by 1200 Liégeois workmen, conveyed the most familiar images to the English eye.   One of these cars was a complete battery, with guns in position and cannon-balls stacked near them.   There were also, if I recollect aright, swords, pistols, and muskets. In fact, it might have been a portion of a fortified town.   The general effect was equal to the care bestowed on the detail.

From the balcony of the Palace the scene was striking.   The high green hedges and thick limes of the Park, studded with flags and medallions attached to gilt staves, formed a picturesque background. The space in front was wide. Looking to the right the long *cortège* and the magnificent cars wound round the front of the Prince of Orange's palace, which was covered with spectators. On it came, to appearance interminable, blending the bright colours of the different groups. The cars halted for a moment before the King, while their predecessors turned under the arch at the entrance of the Palais Royal. The brightness of the day—calling to mind a southern climate—the whiteness of the buildings, the vivid tints of the verdure, the enthusiasm of the crowd, the music of the orchestras, combined to produce a scene which will perhaps never be rivalled.

Here was collected in the capital the whole loyalty and attachment, and the great proportion of the population, of the entire kingdom. When one remembers that, with the exception of the remission of railway fares, the pageant, of which the cost must have been enormous, was provided without any assistance from the Government, some estimate may be formed of the intensity of feeling existing in a practical and naturally rather phlegmatic nation.

The King, in his great friendship for Lord Westmorland, invited the Mission to accompany him in his progress through the kingdom ; but this invitation it was considered wise to limit to Bruges. In that historical town the *fêtes* were well adapted to its past, and the same enthusiasm, governed by the same order, was prevalent.

There was one beautiful ceremony which took place in the Chapel of the *Sacré Sang*. The illuminations were splendid, outlining the buildings, which, at Bruges, are very remarkable. My former acquaintance with the town enabled me to find an old circulating library, where I procured a much-battered copy of Grattan's novel, *The Heiress of Bruges*, a charming book. This I obtained at the request of the Princess Charlotte of Belgium, who was travelling with her father, and whose later misfortunes as Empress of Mexico constituted a great tragedy. We returned for a day or two to Brussels, and then Lord Westmorland took leave of the King.

The conversations that took place between His Majesty and Lord Westmorland were excessively interesting, as both had been actors in the early politics of the nineteenth century. Lord Westmorland had been nearly connected with the Duke of Wellington, and all the incidents in which the Duke took part were familiar to him. In Chapter XIX. respecting Elba, it will have been seen that Claude Holard was recommended by the Duke to Lord Westmorland—then Lord Burghersh—at that time Minister in Tuscany. Lord Westmorland, who was a general in the army as well as a diplomatist, was acquainted with all the *dramatis personæ* of the century, and both the King and he spoke of them as familiar friends.

I had first known Lord Westmorland at Florence.

He came there from Vienna, to which Court he was then accredited.

Amongst the Ministers with whom we travelled, I saw a good deal of Monsieur Deschamps, the head of the Clerical Party, whose brother was a Cardinal and Archbishop of Malines. He was Prime Minister at that time. I also knew well Monsieur Nothomb, who held a portfolio in the same Cabinet.

I had many occasions of conversing with His Majesty, who was excessively kind and open with me. I was much struck by the common sense and depth of his remarks on subjects both great and small, and easily understood the position which he then occupied as counsellor of most of the Governments of Europe. Later I met him one day in the garden of St. James's Park. He at once stopped me and spoke for some time on subjects of great interest.

Since that time I have had frequent opportunities of seeing the present King of the Belgians, as well as the Comte de Flandre, who, until his death, was always exceedingly kind to me, inviting me to his house in Brussels. The last time I had the honour of seeing the present King was at Madrid. He summoned me to his hotel, where he was living in a species of half *incognito*. The reason of his sending for me was to give me a letter for Queen Victoria, to whom he told me he was in the habit of writing every Sunday.

I think it may be interesting to add to this summary the despatch addressed by Lord West-morland at the time to Lord Clarendon :—

MY LORD—I received a visit from Monsieur de Vilain XIIII., the Minister of Foreign Affairs, who stated that he was commissioned by His Majesty King Leopold to announce to me that he had named me a Knight Grand Cross of the Belgian Order of Leopold, and that he had appointed my son, Lord Burghersh, and Mr. Wolff to different grades of the same Order.

I replied to Monsieur de Vilain XIIII. by the expression of my most grateful acknowledgments to the King for this most distinguished mark of his considerate favour, but I also stated that I was enabled only to accept it under the reserve of Her Majesty's approval, which, being subject to established regulations, might be refused to me. Monsieur de Vilain XIIII. replied that His Majesty was perfectly cognisant of those regulations, but that he conceived the peculiar nature of my Mission would be an exception to them ; that these regulations had been set aside in the case of the Duke of Devonshire when he attended the Coronation at Moscow, and that other exceptions had since been made ; but he believed that, the special Mission upon which I was now employed being from the Queen to her Uncle, and upon an occasion such as the present which never could occur again, Her Majesty would grant the leave to accept and wear his Order, to obtain which he should himself make a most special application.

The next day I received the insignia of the Order, and I afterwards waited upon His Majesty and expressed to him my most sincere obligations and my gratitude for the high honour he had conferred upon me, and which (if permitted by Her Majesty) I should wear with the pride which it merited as a signal proof of his favour.

His Majesty, in the most gratifying language, assured me of the pleasure which he felt on being able to confer upon me this proof of his esteem and affection, and assured me that he would write with so much interest to Her Majesty the Queen for her permission that I might accept his Order, that he felt satisfied he should obtain it.

Under these circumstances, I can only recommend myself to Your Lordship's favour.  In that recommendation I will also beg to include my son, Lord Burghersh, and Mr. Wolff, who are attached to my Mission.

After this Mission, Lord Westmorland introduced me to his sister, Lady Jersey, who, like Lord and Lady Westmorland, was always excessively kind to me.

# CHAPTER XXII

THE year 1857 was rather an eventful one.    In all
my remarks I have avoided as much as possible
everything in the shape of political discussion.    I
am writing, therefore, in a perfectly neutral spirit
when I point out that what happened in that year
gives evidence of the sympathy of the House of
Lords with popular feeling.

A great debate took place in the House of
Lords on Lord Derby's motion to censure Dr.
Bowring, Governor of Hong-Kong, and Plenipotentiary in China.    The motion was rejected by
a majority of 36.    Almost at the same time a
similar motion was introduced in the House of
Commons, and there carried against the Government by 16 votes.    I heard Mr. Gladstone's
wonderfully eloquent speech on that occasion, in
which the following passage occurred :—

The subordinate officers of England, in a remote
quarter of the globe, misconstrued the intentions of their
country.  They acted in violation of their principles of

252

right.   The Executive Government failed to check them.
The appeal was next made to the House of Lords, and made
as such an appeal ought to be made, for the cause was
worthy of the eloquence, and the eloquence was worthy of
the cause.    It was made to nobles, and it was made to
bishops, and it failed.     But it does not rest with subordinate officials abroad, it does not rest with the Executive
Government, it does not rest with the House of Lords,
finally, and in the last resort, to say what shall be the policy
of England, and to what purpose shall her powers be
directed.    Sir, that function lies within these walls.    Every
member of the House of Commons is proudly conscious that
he belongs to an assembly which, in its collective capacity,
is the paramount power of the State.    But if it is the
paramount power of the State, it can never separate from
the paramount power a similar and paramount responsibility.
The vote of the House of Lords will not acquit us.    The
sentence of the Government will not acquit us.    It is with
us to determine whether this wrong shall remain unchecked
and uncorrected.

Thereupon a dissolution took place; but it
resulted in a triumph for the Government, and
they returned to office in April with an increased
majority.    Parliament was prorogued on the 28th
of August by commission.    Later in the year, however, it was again called together by a monetary
crisis of great severity, which required to be dealt
with immediately.

The year was remarkable for the breaking out
of the great Mutiny in India.    The conduct of
the Government in suppressing it was commented
upon with much severity, as displaying want of
energy.    By the end of the year, however, the
position in India, though still very critical, was

254 . ORSINI'S ATTEMPT CH.

considered to be assured. The East India Company's government of that country was abolished, and India was transferred to the direct government of the Crown. Meanwhile, the Indian question was not the cause of the downfall of Lord Palmerston's Government. No doubt, as Lord Fitzmaurice has mentioned in his *Life of Lord Granville,* "a variety of circumstances combined to diminish the popularity of Lord Palmerston. He was considered by some to be over-confident and jaunty, and the immediate following of the Prime Minister had shown unnecessary bitterness to those who differed from them. Several unpopular appointments had been made, one in particular to a high office of State."

The attack of Orsini on the Emperor of the French, on January 14, led to the introduction of a Bill by the Government on February 20, 1858, known as the Foreign Conspiracy to Murder Bill. There had been very violent articles in the papers of both countries, and some addresses by colonels to the French Emperor, published officially, were supposed to be insulting to England. Lord Clarendon, the Foreign Minister, for reasons which were probably sound, had not answered a despatch addressed to him by the French Ambassador before the Foreign Conspiracy Bill had been introduced. This may or may not have been an error of judgment, but it was seized upon as being a mark of the subserviency of Lord Clarendon to the French Government.

Consequently, Mr. Milner Gibson brought forward a vote of censure. Great doubts existed at first as to whether the motion would be carried ; but the different elements against the Premier, and the causes already mentioned, were too strong. The Government was defeated by a majority of 19. The Cabinet resigned, and Lord Derby was entrusted with the formation of a new administration. Lord Malmesbury was appointed Foreign Secretary ; Sir Edward Bulwer Lytton was named Secretary for the Colonies, and my relative, Mr. Spencer Walpole, was named Home Secretary. It was at first decided that I was to be Private Secretary to Lord Malmesbury, with Mr. Dashwood as précis-writer ; but Mr. Bidwell having put in an official claim for the appointment, Lord Malmesbury split the two appointments into three. Mr. Bidwell was named Private Secretary, I became assistant, and Mr. Dashwood précis-writer.

I was very glad to get out of the ordinary routine of office life ; but my experience confirmed the old proverb, "Two is company, three is none." The division was the cause of constant misunderstanding, though for some time I remained very happily with Lord Malmesbury, carrying out the business he gave me, I hope, with success.

At that time I saw a great deal of Sir Edward Bulwer Lytton, and stayed frequently at Knebworth. He was good enough to consult me at different times concerning the Ionian Islands, as I had had occasion to study the question, both in the Foreign Office and during my various journeys to the Mediterranean.

It may be considered interesting to reproduce from a manuscript in my possession the opinions of an unobtrusive but highly respected politician on some members of the new Government :—

The Earl of Derby, K.G.—The second Earl of England —a man of whom it was said by a foreigner, that he wants nothing.

His position, as Captain of the Conservative Party, was acquired at a period when that party, elevating a tax into a principle, had quarrelled with a Chief who had sacrificed his party by the mode rather than the substance of an expedient.

In many respects Lord Derby is well qualified for the lead of a powerful aristocratic phalanx. High-born, eloquent, polished, and even dexterous, with a sense of chivalry and of ridicule equally acute, his qualifications for leadership are prominent in this brilliancy. But in some qualities he is deficient. Confident in his natural station, he is, or affects to be, indifferent to the lure of office. To this tendency the Conservative Party owes the fatal blunder of 1855, the loss of the only chance of retrieval which has occurred since 1846, or of official tenure to be counted by years rather than months. He disdains the arts by which office can alone be attained and kept in a Constitutional State.

Though literary himself, he despises the fugitive press, nor is he willing to lend a helping hand, or to extend his social intimacy to any but those whose quarterings place them on his own level. Besides this, he has one great defect from which few men of talent are exempt. He cannot perceive the dangers to which his popularity is exposed by an irony which can neither be understood nor appreciated by mediocrity, which seldom is humorous.

The Right Hon. B. Disraeli, Chancellor of the Exchequer, is a man totally different in character and aspiration. Mr.

Disraeli lives for politics.    In them he breathes and has his
being.    By them alone has he attained a leading position,
and without them every occupation is gone.    Patient, long-
suffering, but of small gentleness, he has achieved a position
without precedent by a stony road which none before him
had trodden.    Self-contained, taciturn, and by art, if not
by nature, unsociable, impatient of advice, he has earned the
respect of some, the hatred of many, and the devotion of a
few.    He is the self-made Minister of a despotic state
turned loose in a Constitution which he uses without loving.
With some he is the hope, with others the despair, and with
all the necessity of his party.    His career has been one of
will, unswerving in its intensity, based on the selfishness and
weakness of politicians, and the power of his own intellect,
rather than on the broad truths of human society.    Seeking
for hidden motives where none exist, he glories in the
mystery which creates distrust and the reserve which repels
attachment.    He has no love, no hatred, except as an
instrument.    For him office or opposition are the sole
elements and objects of political life.    His vast erudition
and considerable eloquence are the projectiles of polemic ;
his subtle vigilance its outworks.    For him there is no
gradation between action and indolence.    In office he
initiates no legislation.    As Minister or Critic, he is merely
the champion, the pilot or the avenger of his party.    But not
even bankruptcy could cancel the liabilities of the Conservative Party to Mr. Disraeli.    They are as indelible as the
gratitude of a child towards its parent, of a drowning man
to his salvor, of the lion to Androcles.    He found it dispersed, betrayed, without a refuge, with scarcely a wish.
He has nursed it with the fierce watchfulness of a tigress
defending her young.    The party had dwindled into a
faction.    Its numbers, like the Italian Legitimists, would
soon have rallied to new combinations, or fought singly like
the brigands of Southern Italy, till they were captured or
killed.    Without veterans, and without recruits, its very
name would have died out from political combinations, had
not Mr. Disraeli made himself a career by restoring its own
broken columns.

In one respect Lord Derby and Mr. Disraeli are alike. They may command the fidelity of their party, and even the support of Parliament. They can never fire the enthusiasm of the country.

The Earl of Carnarvon, Secretary of State for the Colonies, is not without experience in his Department, nor devoid of Parliamentary tact. Under Lord Stanley and Sir Edward Lytton, he acquired during Lord Derby's second administration some knowledge of ministerial life, and, at second hand, some insight into the feelings of the House of Commons. A laborious student, and a finished scholar, his acquirements, to a great extent, make up for his want of originality, while a desire of success may compensate the absence of any striking ability. On the whole, he is a good average Minister, though his early succession to the peerage, and a shy supercilious demeanour, will prevent his achieving the foremost rank, or becoming a party leader.

The Right Hon. Spencer Walpole, Home Secretary, is a man of whom no one can speak ill. A distinguished scholar, a profound lawyer, with a considerable knowledge of the world, and a judgment sound, if not powerful, he will always command the respect and affection, if not the implicit confidence, of those with whom he deals.

I think there must be some mistake in the date of this paper, as Lord Carnarvon was at that time, I think, only Under-Secretary of State. Mr. Spencer Walpole I knew very well. He was one of the most upright men I ever came across, and everybody had confidence in him. He was trustee for more people than I can recollect, and his death was a great loss to many.

About this time misfortunes overtook M. de Lamartine, and people in all countries endeavoured to unite in assisting him. Sir Edward Lytton wrote a letter to M. de Lamartine, which I regret that I do not possess, but the reply to it is still in my keeping, and I give it herewith :—

Monsieur et illustre ami!—Votre lettre n'est pas de ce siècle ; elle devrait être datée de l'antiquité ! Puisse la postérité la lire ! Mais combien l'avenir n'aura-t-elle pas à rabattre des termes dans lesquels vous parlez de ma vie ! Vous vous êtes trop souvenu de cette maxime des bons cœurs : *Flattez les malheureux!*

Je suis très malheureux en effet. Je ne cherche point à le dissimuler à moi-même ou aux autres. Quand une souscription de cette nature n'est pas un éclatant honneur, elle est une éclatante humiliation. Je sais bien que l'humiliation n'est pas la honte, mais elle en est l'apparence. Elle fait baisser la tête devant les hommes, sinon devant Dieu. Il faut, croyez-moi, que j'aye des motifs bien obligatoires, bien sacrés, et bien supérieurs à ceux qu'on m'attribue pour ne pas retirer mon nom de tout ce bruit autour d'un obole !

La France ne me doit rien. Je lui dis vingt fois, je n'ai rien fait pour elle que ce que beaucoup d'autres ont fait avec moi, chacun dans leur rôle, et ce que tout autre à ma place eût fait mieux que moi. Je me trompe cependant. J'ai fait quelquechose. Je l'ai passionnément aimée. Je l'ai aimée non seulement dans sa grande individualité nationale, mais je l'ai aimée dans chacune de ses classes, et, pour ainsi dire, dans chacun des individus dont cette grande famille de la patrie se compose. Si l'on m'avait dit alors que le premier ou le dernier de ses citoyens allait être chassé de son foyer (château ou chaumière) faute de quelque million ou de quelque centime pour le racheter de l'expropriation, ce citoyen eut-il été mon ennemi politique, le ciel m'est témoin que je lui aurais adressé avec ma respectueuse attendrissement la dîme de mon cœur !

Des classes injustement hostiles en France n'ont pas jugé à propos de faire pour moi, à la voix de mes amis, ce que j'aurais fait pour elles ; mais elles ont payé l'occasion bonne pour se venger après dix ans du mal que je ne leur ai pas fait. J'accepte. Elles me méprisent sans en avoir le droit. La France sçait bien cependant que la partie n'est pas égale, car je n'aurai jamais à mon tour ni la volonté ni le droit de mépriser mon pays !

Quant à l'état, je me suis fait une loi de ne lui rien devoir comme homme privé, sous tous les régimes, dans tout le cours de ma vie. Je ne me départirai pas de cette loi à la fin de ma carrière. Le gouvernement est intervenu dans cette circonstance envers le comité de mes concitoyens de Macon, en termes d'une excessive obligeance. Je pouvais les sentir. Je ne devais pas y répondre. J'aurais admis ainsi un caractère politique dans une souscription de cœur et non d'opinion. Ce ne pouvait être ni ma pensée, ni celle du gouvernement. Il ne me devait que sa neutralité.

J'apprends par vous qu'en Angleterre un comité, composé d'hommes d'état, d'orateurs, d'écrivains illustres, veut bien me témoigner un intérêt international. Exprimez-lui ma reconnaissance. Je ne me trompe pas, comme quelques publicistes français se trompent, sur la signification de ce comité. Ce n'est pas un reproche. C'est un concours à la France ; c'est l'alliance des états que l'Angleterre veut illustrer une fois de plus par l'alliance des cœurs. La seule chose, en effet, que l'Angleterre puisse avoir l'intention de récompenser en moi, c'est le culte constant et avoué de cette paix plus glorieuse pour les deux nations que leurs plus belles victoires, car c'est la victoire de leur bon sens sur des rivalités surannées qu'il faut laisser, sans les remuer, au fond de l'histoire, comme la mauvaise lie des vieux tems !

Recevez, Monsieur et illustre ami, l'assurance de ma haute considération.          LAMARTINE.

Paris, 14 *juin*, 1858,
   43, rue ville l'Evêque.

# CHAPTER XXIII

DURING 1858, Fuad Pasha, who was at the time, I think, Grand Vizier in Turkey, came to England. Lord Malmesbury was in Scotland, in attendance on the Queen; but Lady Bulwer, who was in England, the wife of Sir Henry Bulwer, then Ambassador at the Porte, was anxious that he should be well received. It was unfortunate that Lord Malmesbury should be absent at such a time, and Sir Edward Lytton therefore gave a party at Knebworth, to which Fuad Pasha was invited, and I was instructed by Lord Malmesbury and Sir Edward Lytton to place myself at his disposal. This led to an acquaintance which later circumstances proved very confidential.

During the Pasha's stay in England, he was in the habit of visiting a lady whose husband was much mixed up in Turkish matters, but who herself was not a woman of any great tact. She

261

thought it witty to ask Fuad Pasha how many wives he had. He generally evaded the answer; but on one occasion she repeated the question very bluntly in the presence of others. Fuad Pasha replied, " The same number as your husband—two. The only difference is that he conceals one of his, and I do not."

I recollect this same question being put to a Turkish naval lieutenant, who commanded a launch placed at my disposal at Constantinople by the Sultan. He was asked by a young Secretary how many wives he had, and replied, in English, " I have only one. I find that quite enough ! "

Towards the end of 1858 there was a readjustment of the office of Private Secretary, and it was agreed between Sir Edward Bulwer Lytton and Lord Malmesbury that I should become Private Secretary to the former; but that for special circumstances I should always give such assistance as was in my power to the Foreign Secretary.

I found that the work of the Colonial Office was extraordinarily different from that of the Foreign Office. In the latter, business requires quick despatch ; in the former, great deliberation. There are few sudden emergencies under the Colonial Office, and the work is done very much according to precedent, whereas in the Foreign Office unprecedented events frequently occur. The Heads of Departments in the Colonial Office, therefore, often obtain much more influence and authority than in the Foreign Office. At that time several men of great capacity had charge of the Departments. One was Sir George Barrow, whose father had been Secretary to the Admiralty. Others were Mr. Blackwood, a brother of Sir Francis Blackwood, and related to Lord Dufferin, and Mr. Cox, who was always peculiarly dressed. In the morning he used to wear a tail-coat, and a single glass in his eye, to which no string was attached. Their work was rather that of Ministers on a small scale than of subordinates in a Department, and their decisions were rarely altered, for they had all the circumstances at their fingers' ends. Mr. Herman Merivale was Under-Secretary of State, a man of great knowledge and experience, and well replaced, when necessary, by Mr. — later Sir Frederick — Elliot, the Assistant Under - Secretary of State.

One of the foremost Heads of Departments was Sir Henry Taylor, the poet, author of *Philip van Artevelde*. He was also a great authority on Colonial subjects. The ease with which the work was done in those days is shown by the fact that Sir Henry Taylor was allowed to live principally out of town, his work being sent down to him every day by post. I knew him at Bournemouth, where he had a house, and where he carried on his Colonial Office business. On more than one occasion I believe he was offered an Under-Secretaryship of State, but declined it for fear of his liberty being restricted. He had married a daughter of Lord Monteagle, a sister of Mr. Spring-Rice, whom I have mentioned elsewhere and who was a great friend of mine in the Foreign Office.

Another prominent member of the Colonial Office was Mr. Dealtry—a son of the celebrated Archdeacon. He, for a long time, managed the affairs of the Australian Department.

As Assistant Private Secretary I was fortunate enough to obtain the services of Mr. Arthur Birch, then a clerk in the Colonial Office. I had some intimate friends in his family. He subsequently held several important appointments in the Colonies, for which he received the K.C.M.G. He is now the West End representative of the Bank of England.

One of my pleasantest recollections of the time when I was Secretary to Sir Edward Lytton was that of taking a tour with him through the Lake Country. He was well versed in its history, and in the poetry of the Lake School.

During my term of office as Secretary to Lord Lytton, I naturally made the acquaintance of many distinguished colonists. Amongst them was Sir Charles Nicholson, who had settled in Australia as a physician. He held office more than once, and, when Queensland was established, he accompanied the first Governor to that Colony, and was made Speaker of the House of Assembly. Sir Charles was the premier baronet of Australia.

I also made the acquaintance of Sir George Macleay, who came of a scientific family. His father was Colonial Secretary of New South Wales, and had founded the Linnæan Society. I believe it was he who gave Botany Bay its name.

Sir George Macleay had some interesting anecdotes respecting the Australian natives, whom he described as very intelligent. He visited one distant part of the Colony by steamer. There he found that the inhabitants had recently been instructed in the doctrines of Christianity ; but they all believed that the history of the New Testament was going on still and that the principal persons were still alive. When the steamer came to the landing-place, the natives came up and said to the Captain, "How do, Captain ? All well at Sydney ? How's the Governor ? And how's 'Postle Paul ? "

On one occasion, when riding, Sir George saw in the distance some one who afterwards turned out to be a clergyman. He asked his native guide who the gentleman was, and received the reply, "Him white man—belong to Sunday. Put his shirt outside trouser and talk long corrobery 'bout debble-debble."

It appears that the cattle browsing in the Australian bush have a very keen scent for natives, of whom they are afraid. One day, when Sir George was riding with his guide, he saw in the distance a drove running away for no apparent reason. He said to his guide, "Why are those cattle running away ? " The native replied, " Me 'tinkee."

There was an Australian millionaire whose

fortune was said to have been accumulated in the following manner. Being in Australia at the time of the discovery of gold in Victoria, he at once went to live in the city, later on known as Melbourne, and took a house next door to the Bank, where all the gold was stored that came from the mines. He proceeded to dig a tunnel between his cellar and the cellars of the Bank where the gold was stored, and at once accumulated a very large fortune.

Another man, G——, a contractor, married a remarkably able woman, who for a long time held rather a prominent position in London, in certain political and financial quarters. The origin of his fortune was as follows. At the time of the gold being found in Victoria, he went there with his wife, after obtaining an ordinary letter of introduction from Messrs. Rothschild to some influential persons at Melbourne. He observed that the whole city, then becoming so important, was unpaved. Presenting himself to the authorities, who believed him to be an agent of Messrs. Rothschild, he asked to be trusted with the contract for paving the town at a certain price. The authorities inquired where they should find the money to pay him for the work. He said, "Leave that to me," and the contract was signed. He then found a contractor willing to execute the works for a certain sum, less than that stipulated for with the municipality.

His next step was to bring out a loan, to be

repaid by the municipality out of the money
destined for the contract. This loan was eagerly
taken up by persons in Melbourne itself, who, at
that moment, had no means of investing their
savings, and G—— left Melbourne, within a fortnight of his arrival, with a profit of about forty
thousand pounds.

Sir Edward Lytton used frequently to ask
Colonial visitors to stay with him. I remember
that one particular guest, who had never been in
England before, but was well versed in English
literature, turned out at the end of his visit to
be under the impression that Knebworth was
Kenilworth.

Amongst others whose acquaintance I made at
Sir Edward Lytton's house was Mr. Dallas, the
United States Minister, who, with his family, came
there frequently. Sir Edward Lytton was greatly
admired in America. He had a somewhat close
connection with that country from the fact that
his brother, Sir Henry Bulwer, had passed a long
time as Minister at Washington. As has been
mentioned elsewhere, he was one of the authors
of the Clayton-Bulwer Treaty.

I once heard Mr. Dallas make an excellent
speech at an Agricultural Dinner at Stevenage.
Before that occasion, I had never heard any
American eloquence; but it struck me, though
somewhat peculiar, as very forcible. Mr. Dallas
used to make a pause after every word, and,
after a certain time, this habit had the effect of

emphasising to a marked degree the opinions he wished to expound.

An American Secretary, a cheery and rather rollicking young man, came to Knebworth at the same time as a certain clergyman, remarkably self-complacent, of the genus known as "squarson." The contrast between the two guests was remarkable. On one occasion, the squarson, standing with his back to the fire, delivered himself of some pompous remarks. "I was going through Paris," he said, "and I saw a placard announcing that a gathering of Americans was to be held in the neighbourhood. I attended the meeting, and," turning to the American, "you must acknowledge that the occasion was one to draw forth all the eloquence of American hearts. It was the death of Webster." The American replied, "Yes, sir. I agree with you. Mr. Webster was a very jolly old fellow."

Another American gentleman, during this visit, also gave me two specimens of his native humour. Some people were travelling on a steamer in America, and there was a man on board who came from the West. My friend said that there was always some joke about Westerners, and one man—thinking himself humorous—went up to this passenger and said, "You don't remember me? I come from your neighbourhood." The other replied, "Oh, I remember you well. I recollect when you was born. Your mother had twins— a boy and a monkey. The boy died."

Another anecdote was of a public functionary in high office who went to make enquiries about a new settlement that was to be founded. He asked the Head what was most wanted. The reply was, "We require water, and a little good society." The functionary answered, "That's what hell requires."

During 1858 a marriage was arranged between the eldest son of the King of Prussia and the Princess Royal of England. This was the first wedding that took place of any of the children of the Queen, and the rejoicings in England were great.

In March a Treaty of Peace was signed between Great Britain and Persia, putting an end to the war which had been going on for some time. It had been brought about by the following letter from the Shah, which, together with others written by his Ministers, was considered offensive to the British Minister.

*December* 1855.

Last night we read the paper written by the English Minister Plenipotentiary, and were much surprised at the rude, unmeaning, disgusting, and insolent tone and purport. The letter which he before wrote was also impertinent. We have also heard that, in his own house, he is constantly speaking disrespectfully of us and of you, but we never believed; now, however, he has introduced it in an official letter. We are, therefore, convinced that this man, Mr. Murray, is stupid, ignorant, and insane, who has the audacity and impudence to insult even kings! From the time of Shah Sultan Hossein (when Persia was in its most disorganised state, and during the last fourteen years of his life, when by

serious illness he was incapacitated for business) up to the
present time, no disrespect towards the Sovereign has been
tolerated, either from the Government or its Agent.   What
has happened now, that this foolish Minister Plenipotentiary
acts with such temerity?   It appears that our friendly Missions are not acquainted with the wording of that document ;
give it now to Meerza Abbas and Meerza Malcum, that they
may take and duly explain it to the French Minister and
Hyder Effendi, that they may see how improperly he has
written.   Since last night till now our time has been passed
in vexation.   We now command you, in order that you may
yourself know, and also acquaint the Missions, that until the
Queen of England herself makes us a suitable apology for the
insolence of her Envoy, we will never receive back this her
foolish Minister, who is a simpleton, nor accept from her
Government any other Minister.

Three Canadian statesmen came to England
in 1858 to study certain points.   They were Mr.
Cartier, Mr. Ross, and Mr. Galt, who was a son of
the celebrated author.   All three had held high
office in Canada.   They were invited to stay at
Knebworth, and, at a dinner given by Sir Edward
Lytton, they made most interesting speeches, in
which they laid claim to being the advisers of the
British Crown for Colonial affairs.   Subsequently
to this, I think, Sir John Rose was named High
Commissioner for Canada.   The rapid progress
made by that country may be said to have begun
with the visit of these Canadian statesmen.

The year 1858 was remarkable in the Diplomatic
Service through the appointment of Marshal
Pélissier as French Ambassador in London.   The
period was also one of interest owing to the foundation of British Columbia.   An expedition of Royal

XXIII FAREWELL SPEECH 271

Engineers was organised to go there. On their embarkation Sir Edward Lytton made a speech, which has never till now been published, and which, to my mind, was one of the best he ever delivered :—

Soldiers! I have just come to say to you a few kind words of parting.

You are going to a distant country, not, I trust, to fight against men, but to conquer nature; not to besiege cities, but to create them; not to overthrow kingdoms, but to assist in establishing new communities under the sceptre of your own Queen.

For these noble objects, you, Soldiers of the Royal Engineers, have been specially selected from the ranks of Her Majesty's armies. Wherever you go, you carry with you not only English valour and English loyalty, but English intelligence and English skill. Wherever a difficulty is to be encountered, which requires in the soldier not only courage and discipline, but education and science, Sappers and Miners, the Sovereign of England turns with confidence to you. If this were a service of danger and bloodshed, I know that on every field, and against all odds, the honour of the English arms would be safe from a stain in your hands; but in that distant region to which you depart, I hope that our national flag will wave in peaceful triumph, on many a Royal birthday, from walls and church-towers which you will have assisted to raise from the wilderness, and will leave to remote generations as the bloodless trophies of your renown.

Soldiers! you will be exposed to temptation. You go where gold is discovered—where avarice inflames all the passions. But I know that the voice of duty and the love of honour will keep you true to your officers, and worthy of the trust which your Sovereign places in her Royal Engineers.

On my part, as one of the Queen's Ministers, I promise that all which can conduce to your comfort, and fairly reward your labours, shall be thoughtfully considered. You have heard from my distinguished friend, your commanding officer, that every man amongst you who shall have served six years in British Columbia, and receives at the end of that time a certificate of good conduct, will be entitled—if he desire to become a resident in the Colony—to thirty acres of land, aye, and of fertile land, in that soil which you will have assisted to bring into settlement and cultivation.

In the strange and wild district to which you are bound, you will meet with men of all countries, of all characters and kinds. You will aid in preserving peace and order, not by your numbers, not by mere force, but by the respect which is due to the arms of England, and the spectacle of your own discipline and good conduct. You will carefully refrain from quarrel and brawl. You will scorn, I am sure, the vice which degrades God's rational creature to the level of the brute— I mean the vice of intoxication. I am told that is the vice which most tempts common soldiers. I hope not, but I am sure it is the vice which least tempts thoughtful, intelligent, successful men. You are not common soldiers—you are to be the pioneers of civilisation.

Nothing more counteracts the taste for drink than the taste for instruction. And Colonel Moody will endeavour to form for your amusement and profit, in hours of relaxation, a suitable collection of books. I beg to offer my contribution to that object, and I offer it, not as a public Minister, out of public monies, but in my private capacity as a lover of literature myself, and your friend and well-wisher.

Farewell! Heaven speed and prosper you! The enterprise before you is indeed glorious. Ages hence, industry and commerce will crowd the roads that you will have made; travellers from all nations will halt on the bridges you will have first flung over solitary rivers, and gaze on gardens and cornfields that you will have first carved from the wilderness. Christian races will dwell in the cities of which you will map the sites and lay the foundations. You go not as the enemies but as the benefactors of the land you visit, and children unborn will, I believe, bless the hour when Queen Victoria sent forth her Sappers and Miners to found a second England on the shores of the Pacific.

# CHAPTER XXIV

Ionian Islands—Tenure of Islands—Sir Thomas Maitland's Constitution—Ionian titles—*The Three Constitutions*—Desire for union
with Greece—Constant friction—Legislative anomalies—Consular
jurisdiction—Mr. Gladstone's Mission.

GREAT difficulties had arisen in the Ionian Islands,
owing to the anomalous character of our hold
upon them. When, by the Peace at the end of
the Napoleonic Wars, the Ionian States were
placed under the protection of Great Britain, it
was found very difficult to adjust conditions under
which the new system was to be carried on.

The tenure of the Islands by England was of a
most curious character, and made up of contradictions. It was derived from the Treaty of Paris,
but in somewhat vague language, and did not give
to the British Government that absolute and direct
control exercised over the Colonies of England.
With the object, however, of assuming authority by
indirect means, Sir Thomas Maitland constructed a
constitution whereby the Lord High Commissioner
practically enjoyed a good deal of power. It was
a constitution which in his hands, and with his
skill, had produced good results.

In a letter to Lord Bathurst, dated September 10, 1817, Sir Thomas Maitland said that the Constitution would want what his brother, Lord Lauderdale, called a "shall and will doctor," and this was found in Sir Thomas Maitland himself. He fully appreciated both the defects and the virtues of the Ionians. In the *Life* of him, written by Mr. Frewen Lord, Sir Charles Napier is reported as saying of them at that time :—

> The merry Greeks are worth all other nations put to-gether. I like to see them, to hear them; I like their fun, their good-humour, their paddy ways. . . . All their bad habits are Venetian; their wit, their eloquence, their good-nature are their own.

Sir Thomas Maitland borrowed from the policy of the Venetians, when they held the Islands, of appealing a good deal to the vanity of the subject race. The Venetians had made a regulation whereby it was possible to confer the degree of Doctor on Ionians, without examination. This was much appreciated, and, though the Venetians took no titles themselves, the islanders were freely raised to the rank of Count. Officials were entitled to enjoy the most flattering adjectives, such as "The Most Excellent," "The Most Illustrious," "The Most Honourable," according to their rank. The President of the Senate was styled "His Highness." When the Order of St. Michael and St. George was founded, the first idea was to call it the Order of St. John of Jerusalem, or of St. Spiridion; but its present name was adopted, and the Order is now given to the King's Colonial and Diplomatic servants.

I have a book called *The Three Constitutions*, describing the government of the Ionian Islands. The constitution under the Russians, in 1800, which was, I believe, the work of Count Capo d'Istria and Count Mocenigo, two Ionians in the Russian Diplomatic Service, realised in its first article the aspirations of the Ionians :—

La Repubblica delle Sette Isole Unite è una ed Aristo-cratica.

The next constitution was drawn up on the French occupation of the Islands in 1807, by General Berthier, who was Governor-General and Commander-in-Chief; and the third, which was still in vigour in 1858, was promulgated by Sir Thomas Maitland in January 1817. This constitution presented the appearance of very wide liberties, which were merely kept in check by certain manipulations of the constituencies electing to the Legislative Assembly ; but, as a fact, the Lord High Commissioner exercised great control over the electoral lists. This constitution had, no doubt, effected great good by releasing the peasantry from the arbitrary control of the old nobles. Certain modifications were made by Lord Seaton in 1847. His reforms, by cutting away the modifying pro-visions, converted theoretical liberties into real ones, and almost into license. The Ionians, however, had never been reconciled to their subjection to

England.　At the time of the Greek Revolution, they became very much excited when they thought that the action of the British Government evinced a tendency to support attacks against the Greeks. Their leading idea was to become part of the Greek kingdom, and nothing short of this would in any way satisfy them.　It was plain, therefore, that, owing to constant friction with the Ionian Legislature, the constitution required reform.

Great difficulties presented themselves on financial questions, which could only be settled with the good-will of the Assembly.　Still further questions arose as to the relations of the Ionian Islands with foreign subjects; for the Ionians did not think they were in any way bound to further the foreign policy of the British Government, or to abstain from acts which might embroil England with foreign countries.

The immediate cause of the difficulties in 1858 was the fact that the municipal authorities had interfered to prevent the supply of provisions to some Turkish troopships which had stopped in the harbour.　It is useless to go into the details of this question, though it was evidently one of extreme gravity, for the contention was that this refusal on the part of the municipality of Corfu could not be controlled by the Protecting Power.

The dilemma seemed almost insoluble.　It was clear that the Ionian Islands stood in great need of reform.　Finances were getting into disorder, and constant slight collisions occurred between the Protecting Power and the islanders.

There were some curious anomalies, too, in Ionian legislation. The land laws required much revision. The law of succession was very complicated, and mortgages were the rule and not the exception. Besides this there were certain rights, which existed nowhere else, and which came down from the times of the Venetians.

More than one Venetian noble among the *signori* of the islands had rights to certain portions of the lands or their produce ; some to a half, some a third, some a fifth ; but all leading to complications. Thus, on occasions of death and succession, the following anomalous position often presented itself.

One great source of wealth in the island of Corfu was oil. Sometimes a man would die possessing the right of obtaining what he could from certain olive-trees belonging to a landowner : this right was probably mortgaged. There were other persons who had a perpetual tenant right, who were called *coloni*, and they might cultivate these trees on paying a portion of the produce to their owner. The *coloni* also had mortgages. Sometimes a tree, by the minute subdivision of property, was found to belong to several persons, and this would be the position. As a whole, the tree belonged to A., and was mortgaged to B., with perpetual rights of cultivation belonging to C. A. had a mortgage on the property, which belonged to him from the payments of the *coloni*.   The *colono* had a mortgage, and there was a fourth party who had the perpetual right of purchasing the fruit from the *colono*, and this perpetual right was also mortgaged.   At times ownership was limited to the branch of a tree.   It was impossible to clear up these points, as the Legislature refused to interfere.

By the Constitution, the Legislature was summoned of right every two years for three months, during which time they were supposed to produce a new budget; but if the discussion was not finished by the end of the three months, the session terminated, and, by the existing rule, the last budget was *ipso facto* re-enacted.

The great difficulty in obtaining the budget was owing to the jealousy of the different islands. Zante would say, "Cephalonia has this: why should we not have that?" and it very often ended in what the Americans call "log-rolling"; that is to say, Zante would say, "We will vote for your having an hospital, if you will vote for giving us a pier."

Matters were rather complicated by the reports of many military officers who declared that the Ionian Islands were of no great value strategically. Enormous sums had been spent on the fortifications of Corfu; but it was said that by one approach no enemy could be prevented from reaching the town. Large sums were due to the Protecting Government, and an annual sum of money devoted to the payment of the British officials was gradually dwindling away.

Questions had also arisen as to consular jurisdiction over Ionian subjects. As is well known,
differences between British subjects in Turkey, and
even crimes, are adjudicated upon by consuls, who
administer justice according to the laws of their
own country. The Ionians, hitherto, had been
subject to the same jurisdiction, namely, to that
of the British consuls, who adjudicated according
to the laws of England. A pretension, however,
had been recently put forward that British consuls
should administer justice to Ionian subjects according to Ionian law. This they based on an article
of the Constitution which said, "British consuls
in all foreign states, without exception, shall be
considered to have the character of consuls and
vice-consuls of the United States of the Ionian
Islands, and the latter shall have the right to their
fullest protection." As by this article it appeared
that the British consuls did not administer justice
to Ionian citizens as British but as Ionian consuls,
the Ionians based on it their claim to be judged
by Ionian law. This right was subsequently
admitted, and here a curious circumstance occurred.
By the Constitution, the Lord High Commissioner
and the Senate—which consisted of five and their
President—were authorised, at a time when Parliament was not sitting, to enact laws called *atti di
Governo* — acts of Government — which had the
validity of law until the next meeting of Parliament. The discussion of the rights of the Ionians
lasted for a long time, and I once had to pay a visit

to Constantinople, where a complicated question
had arisen, owing to a decision given by a British
consul in the Principalities. At length it was
decided to publish an *atto di Governo* to settle the
matter ; but this, unfortunately, was completed
only immediately before the annexation of the
Islands to Greece, and therefore was what is called
in French *un coup d'épée donné dans l'eau.*

When the crisis in the Ionian Islands arose in
August 1858, Sir Edward Lytton induced the
Cabinet to adopt the most conciliatory attitude
possible. It was the wish of the Government, he
wrote, " that the Ionian people should be, without
delay, convinced of the earnest desire of the
Government to see the genuine interests of the
Islands advanced by the removal of whatever
defects in their institutions might impair the
desired harmony between the Ionian Legislature
and the Protecting Power." It was therefore
considered advisable to invite Mr. Gladstone to
undertake a Mission to the Ionian Islands, with
a view to adjusting the differences, if possible,
between the Protecting Power and the people
protected. His appointment to assist Sir John
Young, the Lord High Commissioner, was
announced to the latter in a long and weighty
despatch from Sir Edward Lytton, of which the
following is an extract :—

In all these disputes I have failed to perceive anything
that the forbearance and good sense of authorities in office,
so dignified and responsible, might not readily adjust, while

there is much that any harsh or hasty action on the part of the Protecting Government might aggravate into lasting discords.

If, on the other hand, I am to take a more serious view of the dissensions which have been submitted to my judgment, I might inquire whether their origin may not be traced to certain defects in the Ionian Constitution, which the Constitution itself enables the Legislature to remove.

These are the general principles and sentiments entertained by Her Majesty's Government with reference to the pending questions which at present agitate the Ionian mind, and which of course so materially augment your official difficulties and responsibilities. With a view to assist you in discharging the trust committed to you, and also to derive the great advantage of a weighty opinion on Ionian affairs, pronounced by a statesman who belongs to his country rather than to any party in it, who has already occupied, with marked distinction, the highest offices of the State, whose mind has grasped foreign as well as domestic questions with equal vigour and success, and whose renown as a Homeric scholar will justly commend him to the sympathies of an Hellenic race, Her Majesty's Government have resolved on despatching the Right Hon. W. E. Gladstone as a Special Commissioner to inquire into and report on the whole state of government in the Ionian Islands, and on the political relations between the Protecting Power and the people, so, let me hope, as to lead to the equitable and constitutional adjustment of every existing difficulty.

You will not fail to observe in the choice of Mr. Gladstone, a gentleman not unknown to you in public and private life, the intention of Her Majesty's Government to place the most generous interpretation upon the policy which you have pursued, to strengthen your hands by every legitimate means, and to manifest to the Ionian people that the interests and welfare of their islands are in this case receiving that special consideration and investigation which have been bestowed in somewhat similar political emergencies on some of the most ancient and important dependencies of the British Crown.

# CHAPTER XXV

MR. GLADSTONE was well qualified for the mission
confided to him.  He had a thorough knowledge
of Italian, the language commonly spoken in the
Ionian Islands, and his reputation as a statesman
and as a Hellenic scholar was very great.  It
would have been impossible to find a representative
of England whose personal qualities were more
adapted to the nation with which he was about
to negotiate.  He was appointed Lord High
Commissioner Extraordinary, and started early in
November, accompanied by Mrs. and Miss Gladstone.  He had with him as Secretary to his
Mission Mr.—afterwards Sir James—Lacaita, a
Neapolitan gentleman well known in literature,
and a great friend of Sir Antonio Panizzi.  Mr.
Gladstone was also accompanied by Mr. Arthur
Gordon — now  Lord  Stanmore — a son of Lord

Aberdeen, the Premier under whom Mr. Gladstone
had served so long, and who himself has since
occupied, with great success, the highest Colonial
positions.

During the time of the preparations for the
Mission, I saw a good deal of Mr. Gladstone, as
he constantly came to my room at the Colonial
Office to meet persons who were invited to give
him information. Amongst others came Sir
Henry Storks. He had passed several years in
the Ionian Islands, when serving in the Army,
and having been, I believe, married to an Italian
lady, spoke that language with great ease and
fluency. He thought himself rather a conqueror,
and on one occasion he told Mr. Gladstone that
one could only deal with the Ionians through the
women. Mr. Gladstone answered that on that
account he would take with him some of the
ladies of his family.

Very shortly after the departure of the Mission,
an event occurred of the greatest possible inconvenience, namely, the publication of two despatches
on the Ionian Islands, containing proposals made
by the Lord High Commissioner, Sir John Young.
This created much perturbation. They had been
printed for the use of the Cabinet, and a number
of copies were lying on the table of an official in
the Colonial Office, covered by a letter-weight.
A friend of this official happened to come and
see him, and, being left alone, abstracted a copy
from the heap of papers, his eye having been

attracted by the words "Ionian Islands" and "Secret and Confidential," which evidently indicated matter of great interest on a subject very much before the public.

The proposal contained in these despatches from Corfu was that steps should be taken to preserve for England, as a colony, the islands of Corfu and Paxo, and to abandon the protectorate of the southern islands. In answer to this recommendation, Sir Edward Lytton had replied that the British Government could not admit the possibility of "an enforced abolition of the constitution conferred by charter, without the consent either of the Legislature, or that of the Powers of Europe, to such a revisal of the Treaty as would give the protecting sovereign rights which the Treaty does not at present legally sanction."

This extraordinary violation of confidence gave me a great deal of anxiety, as some persons ill-naturedly insinuated that the publication had been purposely effected by the Government with a view to damaging a political opponent. I was in consequence instructed to write the following letter to the *Times* :—

I am directed to inform you that the recent publication of two despatches from the Lord High Commissioner of the Ionian Islands took place without the knowledge or sanction, direct or indirect, of Her Majesty's Government, and that from the time of their appearance strict inquiry has been in progress into the manner in which they became public.

Mr. Strachey, précis-writer at the Colonial

Office—a man of great ability, who had been in India—and myself spent literally days and nights in ascertaining how these papers had become public.

We had almost given up the search in despair when we at last learnt the truth, almost by accident. One evening we went to the office of the newspaper which had published the despatches in question, and there we met a gentleman of considerable importance. We explained to him how hard it was that we should not be able to obtain the information we required, as it caused doubts to be entertained of persons who were quite innocent. He thereupon gave us some clue as to the names of the informant, which were peculiar. He would not tell us the actual names, but said he had done all he could by giving us this intimation. The next day, on going to the Colonial Office, we found that the official from whose table the papers had been abstracted had informed Mr. Elliot, the Under-Secretary of State, that he suspected Mr. Wellington Guernsey, a friend of his, who had been in his room the day that the papers were lost. The name tallied with the indications given us at the newspaper office, and thus the mystery was cleared up.

The prosecution of Mr. Wellington Guernsey ended in his acquittal, on the ground that the papers and print had no intrinsic value. This view, put forward by the defendant's counsel, was combated by the Judge, Baron Martin, but adopted by the jury. The counsel for the Crown were the Attorney-General, Sir Fitzroy Kelly, and Mr. Serjeant Ballantine. It was said that the jury had resented the employment of so big a gun as the Attorney-General.

A great part of my time was engaged in keeping Mr. Gladstone informed of minute events that occurred in conjunction with his visit to the Ionian Islands. Much tittle-tattle was raised in England on account of a report that Mr. Gladstone, following the example of all the Greeks, had kissed the hand of a Greek Archbishop. Disagreeable innuendoes were made public, and Sir Edward Lytton thought it advisable that, in my letters of gossip, I should call Mr. Gladstone's attention to these matters, in case they had been exaggerated. He replied to me as follows on the 7th of February 1859, from Corfu :—

The charge against me in the second paragraph is true. I hope, however, that Sir E. Lytton will not, in his consideration for me, entangle himself in such a matter ; but, as he knows nothing now, will continue to know nothing on the matter of fact, and will say that the subject did not enter into his instructions or my despatches, and that he presumes I shall be at home in two or three more weeks to answer for all my misdeeds. In this case you would, I presume, simply keep to yourself my avowal.

On the 13th of January he had written to me as follows :—

Your letter was very acceptable, and I hope you will send me another without any apology.
.It contained important news connected with my Mission ;

for if as you say the Cabinet met on the 10th (telegram said 12th) I may have Mr. St. John here next Monday with the result, and may reply by our quick mail of Tuesday. We have a messenger from Vienna come to-day, whom we shall keep in pickle until then.

I have not got your *Herald*. I have written to Lord Carnarvon about the telegrams.

From what you say, "Charles & George" will not make a good dinner except for men with an appetite. I have no means of knowing, at present, how that stands. But I should think there would be no extreme keenness to prevent the Government from playing its card, whatever it may be, on Reform. It is a subject that yields few trumps or honours.

The deaths you mention are very touching, and they have been accompanied with others of much interest to us.

Our winter is now become clear and cool. Mr. Lacaita has, however, had a smart attack which his zeal has not permitted him to nurse with sufficient care.

Though the telegram of Friday (7th) told us Sir J. Young was recalled, he has not had any letter to-day to that effect. Our letters are up to 5th.

Mr. Gladstone made a tour through the Ionian Islands, and returned to Corfu on Christmas Day. On the 5th of February he went in state to the Senate, and in the course of his speech suggested a number of reforms, while adding that Her Majesty refused to abandon obligations to which she was bound by the Treaty of Paris.

The *Times* wrote of "Mr. Gladstone's blandishments, carried beyond the bounds of dignity and common sense. He leaves Corfu, after throwing down a heap of suggestions on the table of the representative assembly." The Press, on the whole, was very much opposed to Mr. Gladstone's Mission. On his return he was offered the Grand

Cross of the Bath.   Among his reasons for refusing it he made use of the following quaint expression : " I am an old bachelor of the commonalty."

The suggested reforms may be summed up as follows : the improvement of Ionian institutions by extending the sphere of the Ionian element, and contracting the sphere of the British ; the establishment of a ministry open to the influence of the Chambers, combined with the effective appropriation to the Assembly of what is termed the power of the purse.   It was also proposed that on a joint address from the two Chambers, praying for the removal of a Ministry, it should cease to hold office ; that all acts of the Lord High Commissioner should require counter-signing by a responsible Minister ; that the Lord High Commissioner should be responsible to Ionian authority ; and that the Ionian Parliament should be permitted to lodge complaints against the Lord High Commissioner.

Though these proposed reforms were of the widest possible character, the Ionian Parliament pronounced them inadmissible, and again demanded freedom and union with Greece.   Mr. Gladstone had aimed at establishing a state of things similar to that of a self - governing British colony ; but the conditions and the mutual relations between Great Britain and the Ionian people had no precedent.   The Ionians were not bound by any natural allegiance to the Protecting Power.   They had been handed over by the vote of a Conference,

held when the world was under very different
conditions, and before that, they had been under
the dominion of various other nations.  It was
impossible for them to feel enthusiasm for the
British.  Everywhere matters were progressing in
the sense of liberty and national consolidation.
Greece had been made free, and Italy was in a
state of insurrection.  Either of these two countries
— particularly Greece — would have been more
congenial to the Ionian nature.

In refusing Mr. Gladstone's proposals, it was
evident that the last offer had been made and
rejected, and that nothing would satisfy the islanders
but complete liberty and union with Greece.

An Ionian gentleman once said to me : " How
can we be happy when the principal language
spoken in the island is a foreign one ? when we
have to look upon every British soldier as our
political master ?  No doubt Great Britain has
given us a great many of the material appliances
of civilisation.  She has made roads for us ; but we
do not want roads.  We would rather have tracks
over which our horses and mules could convey our
produce.  There is a great deal of society in the
island ; but we do not want society.  We prefer
remaining in our homes in the country without
being obliged to dress for dinner.  And those of
us who have ambitions, and require a higher
political and social atmosphere, would be better
contented if they could carry out their aspirations
in Greece, and belong to a nation which certainly

has had a great past, and which may renew in the future the traditions of its history. We consider that the Ionian people are subject to an abnormal state of things. We are obliged to accept the orders of a foreign Government, and that simply because it is the desire of the Powers of Europe that we should not form part of the Greek kingdom."

Mr. Gladstone left Corfu to return to England on the 26th of February 1859, Sir Henry Storks, the new Lord High Commissioner, having arrived three days previously. It may be seen, from what I have already said, how difficult was the task of the administration of the Ionian Islands.

In 1859, the Government brought in and were defeated on their Reform Bill. On April 1 of that year, a Cabinet was held to decide whether the Government should retire at once, or dissolve previously. Sir Edward Lytton was for immediate resignation; but, at the Cabinet in question, he was overruled, and it was determined to dissolve. Sir Edward thereupon wrote a memorandum in the following words. This he specially gave to me, and is still in my possession :—

DOWNING STREET, *April* 1, 1859.

Remember my words! From this day dates a change that in a few years will alter the whole face of England. From this day, the extreme Liberals are united. The great towns will be banded for democracy, and democracy in England is as sure as that we are in this room. Nothing like this day since Charles I. did much the same as we are doing.

PALAIOKASTRITZA, CORFU.

Previously to the defeat of Lord Derby's Government, I had been named to succeed Sir George Bowen as Secretary to the Lord High Commissioner of the Ionian Islands. Sir George, who was a great Greek scholar, had been appointed Governor of the new colony, which, by the express wish of Queen Victoria, had been called Queensland. On this occasion I received the following very kind letter from Mr. Gladstone :—

I congratulate you very sincerely on your appointment. I am confident both that you will discharge exceedingly well the direct duties of the office (you may, however, find some difficulty at first with the modern Greek) and that you will carry into them and into your whole course the spirit of which it is so desirable that every Englishman in office should set an example.

I presume you will not go out for some little time, and I hope to have opportunities of seeing you before you go.

Sir Henry Storks brought with him to Corfu two *aides-de-camp* : one was Major Peel, the son of General Peel. He had been wounded in the Crimea, and consequently at times suffered dreadfully from rheumatic attacks. The other was a young gentleman named Strahan, of the Artillery, who had been chosen by Mr. Gladstone as his A.D.C. from hearing an account of his proficiency in Greek. On the departure of Major Peel, who was promoted to a staff appointment in England, Lieutenant Evelyn Baring was named his successor. After a brilliant career he is now Lord Cromer. Strangely enough, his first achievement in the public service was of a financial character. When he arrived at Corfu, as a subaltern of Artillery, the accounts of the Artillery mess were found to be in some disorder. Lieutenant Baring was asked to undertake the management. He did this so well as to pave the way to his administrative reputation.

General Sir George Buller commanded at Corfu. He was married to a daughter of Sir John Macdonald, the Adjutant - General in London. His military secretary was Colonel Leicester Curzon, a man thoroughly honourable and amiable, and a universal favourite. He ended his life as General Leicester Smyth, having changed his name, and at one time commanded the forces at the Cape of Good Hope. General Buller's other A.D.C. was Mr. Arthur Ponsonby, to whom I have already alluded as being an old friend of mine, and a member of a family with which I had been long acquainted.

Mr.—later Sir Henry—Bulwer, a nephew of Sir Edward Lytton, was appointed Resident, first at Paxo, and then at Cerigo, the ancient Cythæra. Before that he had been Secretary to the Governor of Prince Edward Island. On the annexation of the Islands he received a Colonial appointment, and was Governor, with great success, of several important dependencies, the last of them being Cyprus.

# CHAPTER XXVI

WHEN I assumed my office in the Ionian Islands,
there were many questions, not strictly speaking
political, to which I was asked to turn my attention. Sir Henry Storks was fond of occupying
himself with detail, and he was anxious that I
should devote my studies, as far as possible, to
the development of those resources of the country
which were available, irrespective of conflicting
politics or current administration. With this object,
Sir Henry Storks issued several Commissions of
which I was a member.

In the first instance, on March 3, 1860, a Commission was formed for enquiring into the financial
and fiscal system of the Ionian States, with the
view of preparing for submission to Parliament a
scheme for the more equal adjustment of the public
burdens. It ended in the preparation of a report
which might have been of value, had we continued
the occupation of the islands.

The fiscal system of the Ionian States had

hitherto principally relied on import and export duties. From these sources, together with some revenue from the sale of stamps, the monopoly of salt and gunpowder, post office, port and health dues, the income of the country had been chiefly derived.

The average revenue of the last twenty years, general and municipal, had been £172,000, and during the same period the expenditure had amounted to £182,000. Debts owing by individuals to the Government amounted to no less a sum than £200,000.

The collection of the rents from municipal property in Corfu showed a deficit. That property might have yielded a considerable sum ; but tenants of municipal houses frequently declined to pay rent until judicially forced to do so, and social ties, so strong in a small community, generally deterred the authorities from resorting to so stringent a measure. The same might be said of the water. Pure water was supplied to the town of Corfu for a certain payment; but receipts from this source amounted barely to £700 a year, of which some £400 was paid by the British garrison, or about one-seventh of the population.

The gross debt of the State was £298,000, of which £90,000 was arrears of the military contribution due by the Ionians to the Protecting Power.

It was thought that the duties on currants, one of the staple products of the Islands, demanded

reduction.   The only country which competed with
the Ionian Islands in the production of currants
was   Greece.    Export   duties   in   that   country
amounted to twenty drachmas, or 14s. 2d. sterling,
per 1000 lbs.; and the Commission was of opinion
that, considering the superior quality of the Ionian
fruit, and the greater facilities for its conveyance,
the Ionian currant-duty might be assimilated to
that of Greece and be fixed at 14s. 2d.   It was
also thought that duties might be levied on oil,
wine, sugar and tobacco.   In fact, by an adjustment of these different sources of revenue, it was
considered that the annual deficit might be met.

I   was   sent   home   in   1860   to   submit   to   the
British   Government   the   proposed   changes   sug-
gested by the Financial Commission, and also to
be of use in the passage through Parliament of a
Bill for legitimising British marriages in the Ionian
Islands.

When   the   occupation   first   took   place,   the
object had been to assimilate everything in the
Islands to the condition of a British Colony, and no
law had been passed regulating marriages between
British subjects.    When in the Foreign Office,
I   had   been   employed   on   the   Consular   Marriage
Act, passed in 1849, and I was struck with
the necessity for a similar Act for the Ionian
Islands.    These Islands, not being a British possession, were not subject to British law, and as
there was no consul or diplomatic representative
from England, there was no Act which regulated

such marriages. Although no question had been raised as to the validity of past marriages, it was considered desirable to establish a system, and to acknowledge the validity of all marriages previously contracted. One couple were most unfortunately situated : they had married and, ascertaining that the marriage was not valid, had separated and married other persons. They displayed great anxiety lest the Act should validate their first marriage, and thus make them retrospectively bigamists.

At the time of this visit of mine to England, I was also appointed Delegate for the Ionian Islands to the International Statistical Congress then held in London, under the presidency of Prince Albert and Lord Brougham. Lord Brougham I had known previously at Holland House, where I met him more than once ; but it was the only occasion on which I had the honour of speaking with the Prince.

On my return, I was accompanied by Sir Edward Lytton, to whom Sir Henry Storks had offered the use of his country house, called the "Casino," as he very much wished to see the Ionian Islands.

Sir Edward Lytton's conversation was extraordinarily interesting, and his studies were most varied. There seemed to be scarcely a subject of which he had not some knowledge, and often a profound one. There was one story that he had read in some book which he never was able to find again.  It was of a man who lived to an advanced age.  Wishing to be perfectly free, he summoned his children and said, " I do not wish to be troubled with you any longer.  I shall divide my property among you, reserving a certain portion for myself.  You need never expect that share, as I shall leave it to the Church.  All I want is to be left alone."  He then practised the life that he thought conducive to longevity, and finally attained the age of 150, when his teeth and hair grew again.  Elated by these circumstances, he married, but died almost immediately. Sir Edward Lytton said he found this story in an old book, and I recollect that he and I took great pains to discover it.  I wrote to Sir Antonio Panizzi, who was one of the people most likely to know ; but he did not recollect the story, and I have never been able to find it.

Occult matters always interested Sir Edward Lytton deeply, and through the instrumentality of Sir Patrick Colquhoun, one of the Judges, who spoke Greek fluently, he interviewed some fortune-tellers who explained their methods of procedure.  One of these was to go at night into a shallow part of the sea, where, strange to stay, they stated that they were severely beaten by the Naiads.  It is curious how long this tradition survived in a Greek community.  The most popular book circulated in Greece was the legendary history of Alexander the Great.  It attributed to him extraordinary and sometimes supernatural adventures.

Sir Edward Lytton's feeling for the occult may
be seen principally in his novel of *Zanoni,* as well
as in one or two others of his works, notably *The
Strange Story.*   He had learnt very thoroughly
one of the four compartments of necromancy,
namely geomancy.   These compartments are aero-
mancy, the signs of the air, which foretells the
future by the flight of birds ; pyromancy, whereby
the future is found in the position of burning
coals ; hydromancy, in the circles formed when
stones are thrown into water in a particular
manner ; and geomancy, the art most practised at
the present day, which refers to a forecast of the
future by means of dots made in the sand.   It is
mentioned by many English writers—by Chaucer
and Dryden—and is at present largely practised
in China, in the Soudan and in Egypt, where
its practitioners may daily be seen making signs in
the dust at the corners of the streets.   Instead of
making marks on the earth itself, it has been the
habit in Europe—one may say for centuries—for
the marks to be made by pen or pencil on a sheet
of paper.   Sometimes, indeed, dice have been used,
but this is not a favourite method.   Several books
on geomancy have been produced at different
periods.   I am in possession of three.   One,
which I think is the best known, is *La Geomance
du Seigneur Christofe de Cattan, Gentilhomme
Geneuois.   Liure non moins plaisant et recreatif,
que d'ingenieuse inuention, pour sçauoir toutes
choses, presentes, passees, et à aduenir.   Auec la*

*Roüe de Pythagoras. Le tout mis en lumiere par Gabriel du Preau ; et par luy dedié à monsieur Nicot, Conseiller du Roy, et maistre des Requestes de l'hostel.* It was published in 1567, under privilege from the King, which is given in full. Another was published in 1657 by the Sieur de Peruchio. I have also a very curious one in manuscript. It was written by the astrologer of Diane de Poitiers and is in black-letter. On the outside of the book is her device of three crossed crescents.

The great professors of the art assert for geomancy the widest possible extension to all subjects :—

Vita, lucrum, fratres, geniti, nati, valetudo,
Uxor, mors, pietas, regnum benefactaque, carcer.

These two hexameters give a name to each of the twelve houses.

This was the distraction that Sir Edward Lytton often sought in the intervals of business and study. Seeing that I was very much interested in the subject, he gave me at Corfu a summary of the art whereby I was enabled to study the rudiments, while waiting for the purchase of the principal authorities on the subject. Whether true or not, the study is very interesting. It may not be inappropriate here to copy Sir Edward Lytton's *Memorandum*, as it also gives a general knowledge of the system. Before doing so, however, I think it desirable shortly to explain, from the books I have mentioned, the means by which this system of divination is carried out.

"Geomancy," according to M. de Cattan, "is a science and an art which consists of points and lines representing the four elements and the stars and planets of the sky. . . . The instruments of this art are pen, ink and paper, or a small stick, and earth, dust, or well-cleaned sand. This method was used by the Chaldeans, Persians, Hebrews, and Egyptians before ink and paper were invented. The science therefore retains the name of geomancy. At present the best system of practising it is with pen, ink, and paper ; to use one's fingers or beans or grain, as is done by the women of Boulogne who want news of their absent friends, and as is still done in Italy, does not please me, nor is it certain in its method. . . . When the questioner makes the dots to form his figure, he must only think of the question for which he makes that figure. First he must make four lines of dots to resemble the first fingers of the left hand, but without counting. Nevertheless he must be sure that he has made at least fourteen dots in each line. The first will be long, like the first finger, called the ' index ' ; the second longer, like the second finger, named the ' medius ' ; the third shorter, in the manner of the third finger, called ' medicus ' ; the fourth smaller than all the others, like the little finger, called ' auricularis ' ; and thus he must form sixteen lines divided into four sets as above. He must not move his hand from the paper, or from the table, earth, or sand which he may be using, until he has finished the sixteen lines, keeping in his heart, while moving his hand, the question for which the figure is made." In each group, the first line is dedicated to fire, the second to air, the third to water, and the fourth to earth. When the figure is complete, each group of four lines is dedicated in a similar way to the four elements.

The figure is then constructed in the following manner, and the explanation will be clearer if reference is made to Lord Lytton's experimental figure (see p. 317). When the lines are made, the number of dots in each line is to be added up, and if the result is an odd number, one dot is to be placed at the end of it ; if an even number, two dots. The first figure on the right-hand side comes from the first group of four lines, the second from the second, the third from the third, and the fourth from the fourth. In order to make the second group of figures, take the dots laterally from right to left of the first four figures, and repeat this process by taking laterally the dots of the second, third, and fourth lines. You thus obtain eight so-called " Houses." To make the ninth and tenth, add together the dots of the first and second, and of the third and fourth houses respectively, marking odd and even as before. To obtain the eleventh house, add together the dots contained in the fifth and sixth houses, and the twelfth house by adding the dots contained in the seventh and eighth.

Having thus formed twelve " Houses," you obtain two " Witnesses.' The witness on the right

is formed by adding together the dots of the ninth
and tenth houses, and the witness on the left is in
a similar way produced by the eleventh and twelfth
houses.   The "Judge" is formed by the combination of the two witnesses.

# CHAPTER XXVII

## LORD LYTTON'S MEMORANDUM

### GEOMANCY

THE figures :—

| Acquisitio | Fortuna Major | Fortuna Minor |
|---|---|---|
| . . | . . | . |
| . | . | . |
| . . | . | . . |
| . . | . | . . |

| Dragon's Head | Dragon's Tail | Lœtitia | Tristitia |
|---|---|---|---|
| . . | . | . | . . |
| . | . | . | . . |
| . | . | . . | . . |
| . | . . | . . | . |

| Populus | Via | Conjunctio |
|---|---|---|
| . . | . | . . |
| . . | . | . |
| . . | . | . |
| . . | . | . . |

| Puer | Puella | Carcer |
|---|---|---|
| . | . | . . |
| . | . . | . |
| . . | . | . . |
| . | . | . |

| Amissio | Albus | Rubens |
|---|---|---|
| . | . . | . . |
| . . | . . | . |
| . | . | . . |
| . | . . | . |

16 *figures.*

303

The good figures generally are :—

```
.   .   .   .   .   .   .     .   .     .
  .     .   .     .   .     .   .     .   .   .
  .     .   .       .   .     .   .     .   .   .
  .       .       .       .   .       .
```
*6 figures.*

The bad :—

```
. .     .       .         . .
  .       . .     .         . .
. .     .       . .       . .
. .       .   . . .     . .
```
*4 figures.*

```
.
. .
.
```
though not bad, is a sign of Mars, and in certain houses signifies quarrel.

The figures more indifferent are : —

```
.     .   .   .     .   .     .
  .     .   .     .   .     .   .
  .     .   .     .   .       .   .
.     .   .     .   .     .   .     .
```

Figures, however, vary in signification, first, according to their House, next, according to conjunctions and aspects, and each has a more peculiar meaning according to the question asked.

There are twelve Houses made by the twelve figures, besides the two Witnesses and Judge.

### SIGNIFICATION OF HOUSES

1st House relates to the personnel of the questioner.

2nd House relates to his house, to things movable, to what may shortly happen ; also indirectly to his affections, wishes, etc.

3rd House relates to brothers, sisters, letters, short journeys.

4th House relates to parents, legacies, the end of life, and the *final* result of things inquired into : generally also to things secret and hidden. It is under Saturn.

5th House relates to children, to pleasures,' to light loves, to society, parties, etc. It is under Venus.

6th House relates to illness, to servants.

7th House relates to marriage, to wife or husband, to a partner in any business or enterprise, and to the special object asked, whatever that may be. For instance, "Shall I see Mr. Jones soon?" or "Is it good to buy that estate?" you would look to the 7th House as forming the direct *object of the question*, though in connection with other Houses more especially devoted to the nature of the objects. The 7th House would thus denote Mr. Jones, or the estate.

8th House relates to death, and advisers of married people and partners ; also wars and public enemies.

9th House relates to clerical matters, clergy, all that relates to religion, also to letters and to *long* journeys.

10th House relates to honours, distinctions, etc.

11th House relates to friends.

12th House—a bad house—private enemies, perils, afflictions ; also beasts, wild or tame ; injury or profit by them, etc. You would look to this House for the question, "Will the horse I have bought turn out well?"

Of these Houses, the strongest and most influential are the 1st, 4th, 7th, 10th. These, in fact, are the four fatal angles in astrology. The Houses most weak are the 3rd, 6th, and 9th. The importance of bad figures is increased when found in the strong Houses; also the importance of good ones.

Some figures, however good, lose their nature and become bad in certain Houses according to certain questions, and *vice versa*. For instance, Acquisitio, excellent in most Houses (especially 1st and 2nd), when in the 8th House signifies Death, if the question relate to a death (more especially if the 6th and 10th Houses have bad figures). Thus, " Shall I gain that property ? "

```
. .
.
. .
.
```

in the 1st House, repeated in 7th House (the House of the object), you have every chance to gain it, provided the other Houses and Judge do not greatly contradict. But, " Will my poor gardener die of this illness ? " Acquisitio in the 8th House would denote " Yes." Suppose in the 6th House (of sickness) there is

```
. .
. .
. .
.
```

in the 7th House the object, that is the gardener,

```
.
. .
. .
.
```

in the 8th Acquisitio ; in the 10th

```
. .
. .
.   (Albus)]
. .
```

the answer would be, " It appears to be dropsy or

vitiated humours," Populus being the sign of the moon direct, which indicates such diseases. It is likely to be lingering, attended with confinement, much weariness and distress, denoted by Carcer in 7th House (House of object). He probably will die of it, but, at last, peacefully and happily,

. .

∴ being in the 10th House, which being in

. .

sextile to the 8th should be always consulted in looking to the 8th House. Now Albus and Acquisitio are in themselves good figures, yet here they are the characters of doom. More on this head I will say in describing each figure, but the best way is to make several schemes, learning the names of the figures as set down above and the general properties, and then I will help to construe them. Practice is essential, and experience modifies mistakes.

In looking at my general figures, you look first at the four angles, viz. 1st, 4th, 7th and 10th Houses, which in much determine the general nature and character of the scheme. For they are very good. Their power counteracts what is bad in the weaker Houses, and *vice versa*.

The next thing to consult is what astrologers call "the conjunction." This in geomancy is found in the immediate neighbour to the figure asked, and the figure that is formed by summing the two together. Thus, "Shall I admit that Roman Catholic into my house?"

2nd House　　　　　　　　　1st House

These two conjoined form ∴　9th House, being

the sum of the two conjoined, and also House of religious matters.　Answer : " You have kind motives in that notion.　You yourself are frank, easy and unsuspicious.　The person you would introduce will be treacherous and wily.　You would be involved in religious differences that would give you vexation and annoyance, and might linger long in effect."　Such would be the answer unless the other figures contradicted or softened it, and the answer is given for these reasons.

The Dragon's Head, the signification of the

sun, is in your 1st House and relates to yourself. It is frank, open, generous in its character.　The Dragon's Tail in your 2nd House is the reverse. The two conjoined make Carcer, which finds itself in the House of Religion and denotes weariness, cunning, hitch, and lengthened trouble.

*Aspects.* —You look next to Aspects, which besides the four great angles—1st, 4th, 7th and 10th—are formed by the figure twice removed (next but one) from that in which the question is asked.　Example : " Will my sister's intrigue be found out, and will my father be angry?"

Suppose Puer    ∴    in the 3rd House (of brothers

and sisters), and you find in the 5th House, next

but one to it    ∴    Dragon's Head, and in the

4th House (House of Parents)   ∴   Rubens, the

answer would be, judging by the aspects in sextile,
viz. the 5th House : "The intrigue will be brought
to light and make great scandal. Your father will be
so furious that he could almost kill your sister." The

answer is given because the    ∴    in the sister's

House, Mars indirect, shows illicit love, liable to
anger. The aspect in the 5th is the sign of the
House which, though usually good in itself, denotes publicity, and, in this question, so posited,
scandal. Rubens is in the father's House — a
sign of deadly wrath.

But a figure is generally told without much
necessity to look at the alternate aspects. The
main decision is formed by the four angular
Houses, the Judge, the Witnesses. The two
Witnesses signify—the first one to the right, things
within you, subjective; the second, things objective.
Sometimes they also signify, the one, the things

for you, the other, the things against. These
varieties of construction depend on the general
experience and skill of the geomancer. The
Judge sums up, and is of immense importance in
deciding the figure, though if the four angles be
good his evil response is not necessarily fatal to
your wish. A good Judge, however, neutralises
much that is bad in the figure. Whenever the
Judge is an odd figure, such as

the scheme is torn up and rejected altogether, and
no one on the same subject should be made that
day, or, at all events, that hour. Better wait at
least a day. Whenever Rubens appears in the
1st House, the figure is not proceeded with, but
destroyed. The same rule for delay in making a
new one applies.

### CHARACTERS OF FIGURES

*Acquisitio,* implies gain, both in money,
in schemes—in the object asked. It is good in
all Houses but the 8th.

*Amissio,* loss, is just the reverse, and not
good even in the 8th House, though not, of itself,

fatal in that.   It is, however, a tolerable sign, of itself, in the 12th House (of enemies), implying that enemies are not strong.   But supposing it were both in the 12th and the 2nd Houses, it would imply that you have an enemy in your own house or immediately about you from whom you will suffer loss.

*Dragon's Head,* is a sign of truth, of open-ness and of gentleness, excellent in the 7th House, as for marriage and the character of wife and husband. In the 10th House (of honours) it signifies distinction, fame, but not positive honours or worldly rank.   For instance,     should be in the 10th of Spenser, who had neither honours nor wealth, but who had publicity and fame.

But      *Fortuna Major,* signifies great good-fortune, or great good-luck ; if in the 1st and 10th Houses, and not otherwise contradicted, it shows a brilliant and fortunate career.   It is good of itself in all Houses—Jove direct.

*Fortuna Minor,* is a movable, unsteady sign.   It is luck, but not permanent luck.   In the 10th House it would show brief and flashy success or honours.   In love and marriage, it denotes hot flames but inconstant.

```
• •
• •      is good, or bad, according to the figure next
• •
```

it with which it forms conjunction—very good, for instance, if next to Fortuna Major, very bad if next to Rubens or Dragon's Tail.   It generally denotes a multitude.   If the question be "Shall I marry

```
                        • •
So-and-So?" and  • •   is in the 7th House, "Yes."
                        • •
```

It is good for marriage, which is supposed to bring people together.   It is bad for a question of love because it is the moon's signification and denotes change.   "Does that woman still love me?"

```
•  •                    •  •
•      8th House         •  •   Populus
                        •  •   7th House
•  •                    •  •
```

The answer by Conjunctio and the figure on the 7th would be: "She is already changing; there is love, but unsteady and fickle."   Populus is good in the House of friends (11th), bad in enemies (12th).   It means, "You have a great many." Good in the 10th, of honours, if other figures are good.

```
•
•      *Via*, is also a signification of the Moon.   It
•
```

is more uncertain than Populus.   It nearly always denotes a going or passing away.   But

in this going away there is some delay or
hitch.　In the 3rd and 9th Houses (Houses of
journeys) it signifies a journey certainly, but perhaps suspended or delayed on the road.　It is
very bad in the 2nd House, indicating loss and
impoverishment; bad in the 7th, whether the
question is on marriage or love ; good, according to
geomancers, generally in the 10th, where they consider it denotes honours, but I have not observed
its effect in that House to be so good as alleged.

*Carcer*, bad in most Houses, vexation and

annoyance in 1st and 2nd, confinement and bringing illness in 6th and 8th Houses ; disappointment
and weariness in society if in House 5 ; unsatis-
factory marriage and love in House 7 ; honours
intercepted and balked in House 8 ; in 12, foes
troublesome and wearing, but not powerful; in
4th House, good for inheritance, and always good
for keeping a secret.

*Puella*, good for gaiety, love, amusement ;

in House 10, promotion or honours through female
influence.

*Puer*, good or bad according to the question :

trouble to hasty loves, and significant of hasty
anger.　Good in war.

*Rubens,* the worst of all figures, except in
war and contention.   Suppose the question were,
" Will war be the end of this negotiation, and if
so will the war be honourable to England or not ? "
Then, Rubens in the 4th House (the end or result
of the thing demanded), if conjoined in the 8th
House to the Dragon's Head,

4th                          3rd

gives          Fortuna Major in the 10th House of

Honour.   Thus Rubens, so conjoined, becomes
of itself favourable.      " There will be war and with
great honour to England," provided the 7th House
(the  object  demanded  about,  viz.  England)  be
good,  and  that  of  enemies  weak.    Suppose,  for

instance, there were          or          in   the   7th

House, and       in   the   12th ;   but suppose in  the

7th House were Via, and  in  the  12th  Fortuna

Major,  and          (the  same)  is  in  the  10th,  and

the Judge were bad, the answer would be : " There

will be war ; England will be defeated. She will
be put to flight (Via). The honours will be to
the enemy." Rubens is worst in the 2nd House.
He signifies violence, treachery, even murder if the
question relate to it.

*Albus*, is the signification of Mercury,
propitious. He is excellent in 1st and 2nd Houses,
good indeed in all ; in the 10th signifies honours
through literature, art, or oratory. He is mild
and a lover of peace.

*Conjunctio*, bad in the 1st and 2nd Houses,
usually there denotes impoverishment ; but much
depends on the figure next him and in the 7th
and 10th Houses. He denotes the bringing people
and things together—reconciliation of friends and
enemies, recovery of things lost. In the 8th House
he is worse than even Acquisitio, and denotes
Death if the question relate to death ; but if to
marriage or partnership, not so. The 8th House
is that of advisers to married people or partners,
and if the question were, " Will my husband be
advised to be reconciled to me, or my partner to
forego litigation ? " Conjunctio in the 8th House
would be good.

*Dragon's Tail*, bad in all Houses, except in

questions of war, of success in illicit love, and in getting out of some horrid scrape. It is hasty, perfidious, secret, very bad in 1st and 2nd Houses.

*Lætitia*, is a sign of content and pleasure, not very profound nor constant. In the 5th House it is excellent, but if the question be, "Will the woman I love be constant?" it would be unfavourable, as it implies a certain cooling of affection. It is the signification of Venus retrograde.

*Tristitia*, on the contrary, though a very bad sign in most things, signifying melancholy and disappointment, is the best of all signs to a lover in answer to a question of constancy. If, for instance, you ask, "Will my marriage with So-and-so be happy?" Tristitia in the 7th House would reply, "No, wretched." But if you ask, "Is my wife or sweetheart constant and true in my absence?" then Tristitia in that same 7th House answers, "Yes, most constant, and miserable at your absence." Thus the same figures in the same Houses vary in signification according to questions asked, as well as according to aspects and conjunctions.

If the above be carefully studied and learned, the Art is begun, and the rest depends much on practice, and somewhat on a talent for generalising and harmonising details. I say nothing of a peculiar

gift; but some are naturally more lucky in conjecture than others.

EXPERIMENTAL FIGURE

Will England go
to war with the
Emperor Napoleon
III. soon; or within
any reasonable time
deducible from
circumstances at
present in opera-
tion ?

England is, and will be, for some little time varying and fickle in her inclinations. But she will before very long be much more peacefully disposed towards the Emperor. Those immediately in her counsels are for peace. Female influences will be for peace, and religious influences not less. There will be, nevertheless, many noisy and clamorous opponents to a peaceful policy who will have sympathy with the populace. They will fail. Some causes are now at work to produce a much more cheerful state of things and of feeling between England and France than appears even possible at this moment. Singularly enough some act of violence or treachery on the part of some subordinate agent, whether public servant or other subject *in France,* will conduce to a reaction of kindly feeling between the two countries. The Emperor himself is or will be more than ever anxious to cement the alliance : his confidential advisers will heartily agree with him. The alliance will be confirmed. There is much more unsteadiness in the sentiment of England towards friendship with France than in that of the Emperor towards cordiality with England. The Emperor is bent upon it. With this renewed or re-strengthened alliance there will come a something that will soothe our national vanity, a something that will cause demonstrations of rejoicing. But, in substance, the alliance will inflict on us not actual discredit, but a certain loss that will be felt hereafter. The peace thus cemented will be imposed on us by the force

XXVII DESIRE FOR PEACE 319

of circumstances not now foreseen, and by the pertinacious resolve of the French Emperor : its necessity is so strongly implied that even if, in spite of all signs to the contrary, the fickle irresolution or fear of the English, and some popular bravado, should cause sudden hostility, *we* should be quickly the *loser* and as quickly bent on reconciliation. But apparently the people themselves, even when most warlike in talk, are in heart peaceful, and would be the first to denounce their rulers if plunged into quarrel with France.

It will not be long before this change of feeling will make itself known. If a Congress takes place it will greatly tend to reconcile distrustful nations, and either a Congress or some such proceeding will take effect. There will be a great abandonment of military preparations. Financial distress may contribute to this. There will be peace, and a peace policy established in England with all its concomitant measures for good or for evil.

I suspect that the Emperor himself is resolved to pacify Europe ; that he is alarmed at its present aspect ; that he will find an auxiliary to some scheme that may conduce to a general disarmament in the pecuniary difficulties of other nations, and their absolute necessity for retrenchment ; and that in this scheme it is necessary for him to secure the co-operation of England, and that he will secure it. If peace be thus secured, and military preparations thus abandoned, the enemy to England will become her own popular or democratic party, and the end of all will be popular concessions of a nature ultimately very injurious to the country. Such I conjecture to be the loss or damage which "the Judge" in the figure denotes as the result of that peaceful policy which the scheme so notably predicates.

This was written in the autumn of 1860.

# CHAPTER XXVIII

It may be as well here to mention the Wheel of Pythagoras—a mode of divination which, in all the authorities, follows the description of geomancy. It is called the Wheel of Pythagoras or the Wheel of Fortune, but its revelations are limited to one particular question, and do not give a general scheme of life, as is done by geomancy. M. Peruchio gives this example of a question to be asked: "*Marie demande un jour de lundi si Philandre l'épousera*," and to this the Wheel of Pythagoras gives a reply.

The following is the formula given for asking questions :—

(1) A number must be given by the enquirer.

(2) The number attaching to the first letter of the name of the querist.

(3) The number of the planet of the day on which the question is asked.

(4) The number of the day on which the question is asked.

The whole must be divided by 30, and the remainder gives the answer. If there be no remainder, the answer is 30, which is bad.

Subjoined is a copy of the Wheel, and of the numbers belonging respectively to the planets and to the days of the week.

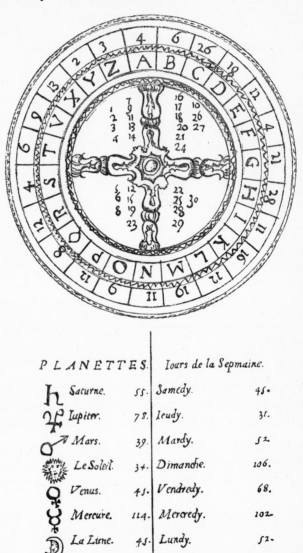

| P L A N E T T E S. | | Iours de la Sepmaine. | |
|---|---|---|---|
| ♄ Saturne. | 55. | Samedy. | 45. |
| ♃ Iupiter. | 78. | Ieudy. | 31. |
| ♂ Mars. | 39. | Mardy. | 52. |
| ☼ Le Soleil. | 34. | Dimanche. | 106. |
| ♀ Venus. | 45. | Vendredy. | 68. |
| ☿ Mercure. | 114. | Mercredy. | 102. |
| ☽ La Lune. | 45. | Lundy. | 52. |

The system, however, has been extended, and it is said that the answers are positive and correct. As the first number is optional, means have been found of giving it a greater value. Arithmetic being an exact science, a method has been devised of converting into numerals words which when written are ordinary characters of no specific value. In figures, each figure has an independent value. Letters have no independent value. For instance, 1 2 separately have an independent value; together 12 have another value. a and b, however, separately have no signification any more than ab. Therefore by converting a and b into 1 and 2 the precise answer is given to the query proposed. A system has been devised by which words and sentences can be converted into figures. It is, therefore, for each person who wishes to practise this art, to form for himself a vocabulary in words which can be converted into figures. To give an instance :—

The question may be, "Shall I inherit a legacy?" The enquirer, having chosen his own code, proceeds to turn those words into figures. For this purpose we will take Slater's Telegraphic Code, which, if chosen by the enquirer, must be rigidly adhered to.

$$\begin{aligned}
\text{Shall} &= 20520 \\
\text{I} &= 11101 \\
\text{inherit} &= 11871 \\
\text{a} &= 00001 \\
\text{legacy} &= 13130
\end{aligned}$$

Add to this (1) the number of the initial letter of the enquirer's first name: this may be Katharine. This, according to the Wheel, is represented by 16. Then add (2) the number of the day of the week—say, Monday = 52. Add (3) the number of the planet, in this case the Moon = 45. Add all these together, and divide by 30. The number remaining will be seen in the Wheel with its signification.

$$20520$$
$$11101$$
$$11871$$
$$00001$$
$$13130$$
$$16$$
$$52$$
$$45$$

$$30) \overline{56736}$$

$$1891—6$$

The numbers on the left-hand side of the upper part of the Wheel—1, 2, 3, 4, 7, 9, 11, 13, 14—are good: on the lower part of the Wheel—5, 6, 8, 12, 15, 19, 23—are bad. Taking the right-hand side of the Wheel, the upper part, the numbers 16, 17, 18, 20, 21, 24, 10, 26, 27 are good: on the lower part 22, 25, 28, 29, 30 are bad. Some authorities say that the numbers on the left-hand side of the Wheel are slow in execution, whether good or bad, while those on the right side are quicker in operation.

Two instances have made a very strong impression on my mind in reference to occult influences.

In Egypt in 1886, at the time when Mr. Gladstone brought in his Home Rule proposals, I made the acquaintance of some Egyptians, who are great students of the occult. They suggested that a woman called the Sheikha, well known for her powers of divination, should be brought from Alexandria to see me. One evening I met her at a friend's house. All the household was sitting round a brazier filled with live coals. The Sheikha then came in, wearing a very thick *yashmak*, leaning dramatically on the shoulder of a little female slave.

We all sat round the brazier, into which the Sheikha threw a few perfumes—the general preliminary, I find, in the East to all supernatural matters.

I was told, if I wanted any information about myself, to give her something that I had worn, such as a glove or handkerchief. This I did, and she certainly told me some remarkable things about my past. I did not pay much attention to this, however, as I was at that moment well known in Egypt, and matters concerning me might have become public.

I was then informed if I wanted to be told about any one else to give the Sheikha a small silver piece, and at the same time to think of the person I had in view, without mentioning the name to any one. I gave her a two-piastre piece, and inwardly thought of Mr. Gladstone.

The Sheikha said : " This is a man far over the sea, and of great influence and power in the Medjlis [Council]. He is now in office, but he is very sad [*sadness* is the word always used in the East to translate *annoyance*] because he feels that he must soon leave office, and that by an act he has just performed he has done injury both to himself and to his friends."

I then gave her another coin, thinking of Lord Salisbury.

She said : " This man is also far over the sea, and very powerful in the Medjlis. He is not in office now, but he soon will be in consequence of the acts of the other man, who will have to retire. He has been in power before, and he is coming into much greater power now." A term was fixed which proved correct.

After that, I gave her a third piece, and thought of Lord Randolph Churchill.

The Sheikha said : " This man is also very powerful in the Medjlis, and will be more so as he is much younger than the others. He has already occupied a great place, and will soon occupy a still greater one."

I then pointed to the two coins representing Mr. Gladstone and Lord Salisbury, and said : " Which of those two is best affected to this young man ? " In reply, she pointed to Mr. Gladstone's coin.

My belief is that there always was consider-able sympathy between Mr. Gladstone and Lord Randolph Churchill. The day after this in-cident occurred, I wrote an account of it to the latter.

The other incident of the occult which has happened to me is as follows :—

While at Madrid I was very anxious about a person in whom I felt great interest. One day, when about to drive, I went down the staircase of the Embassy. There was a door in the hall leading to a short staircase into the street. As I opened this door, a telegram was brought to me from the solicitors of the person above alluded to, asking me about a most urgent matter, and saying that unless a reply was received at once some very painful circumstances might occur. The tele-graphic address, let us say, of these solicitors was " Rehearsal," while that of my own solicitors we will call " Annual." I went into a small room near the door leading to the chancellery and wrote a telegraphic reply, giving it to my English servant to take at once to the telegraph-office. This he did. I then took my drive, came home rather late, dined, and went to bed between eleven and twelve o'clock.

That night I could not sleep—not with the usual sensation of being unable to sleep, though tired, but with a feeling of complete wakefulness. This went on for some time. Then, all of a sudden, I recollected a story I had heard years ago, relating to Mr. Sturges Bourne, who was Home Secretary under Mr. Canning.

Mr. Bourne, who lived in the Birdcage Walk, was one night affected with this same kind of wakefulness. At last, becoming impatient, he got up, dressed so as to take a walk, and went to the Home Office. He had the key in his pocket, and let himself in, proceeding to his own room. There, on his desk, he found a pardon he had signed that day to remit the punishment of a criminal who was to be executed the very next morning at Maidstone, I believe. In those days there were, of course, no railways or telegraphs. He rang his bell, and desired a messenger to take a postchaise immediately and to drive down to Maidstone as quickly as possible with the pardon. He arrived just in time.

It struck me that something of the same kind might have occurred with regard to the telegram I had despatched.

I rang for my English servant and asked him to whom I had addressed the telegram he had taken the previous afternoon. He said, "To 'Annual.'" It should have been to "Rehearsal."

I wrote another telegram, addressing it to "Rehearsal," and desired my servant at once to go down to the post-office in one of the cabs which roam about the streets of Madrid at night, and, as the Embassy had certain privileges, to ring up the officials and have my message despatched. He came back with my original telegram addressed to "Annual," and a further telegram from "Rehearsal," that had just arrived, urging me in the strongest terms to answer immediately his communication of the morning.

# CHAPTER XXIX

In 1861, a Commission was instituted to enquire
into the state of public education in the Ionian
Islands, with a view to suggesting changes in the
existing system. The whole question was one
with which the Ionians were well acquainted.

At the time when the Islands came under our
protection, Lord Guilford spent a large sum of
money on founding a University at Corfu, which
became the principal educational centre for Greeks.
It had at first been intended to build it in Ithaca ;
but, owing to the influence of Sir Thomas Maitland, the High Commissioner, in whose time the
scheme made but little progress, it was transferred
to Corfu. Lord Guilford for a long time took a
leading part in its management, and it received
considerable assistance from Sir Frederick Adam,
Sir Thomas Maitland's successor, whose administration was most fortunate for the interest of the
Islands.

Some of the best-known writers in Greece had

been educated at Corfu University—amongst others, M. Tricoupis, the famous Greek historian, who was afterwards Minister in London.   I knew him well, and his son, M. Charilaus Tricoupis, who also became Minister in London, and subsequently Minister for Foreign Affairs in Greece.   There were also some very distinguished writers, natives of Corfu, one of whom, Sir Peter Braila, afterwards went to London as Minister; Sir Andrea Mustoxidi, subsequently Archon, or Director of Public Instruction, and Mr. Zambelli, who was well known in Italy as a writer, and who was much appreciated by Mr. Gladstone.   He understood English perfectly.   Another gentleman, much admired in Italy for his literary skill, was the Chevalier Tipaldo Pretenderi.

I may here incidentally mention the curious fact that in Cephalonia there are only two surnames, Tipaldo and Metaxa.   One district is called "Metaxata."   The Tipaldos boast descent from the Crusaders.   In order to distinguish people of the same name, different families adopted what may be called separate nicknames.   There are Tipaldo Pretenderi, Tipaldo Xidian, and many others.

Lord Guilford really conferred an enormous benefit on the Ionian Islands by the foundation of the University, on which it was said that he spent £15,000 a year.   He did all that was possible to revive the Hellenic spirit.   He used to wear ancient Greek dress and sandals, in imitation of Socrates.

A Commission was at this time also issued for collecting and transmitting specimens of the produce of the Ionian Islands to the Exhibition to be held in London in 1862. Of this I was Vice-President, and I went through the Islands with a view to establishing local committees to concur with the Commission. Towards the end of 1861 an Exhibition was held at Corfu of the objects which were to be forwarded to England, and this created great enthusiasm. It was held in one of the large rooms at the University. Juries, both of English and Ionians, were appointed to report on the merits of the various exhibits, and a medal was struck in commemoration of the occasion.

Just before the Exhibition was held in London, I paid a short visit to Florence in order to study methods of exhibiting goods at the Italian Exhibition that was being held in that city. There I again met Sir James Hudson, with whom I was in constant correspondence, and I witnessed the opening of the Exhibition by King Victor Emmanuel. A great feature of this ceremony was the singing of Madame Piccolomini.

I was delegated Commissioner to the London Exhibition of 1862, together with Mr. Marcoran, a son of one of the Judges of the Supreme Court. The Ionian part, for which we were responsible, astonished not only those who visited it, but even the Ionians themselves, who were amazed to find that 177 exhibits had been sent from the various islands. They were very much gratified at the number of medals and honourable mentions they received.

Amongst other exhibits were pieces of embroidery. Ionians excel in this work. The duplicate of a waist-band, which had been made for the Empress of Austria when passing Corfu, was on view. It measured exactly sixteen inches, and was said to have been rather too large for Her Majesty. Embroidered tobacco-bags were also shown. Cereals were exhibited, and many specimens of raw material, stone, and timber. Amongst the jewellery were gold hat-pins, such as the peasants wore, and rings with the emblems of the Seven Islands. One especially interesting exhibit was the mitre of a Greek bishop, beautifully ornamented with gold. Cabinet-work in jujube, acacia, and olive wood were also shown, and tables of inlaid olive-wood, which the Ionians were particularly skilful in making. Medals and honourable mentions were gained for wine and liqueurs. Oil and currants also obtained prizes, as a public recognition of their established commercial value. The honey of the Islands, especially that of Cerigo, received the highest commendation, and the wax, both of Corfu and Cephalonia, met with marked success. One characteristic exhibit was a canoe, of triangular shape, formed of bunches of the old papyrus tied together. These boats are very much used for fishing in the Ionian Islands, in the country districts bordering the sea. I sent one of them to the Kew Museum.

One article, though not prized, that attracted

considerable notice, was the lace made at Cephalonia of the fibre of American aloes. All exhibits
manufactured of this substance were sold, and application was made to procure more articles of the same
material. The Exhibition, in fact, created some
demand for productions from the Ionian Islands.
I have, however, naturally been unable closely to
follow the progress that has since been made.

The success of the whole undertaking, though
great, was much clouded by the unhappy death of
the Prince Consort—who really was the inventor
of exhibitions. The Queen appointed the Duke of
Cambridge as her representative on the international
body, which was composed of delegates from various
nations, to receive the awards of the juries, and afterwards to distribute the prizes.

Many interesting incidents occurred at the time
—amongst others the dinner given by the Colonial
Commissioners to Dr. Lindley, whom the Government had appointed Head of the Colonial Department in the Exhibition. It was attended by Sir
Edward Lytton, and brought forward very promi-
nently the whole of the Colonial Question, which
is now assuming such great proportions. Wine
was exhibited by a German firm which tasted good,
but was said to hold no particle of the grape. On
Mr. Gladstone testing it, he observed that this was
the highest kind of adulteration. The Germans
responded, "We are not adulterers, only chymists."

One of the most amusing features of the Exhibition was the extraordinary English of a certain

most useful person engaged in a subordinate capacity. Once I asked him, in the presence of friends, about some one who spoke with a foreign accent, and who was also employed in the Exhibition. He replied, " They say he is a 'Ungarian ; but my belief is that he's a gallant, gay Lutheran." He meant Lothario.

On another occasion, I asked him if he knew a very peculiar-looking man, walking about the Exhibition, whose face and hair were perfectly white, with pink eyes. He replied, " I do not know him ; but he's a regular Albanian."

Having sold a great many of the Ionian exhibits, I organised a raffle for the remainder, and in this undertaking I was greatly assisted by Lady Palmerston, Mrs. Gladstone, and Lady Salisbury.

During the autumn of that year I received the following kind letter from Lord Beaconsfield :—

HUGHENDEN MANOR, *September* 10, 1862.

DEAR COMMISSIONER—Assuming that your public duties must, more or less, detain you in town, I would suggest that you should, if disengaged, change the air a little for that of the Chiltern Hills, which is invigorating. Would you give us the pleasure of seeing you on Monday the 22nd, and staying with us until the 25th, when Lord and Lady Salisbury, whom you will meet, will unfortunately leave us.

I shall direct this to the International, where, I suppose, it will reach you.—Yours faithfully,      B. DISRAELI.

*R.S.V.P.*

This was the first occasion on which I was a guest at Hughenden, though later on, when I entered more active politics, I more than once had the opportunity of going there. I recollect that one of the favourite places where Lord Beaconsfield used to take his guests was Dropmore, for which he had a great admiration. Lord and Lady Salisbury, whom I had long known in Hertfordshire and elsewhere, I visited frequently at Hatfield. I did not make the acquaintance of the late Lord Salisbury until 1864, after I had left the Ionian Islands.

During the year of the Exhibition I saw a good deal of Mr. Babbage, the great calculator. He was always known for his hostility to barrel-organs, and his name constantly appeared in the papers as prosecuting performers on that instrument. The calculating machine, which he had invented, was exhibited, and he used to explain it himself, until one day he gave up his attendance. I innocently asked him why he was no longer seen at the Exhibition, and he replied that he had been insulted by one of the public. I asked him in what manner. He said that in the midst of his explanation some one had asked him the origin of his hostility to barrel-organs.

One or two houses were constantly open to Mr. Babbage—amongst others that of the Dowager Duchess of Somerset.

In this year I had practical experience of a medium who was making some sensation in London. Mr. Chichester Fortescue, Mr. Kinglake, Mr. Hayward and myself arranged a meeting with him. I cannot say that he produced a great impression on us, and what I recollect best is that he would pronounce the word *vase* as though it rhymed with *face*. I told Mr. Oliphant, then a professed spiritualist, about this sitting, and said that we had not been much struck with the medium. When he heard who had been present he said, " What! You four! It really was not fair upon the poor man. Two would have been quite enough ! "

# CHAPTER XXX

DURING my stay in London I received from Lord Glenesk a most valuable present—the original letter addressed to the People of England, from Varignano, by Garibaldi, after his being wounded at Aspromonte, and when Dr. Partridge had been sent from England to take care of him. This letter, with a translation, was published at the time in the *Morning Post*, but it may not be uninteresting to reproduce it here.

## ALLA NAZIONE INGLESE

Soffrente sotto raddoppiati colpi morali e fisici, l' uomo può con ragione sentire più squisitamente il bene e il male, rigettare quindi alla maledizione i fautori del male, e consacrare ai benefattori affetto e gratitudine senza limite.

Ed io ti devo gratitudine, o popolo Inglese, e la sento quanto è capace di sentirla l' anima mia. Tu mi fosti amico nella buona, e mi continui la preziosa tua amicizia nell' avversa fortuna.

Che Dio ti benedica! La mia gratitudine poi è tanto più intensa, o buon popolo, ch' essa s' innalza debitamente al di sopra del sentimento individuale e si sublima nel sentimento generale dei popoli, di cui tu rappresenti il progresso.

Sì! tu meriti la gratitudine del mondo, perchè tu offri un asilo sicuro allo infortunio, da qualunque parte ti giunga, e tu t' identifichi colla sciagura altrui—la compatisci—la sollevi. Il proscritto francese o napolitano trova nel tuo seno un rifugio contra la tirannide—trova simpatia—trova aiuto perchè proscritto—perchè infelice. Gli Heynau—i ferrei carnefici dello autocrate—non saranno sorretti dal suolo della tua libera patria, e fugiranno impauriti lo sdegno tirannicida dei generosi tuoi figli.

? E che sarremmo in Europa senza il tuo dignitoso contegno? L' Autocrazia colpisce i suoi proscritti nelle altrui contrade ove la libertà è bastarda—ove la libertà è menzogna! Ma si vada a cercare sulla sacra terra d'Albione! Io! come tanti, vedendo la causa della giustizia conculcata in tanti parti del mondo, propendo alla disperazione del progresso umano. Ma rivolgendo a te il mio pensiero mi tranquillo dal tranquillo, impavido tuo procedere verso la meta ove sembra chiamata la razza umana dalla Providenza.

Prosegui il tuo cammino, o Nazione invitta, imperturbata, e sii meno restìa nel chiamare le sorelle nazioni sulla via umanitaria.

Chiama la Nazione francese a co-operatrice tua! Ambe siete degne di marciare, dandovi la mano, alla vanguardia dello incivilimento umano. Ma chiamala! In tutti i tuoi *meeting* risuoni la parola di concordia delle due grande sorelle. Chiamala! Chiamala pure in ogni modo, colla tua voce e colla voce dei suoi grandi proscritti—del suo Vittore Hugo— il Pontefice della fratellanza umana! Dille che le conquiste sono un' aberrazione del secolo—un emanazione di mente non sana! ? E perchè dovremmo noi conquidere la terra altrui, quando tutti dobbiamo esser fratelli? Chiamala! e non curarti se dessa sia temporariamente padroneggiata dal genio del male—essa risponderà debitamente—se non oggi —domani! se non domani—dopo! alla parola tua generosa e rigeneratrice.

Chiama, e subito, i forti figli della Elvezia, e stringili al tuo seno indissolubilmente. I bellicosi figli delle Alpi—i vestali del fuoco sacro di libertà nel continento europeo, saranno teco. E che contingente!

Chiama la grande repubblica Americana. Essa finalmente è tua figlia, sorta dal tuo grembo—ed essa—comunque sia—si affatica oggi per l' abolizione della schiavitù da te generosamente proclamata. Aiutala a sollevarsi dalla terribile lotta che le suscitarono i mercanti di carne umana. Aiutala—e poscia falla sedere al tuo lato nel gran consesso delle Nazioni—opera finale della ragione umana.

Chiama a te quanti popoli hanno libero il volere—e non tardare un sol giorno. La iniziativa che ti appartiene oggi potrebbe non esser piu tua domani. Che Iddio non permetta cotesto!

Chi più gagliardamente afferró quella iniziativa quanto la Francia del '89? Essa in quel punto solenne diede al mondo la Dea Ragione, rovescio nella polve la tirannide, e consacrò tra le Nazioni la libera fratellanza. Dopo quasi un secolo essa è ridotta a combattere la libertà dei popoli—proteggere le tirannidi—sulle rovine del tempio dalla Ragione essa si affatica a puntellare quella mostruosità nefanda-immorale che si chiama Papato!

Sorgi dunque, o Britannia, e non perdere tempo. Sorgi colla fronte alta ed addita alle Nazioni la via da percorrere.

Non più guerra possibile ove un congresso mondiale possa giudicare delle differenze insorte tra le Nazioni! Non più eserciti stanziali con cui la libertà è impossibile. Che bombe! Che corazze! Vanghe e macchine da falciare! Ed i milliardi sprecati in apparati di distruzione vengano impiegati a fomentare le industrie e a diminuire le miserie umane.

Comincia, o popolo inglese, e—per amor di Dio!—comincia la grande era del patto umano e benefica le presenti generazioni con tanto dono. Oltre la Svizzera, il Belgio, &c., che aderiranno subito al tuo invito, tu vedrai gli altri Stati—spinti dal buon senso delle populazioni—accorrere allo amplesso tuo ed aggregarsi.

Sia Londra per ora la sede del Congresso che sarà scelta susseguentemente con mutuo intendimento e convenienza.

Io ti ripeto, che Dio ti benedica!!! E a te possa rimeritare i benefizi a me prodigati.

Con gratitudine ed affetto, tuo,                G. GARIBALDI.

The following note appears at the end of the letter :—

Mon cher Mr. Borthwick—Je vous adresse la lettre que le Général Garibaldi a écrit au peuple anglais.  Je vous prie de la publier dans votre estimable journal et très-repandu.  Il va mieux.  Par le rapport du Dr. Partridge vous saurez comme cette forte constitution de lion a su gagner et vaincre la gravité du mal.

Je vous serre la main affectueusement, et je vous prie d'agréer mes sentiments les plus distingués.

C. Augusto Viechi.

Varignano, *Sept.* 28, 1862.

At this passage of his life, Garibaldi writes in his *Autobiography* with a certain amount of bitterness as to the manner in which he was treated by the Sardinian Government.

It is hateful to me to relate the miseries I had to endure ; but enough were inflicted on me on that occasion to have created disgust even in the mind of a scavenger. . . . It is true that they used those commonplace courtesies which are customary even towards great criminals when led to the scaffold ; but, for instance, instead of leaving me in a hospital at Reggio or Messina, I was placed on board a frigate and taken to Varignano, thus being forced to sail the whole length of the Tyrrhene sea, with the greatest torture to the wound in my right foot, which, though not mortal, was assuredly one of a most painful character. . . . My sufferings were great, and great also the kind care of my friends.  It was the illustrious Professor Zanetti, the *doyen* of Italian surgeons, who successfully achieved the operation of extracting the ball.

I twice saw Garibaldi—but not to speak to him. The first time was in England, and the second while he was driving through the streets of Florence, dressed in a red shirt.

In 1863, I received anonymously the following curious paper, purporting to be a suppressed despatch, the reply of Cardinal Antonelli to statements appearing in the Blue-book, "The Correspondence relative to the Affairs of Rome."

## A Suppressed Despatch

*" The Correspondence relative to the Affairs of Rome," presented to both Houses of Parliament, by command of Her Majesty, containing no mention whatever of an important State Paper, by Cardinal Antonelli, other and less regular channels of publicity are unavoidably sought. In order to mitigate, as far as possible, the inconvenience of a separate publication, a few extracts are prefixed to the Roman Despatch. They will be found to include a summary of Earl Russell's case, in his own written and official words, together with some passages from Ministerial speeches, which appear necessary to render the sequel intelligible.*

*Extract from Earl Russell's Despatch to Earl Cowley, dated Foreign Office, January 19, 1863*

That which happened was as follows :—

Mr. Russell, *on the 25th July* 1862, received unexpectedly from the Vatican a written intimation that the Pope would receive him at twelve o'clock on the next day. Mr. Russell, accordingly, went to the Vatican *on the 26th of July*, and in the course of a conversation of some length the Pope expressed a wish to know whether, if any circumstances should at any time lead him to desire to take refuge in England, he would be well and hospitably received there. To this question Mr. Russell could of course only give a general answer.

From this statement it will be seen that, instead of Mr. Russell asking an audience of the Pope, and at that audience making to the Pope an offer of an asylum at Malta, it was the Pope who sent for Mr. Russell, and it was the Pope who started the idea that he might, under certain circumstances, wish to reside in British territory.

This conversation having been reported by Mr. Russell, *led to the despatch of the 25th of October*, of which I send your Excellency a copy, to be communicated to M. Drouyn de Lhuys, together with some other parts of the correspondence on this matter.

It is right that I should explain that Mr. Russell was not called home from Rome, as the French Ambassador imagined, in consequence of his interview with the Pope ; Mr. Russell simply received a direction to absent himself from Rome on account of his health during the unhealthy season in that city.

*Extract from Viscount Palmerston's Speech on the Address,
February 5, 1863*

Well, Mr. Russell could not, of course, give any other [answer] than that he had had no instructions, but that it was the custom of the English nation to receive, *and hospitably to receive*, all those who might from any circumstances feel it desirable to take up their abode in this country.

*Extract from Earl Russell's Speech on the Address,
February 5, 1863*

*The Pope spoke to Mr. Russell very much of Garibaldi being in Sicily*, and, appearing to have considerable apprehensions of the state of Italy, he asked the question whether, if he sought an asylum in England, he might rely on our hospitality. To this Mr. Russell replied that *our hospitality was well known*, and that we gave asylum to all who sought it. . . . *I was glad to have given that venerable man (the Pope) the comfortable assurance that he might resort to the hospitality of England.*

### The Suppressed Despatch

#### *To the Editor of the " Standard "*

Monsieur le Redacteur—Pour peu que cela soit probable que la dépêche ci-jointe ne se trouve pas dans le recueil présenté au parlement, par le gouvernement de la Reine, j'ai cru vous être agréable en vous adressant une pièce, qui ne sera pas sans intérêt pour le publique Anglais. Je regrette de n'avoir assez maîtrisé votre langue pour pouvoir vous en envoyer la traduction.

Veuillez agréer, Monsieur, l'assurance de ma considération la plus distinguée,

Gorgio Borromeo,
*Légat Apostolique en disponibilité.*

Londres, *le 7 février*, 1863.

#### *Circular addressed to all the Pope's Nuncios Abroad by the Cardinal Secretary of State*

Rome, *January* 30, 1863.

Monseigneur — If overtures lately made to the Holy Father, on the part of the Government of her Britannic Majesty, had not found a place in an official communication from the Emperor of the French to his Parliament, I should not have entertained you with the subject. But that communication, eliciting much discussion, and published on the eve of the meeting of another Legislature, is likely, as we have heard, to provoke counter-statements from the English Ministers, which will have the deplorable effect of exhibiting two friendly Governments at issue on questions of fact. We have, therefore, decided that your Excellency shall no longer be left uninformed as to the nature of the English proposition, although we should have been content to pass it over in the silence with which we received it, and which I shall not characterise here.

It might be enough for me to state that we adhere in general to the account which your Excellency will have found in the French despatches. But, if I be correctly informed, it is intended to oppose categorical contradictions to those reports, and where particular assertions are advanced particular answers are required.

In opposition, then, to the statements above referred to, your Excellency must be prepared to hear it alleged that the negotiation in question originated with ourselves, that the Holy Father himself invited the visit of Mr. Russell, and that, in presence of a civil war, of which Italy was last summer the theatre, we recurred for a contingent refuge to the hospitality of England.

I need hardly stop, Monseigneur, to point out the improbability of such a narrative (*pour relever l'invraisemblance de ce récit*). If, in fact, we had thought it necessary, in the emergency of a Garibaldian insurrection, to appeal to the protection of England—if, in proposing Malta as a residence for his Holiness, her Britannic Majesty's Government were only obeying the generous instinct of their hospitality, how is it that that proposal, which we are supposed to have provoked in August,[1] was not made before November, and that our appeal remained three months unnoticed, until after the emergency was over and the danger past? It was not, certainly, after the defeat of the Southern rebellion,—after Garibaldi himself was wounded and a prisoner,—after the Emperor, by the dismissal of an able Minister, had given a signal pledge of his fidelity to that policy of conservation which he represents at Rome,—that we could be thought to need the shelter of the British flag. If her Majesty's Government had really intended to manifest their hospitality by relieving our necessities, at our urgent entreaty, I cannot do them the injustice of supposing that, during our peril, they would have withheld their proffered asylum, and then ostentatiously pressed it upon us, when a happier day of safety and repose had already dawned upon the Militant Church.

If, in extenuation of such conduct, the absence of Mr. Russell from Rome be adduced, your Excellency will not fail

---

[1] His Eminence, it must be observed, was answering statements of which he had only been informed by rumour. It will be seen by the extracts given above that Lord Russell assigns a still earlier date, that of the 25th of July, to this alleged overture.

to recollect that any other channel of communication might have been employed, without any greater breach of diplomatic usage than is involved in the habitual communications of that agent.   And this leads me to state that the audience which we are said to have initiated, was, in fact, accorded to the express application of Mr. Russell.   In admitting to his presence the unaccredited correspondent of a foreign Government, his Holiness was only giving a proof of that high indulgence of which those who are privileged to approach his person enjoy the daily spectacle, but which, certainly, ought never to be used to impart a colour of truth to imaginary propositions.

Our experience would lead us to anticipate that in seeking to accredit their version of this incident, her Britannic Majesty's Ministers may vaunt the hospitality of their country.   Should this be the case, without caring to appreciate the taste of such language, which, in truth, may be more becoming in the guests than in their hosts, your Excellency will at any rate acknowledge its incontestable opportunity.   Inasmuch as the residence here of an unhappy Prince, the sovereign ally of the Holy Father, has continually excited the animadversion of the English Cabinet, it was permitted to doubt whether England still vindicated for herself the noble right which she appears to deny to others —that of offering a refuge to misfortune.   It is time that the ancient policy of her Majesty's Government, in this respect, should be formally re-asserted, and therefore, Monseigneur, in the case supposed, and in spite of anything inflated in the form, you will note with satisfaction the substance (*le fond*) of such a declaration, and express the hope that we may henceforth be allowed to receive the King of the Two Sicilies at Rome, without exposing ourselves to calumnious appreciation or incurring malevolent reproach.

You are at liberty to read this despatch to ——, and to leave it with his Excellency, in copy.—I am, etc.,

(Signed)   N. CARDINAL ANTONELLI.

# CHAPTER XXXI

WHILE in London in 1862, I contributed—I hope usefully—to start an agitation for lowering the duties on tobacco. I wrote some letters to the *Times*, and thus called attention to the subject, one of great importance to smokers, among whom I ranked in those days.

The duty on cigars was, at that time, 10s. 6d. or 11s. 6d. per pound, while the lower duty of 5s. 6d. was levied on unmanufactured tobacco. There were also various gradations of manufacture which caused a good deal of confusion to the importer. This difference of duty between manufactured and unmanufactured tobacco, while admitting foreign unmanufactured tobacco, placed a heavy tax on cigars.

I consulted M. Michel Chevalier on the subject, and, in reply, he wrote me the following interesting letter :—

PARIS, PALAIS DE L'INDUSTRIE,<br>
*le 2 nov.* 1862.

CHER MONSIEUR—Je vous fais passer le passage du rapport du jury français sur l'Exposition de 1862, qui concerne le tabac, et le régime qui y est appliqué en Angleterre.

ًCe rapport paraîtra dans peu de jours; mais il est bon que vous en ayez la primeur.

Cette partie du rapport a été rédigée par M. Barral, homme très entendu.

Puisque vous avez le moyen de faire attaquer la question par le *Times*, le moment est venu.

En qualité de Président des jurés français, j'ai fait une introduction au rapport, où j'ai touché à cette question du régime douanier des tabacs en Angleterre. Cette introduction paraîtra avec le rapport, dans quelques jours. Il y en a eu un morceau dans la *Revue des deux Mondes*, d'hier, 1er novembre, mais dans le morceau il n'y a pas question des tabacs.—Mille amitiés,

MICHEL CHEVALIER.

Un autre fait singulier doit fixer l'attention.

En Angleterre, la culture seule est proscrite; la fabrication et le commerce du tabac sont libres; et cependant, nulle part le tabac n'est aussi mauvais, même quand on achète les sortes les plus chères. Faut-il s'en prendre à la liberté, et l'accuser de produire des effets inférieurs à ceux du monopole? Heureusement, un examen plus attentif montre que les doctrines de liberté ne sont pas responsables du résultat que nous signalons.

Le régime qui règne en Angleterre est un débris du régime prohibitif, c'est-à-dire du régime qui engendre toujours les plus mauvais fruits. Voici, en effet, quels sont les droits dont les tabacs sont frappés à leur entrée en Angleterre: les feuilles écotées ou non écotées paient 8 fr. 27 c. par kilogramme; les cigares et les scaferlatis (tabacs à fumer fabriqués) paient 24 fr. 81 c.; le tabac à priser ou en poudre est prohibé.

Que résulte-t-il d'un tel régime? C'est que la concurrence étrangère n'étant pas à craindre pour la poudre, les fabricants anglais font des tabacs détestables, livrent au commerce des dragues infâmes.

Les frais de fabrication n'étant inégaux pour aucune sorte de tabacs, la différence entre les droits auxquels sont soumises les feuilles et ceux qui frappent les cigares ou les scaferlatis introduits étant considérable, il y a là une prime énorme pour le fabricant anglais, prime qui enlève tout aiguillon à bien faire. Les feuilles écotées ne payant que 8 fr. 27 c., il ne devrait exister qu'un même droit sur les cigares et sur les tabacs à fumer, car le fabricant ne peut invoquer dans la fabrication aucun déchet donnant au tabac étranger une faveur quelconque. Le tarif anglais est donc en complet désaccord avec les règles les plus élémentaires d'une bonne administration ; il semble être une véritable aberration.

I therefore proceeded with the agitation, and had much correspondence with different persons interested in the subject. The result was, to my mind, most satisfactory, for the methods of taxing tobacco were soon entirely altered. Some years later, when in the House of Commons, I obtained a return showing statements of the gross receipts and net produce in respect of the duty on tobacco and snuff for each year from 1841 to 1880, and from this I learnt that, owing to the lowering of the duty, the quantity of cigars imported in 1861 was 438,023 lbs., the net duties received on which amounted to £140,316 ; while in 1880 the quantity had risen to 1,497,341 lbs., and the net duties received in that year amounted to £315,817.

Since the time of my arrival at Corfu, I had been much occupied in the formation of an Ionian Institute, for the examination of all questions connected with the promotion of trade and education. This Society flourished greatly, and contributed largely to the promotion of the General Exhibition. Even those Ionians who were discontented, acted with cordiality in furthering the objects of the Institute. When I first proposed the formation of the Association, I received a most cordial letter from M. Zambelli, which I think may be considered interesting :—

CORFU, *the 7th of Oct.* 1859.

MY DEAR SIR—I have read your paper with due attention. On the whole your plan seems to me most judiciously concocted. The accessories might perhaps require here and there some little change. Therefore I risk the following few remarks.

In article the 1st, containing the definition of the objects of the Academy, and where it is stated that the duty of the members should be to collect information of every kind regarding these Islands, would it not be advisable to extend the scope of their investigations, and say that the past history, the physical resources, and the present condition of the neighbouring Greek provinces should equally become the object of their studies? My reasons for making this suggestion are twofold.

1. Should the literary occupations of our Academy be confined within the narrow boundaries fixed in the proposed article—should it be satisfied with the examination of works *published in these islands* only—its members, I am afraid, would very seldom have any occasion to exert themselves, and the Institution might well deserve one day the compliment paid once by Voltaire to some such institution: "*Bonne et vertueuse fille ; elle n'a jamais fait parler d'elle.*"

2. I consider it as a good policy, that all those who in some way or another represent the protecting nation here, should avail themselves of every opportunity to show that in their endeavours to promote the advancement of civilisation in these Islands, they do never lose sight of the Greek brethren of the Ionians ; and that they hold the national ties which bind together the different Greek populations of Eastern Europe as dear and holy, as have always been to the different Governments of Germany those which connect

the separate German communities to each other.  By such
a constant attention of showing yourselves *Greeks* in all
your tendencies and exertions here, you will soon prepare the
biassed minds of the Ionian people to understand clearly—
what very few now admit—that it is more conducive to the
promotion of the Greek element in the East, and to the
future grandeur of our nation (if God reserves us any), to
have two separate and distinct centres of civilisation in
Corfu and at Athens, rather than a single one, and that it
is a very happy condition, under the present circumstances,
for one of those centres to be sheltered under a generous
and no longer prejudiced protection.  I hope you do not
believe there is any *arrière-pensée* in my hint.  I speak only
out of a sincere sympathy for your nation, and out of a wish
to see an end to the shortcomings of the past policy of your
countrymen in these Islands.  And when I mention my
sympathy, I take for granted that my motives for doing so
cannot be suspected, my only ambition in my present stage
of life, and my deliberate endeavour, being to sink into
utter insignificance.

Resuming my remarks, I am of opinion that, besides the
other objects of the Academy, one of them should be "to
suggest either the publication or the translation of works
intended to promote public education or the diffusion of
useful knowledge."  There is a total want of all such works
in these Islands, and this want accounts, to a certain degree,
for the pitiful state of popular education here.

One of the sections into which the Academy is to be
divided, is styled that of *Practical Science*.  What is, in
your country, the precise meaning of the word *practical*?
According to our notions, each science may be said to
contain two parts, the pure theoretical part, and the
practical one.  Therefore if Practical Science is meant to
signify "Physical and Mathematical Science," or anything
else, some clearer and more appropriate epithet might be
found out.

At last the paragraph purporting that the L.H.C.
should be invited to inform foreign Governments and
learned Bodies of the establishment of the Ionian Academy,

seems to me objectionable in its present form, the idea of such an information being hardly consistent with that humility which becomes an obscure Institution like ours. Therefore it would be quite enough to say, "that the L.H.C. should be invited to obtain for the Ionian Academy from foreign Governments and learned Bodies the same privileges as are accorded to other Institutions of a similar character."

I submit to you these few remarks only to show how much I feel concerned in the full success of your scheme, and this will be my excuse both for the liberty I have taken, and my English.—Believe me, dear Sir, most sincerely yours, N. ZAMBELLI.

To H. Drummond Wolff, Esq.,
    Corfu.

I have in my possession a letter from Mr. Gladstone, in which he said :—

I shall have much pleasure in accepting the honorary office of Vice-President of the Ionian Association.

This post the Association had instructed me to offer. Many persons in England, of all parties, wishing to show their interest in the undertaking, also accepted the honorary office of Vice-President. The Prince Consort graciously accepted the Presidency. I received great encouragement, in particular, from Mr. Herman Merivale, then Permanent Under-Secretary of State at the Colonial Office. He wrote to me, in a letter dated March 7, 1860, as follows :—

First let me say that I shall be really glad to accept the office of honorary Vice-President of your new Society, and feel myself very much flattered by the offer. If I can be at any time of service to it, this will afford me no small pleasure. Time, unfortunately, is what I want most for this, as well as other things. But I shall rely on you for keeping me informed of any opening that occurs to you for which I can be most serviceable.

It has struck me that you might possibly find advantage in offering a vice-presidency to Sir Roderick Murchison, if you have not done so. He is a cosmopolite—his Russian leanings have made him a bit of a Greek—and he is one of the few people who (besides being really flattered even by small honours) have a real disposition to be useful to other folks, and a good deal of resource in finding out how.

Panizzi might also be a good man to enlist in some way, though perhaps hardly to the extent of a Vice-Presidentship.

I received the following letter from Sir Edward Lytton, while he was staying at Corfu :—

I accept with cordial thanks the honour proposed of becoming one of the Vice-Presidents of your Association, and enclose a trifling donation to its funds.

I think the object of the Association admirable, and I trust that it may be vigorously carried out. The glance I have taken of this island has sufficed to convince me of its immense industrial resources, as yet but partially developed. But even in countries like England itself, with abundant capital and eager competition, innovations, however clear may be their beneficial result, encounter many obstacles in the inert force which belongs to prejudice and indifference, to long-established custom and modes of action. There, and still more in communities like that of Corfu, it is only by the patient energy of a few enlightened minds that improvements are gradually enforced upon the many. Such few are the real benefactors of the State. An Association such as yours is the best practical mode to unite their intelligence and encourage their mutual efforts.

I shall feel a lively interest in hearing, from time to time, of the progress made. Once commenced, I trust it will not be disheartened by the difficulties and delays that are inseparable from the career of improvement when it does not depend on the will of an autocrat, but must consult and, to a certain degree, humour the very prejudices it is destined at last to conquer.

One of the first members of the Ionian Institute was the Chevalier Manzaro, a great musical genius, who lived at Corfu. He had composed the music of the patriotic song adopted by the Greek Revolutionaries. Count Salomos, a brother of the Senator of Zante, who had written the words of that song, was another of our original members.

The Senator, I remember, had a great horror of the sea. When going on board the steamer for Zante, he was always accompanied by some friends who came to cheer him up. One day I went with him, and asked what his sensations were.

He said, "*Ho paura.*"

I remarked that the sea was perfectly calm, but he said, "*Anche quando e tranquillo ho paura.*"

Chevalier Manzaro was anxious to promote the study of music in the Institute, in addition to other arts and sciences. He undertook to organise a system, with this purpose.

Greek popular melodies, like those of Italy, are very melancholy. The following are the notes of a song I used often to hear chanted in a low tone :—

Shortly after our return to England, my wife gave a concert at the house in Rutland Gate where

we then lived, exclusively of Greek music.   It was
considered attractive.   Several ladies came from the
Greek community living in London, amongst them
Miss Marie and Miss Christine Spartali.   Both were
of artistic nature, and remarkably handsome.   The
elder one is a great painter of the pre-Raphaelite
school; but I fear that her sister, Christine, is
dead.   She was a remarkable pianist.   Their
father had a residence at Clapham, where he
occasionally gave artistic *soirées*.

# CHAPTER XXXII

Visitors to the Ionian Islands—Princess Darinka of Montenegro—
Friends at Corfu

DURING my stay in Corfu, the island was visited
by many remarkable people, amongst others by
M. de Lesseps.  Both from Trieste and Brindisi to
Egypt, Corfu was always a stopping-place.

I met M. de Lesseps very often after that
time, in Constantinople, Paris, and London.  In
Paris I dined with him more than once.  These
entertainments were most interesting, as nearly all
his children and grandchildren used to dine with
him.  On one occasion I was dreadfully snubbed.
I was asked to take back with me to the Grand
Hotel, where I was stopping, a little American
boy.  In order to make our drive pass pleasantly,
the child said to me, "Did you ever hear a little
boy say 'Twinkle, twinkle'?"  He thereupon
repeated that poem to me word for word.  When
we got to the hotel, I went upstairs with him to
his bedroom, where his grandmother was waiting
for him.  We knocked at the door, and the little
boy said, "This man has brought me home."

Thereupon the old lady, without saying a word, slammed the door in my face.

M. de Lesseps had an old friend in Corfu, called M. Edouard Grasset, the French consul, a most genial and friendly gentleman, who was generally esteemed, and used constantly to smooth down difficulties. He had been an officer in the Greek Revolution, and spoke the language with great facility. A favourite hobby of his was the collection of antiquities : amongst other treasures he possessed a beautiful necklace entirely composed of gold Alexander coins. His anecdotes of the Greek Revolution were excessively interesting. Sir Rowland Errington, whose name will appear later, wrote to me about him as follows :—

You do not mention dear M. Grasset. Do tell him from me and mine that we shall ever preserve the most agreeable and grateful recollection of all his kindness to us.

In 1860, His Royal Highness Prince Alfred came to the Ionian Islands. I recollect that he rode a pony of mine in a paper-chase. His visit created a good deal of excitement, as a cry had been raised that he should occupy the Greek throne. Later on, His Majesty the King—then Prince of Wales—also visited Corfu. Unfortunately I was in deep mourning at the time, and had no opportunity of paying my respects to His Royal Highness.

The late Empress of Austria arrived at Corfu from Madeira in the Queen's yacht *Victoria and Albert*. The Lord High Commissioner, the

President of the Senate, the *aides-de-camp* and myself, went on board and were presented to Her Majesty. She was tall, very imperial, winning rather than handsome in appearance. She spoke English very well to all of us; asked me how long I had been there, and seemed acquainted with the beauties of the scenery. The Empress did not land, but after visiting Govino in the yacht, she left the next day, having stayed for about twelve hours.

The King of the Belgians also visited Corfu. As I have already stated, I had had the honour of making his acquaintance at Brussels.

At another time, Lord Elgin and his staff passed through on their way back from the Mission to China.

Towards the end of our stay, Mrs. Baring, the mother of Sir Henry Storks' *aide-de-camp*, now Lord Cromer, and one of her sons also came to Corfu. Another visitor to the Islands was Mr. Edward Lear. His water-colours of Oriental scenery are well known, as well as his *Book of Nonsense*, which, I think, was the original of what are called "Limericks." Lord Carlingford bought several of his pictures, and so did Sir Thomas Fairbairn. I am also fortunate enough to possess a few. One of the most beautiful scenes he ever painted—Philæ—will, I am afraid, be destroyed by the engineering works. Mr. Lear was an agreeable man, and very much liked by his friends, but a little sensitive.

Amongst other remarkable persons who visited the Islands was the Princess Darinka of Montenegro, whose husband, the Prince, had been assassinated some years before. She came from Trieste. A relative of hers—I believe her sister—had married one of the Counts Roma, a great name in the Ionian Islands.

I was much struck by the Princess' conversation, by her considerable ability and the moderation of her views. She spoke very freely of Montenegro, and did not conceal her desire for the liberation of the Slav race in Servia, Montenegro, and the adjoining districts of Turkey. It was to this portion of the Slav family that she limited her wishes, being anxious not to interfere with the Slav population of Austria, or to be in any way subject to Russia. On this point she seemed very firm. On one occasion I remember she expressed her strong sympathy with the Poles, and I asked her how she could reconcile this feeling with her reputed desire for Russian domination. She replied, " *Plutôt les turcs!* " She went on to say that she was astonished, when conversing with British consuls and others who came to the country, to find how they were penetrated before their arrival with the false impression that Montenegro was entirely in the interests of Russia.

The Princess told me that if her child had been a son, she might have taken greater interest in affairs. She did not deny taking an active part in political matters; but, as they then stood, there did not seem to be any one person with whose fate that of her country could be associated. She spoke very guardedly of the Prince, and expressed regret at his having married an uneducated Montenegrin, and at his having as yet no children. The absence of issue, she said, also stood in the way of the Prince of Servia, and Princess Darinka vaguely hinted that a grandson of Kara George, then being educated in Paris, might afterwards combine the claims of all sections.

The then Prince of Montenegro, as far as I could gather from the Princess' conversation, was of an obstinate character. His secretary and doctor, a Frenchman, used to write his letters, but he himself transacted all business, and allowed no one to influence him.

Of the Turks, the Princess had the same kind of horror I had observed in all the populations of the opposite coast; nor did she seem to have any strong feeling for the Greeks, though she said the Slavs' sympathy for them had been lately on the increase.

The Princess was pleased with the removal of the blockhouses, and hoped for the assistance of England in obtaining access to the port of Spizza.

I remarked that the English people were glad to see the happiness of all races; but that the good-will of England could only be secured by a peaceful attitude. I cited the offer, recently made by Great Britain, to cede the Ionian Islands, as a proof of her willingness to further the fortunes of nations who gave promise of a peaceful rather than of a turbulent future. The Princess replied, " *Oui, les monténégrins sont trop guerriers.*" But she went on to complain of the barrenness and scarcity of cultivable land, and of the difficulty in the way of her countrymen obtaining subsistence by peaceful means. She also lamented the want of education among the Montenegrins, repeatedly saying that the wives and daughters of the principal men, senators and others, were mere peasants who could neither read nor write. I suggested to the Princess that, as a woman, this was exactly the region in which she could be of use, and advised her, on her return to Montenegro, where she was building a house, to take a German or Swiss governess, and to induce the Montenegrins to allow some of their children to be brought up with her own daughter, an interesting child of about four years old. The Princess said that she had already thought of this, and had even proposed something of the kind. The richest, however, were so poor as to be forced to set their children to work almost as soon as they could walk, and their services could not be spared.

The poverty of Montenegro was a constant theme with Princess Darinka. She made no secret of the pecuniary assistance given to the country by foreign states. But for such help, she said, the people would be without bread. France had lately given 60,000 francs, and Austria 30,000 florins. The latter gift she attributed to the instigation of the Empress of the French, who had said to Prince Metternich, "If your Emperor wishes to do anything agreeable to me, let him give something to Montenegro." The Emperor of the French had also given permission to Mr. Quequich, the Princess' brother, to hold a lottery in France in favour of Montenegro, by which she hoped to obtain four or five hundred thousand francs. A portion of this, forty or fifty thousand francs, had been remitted within the last few days.

The Princess spoke of the journey to London of the Princess of Servia, who had political conversations with Lord Palmerston, by which she thought some good had been done. The Princess of Servia, she said, had been much pleased with her reception, though somewhat disappointed at not being able to pay her respects to the Queen without the intervention of the Turkish Ambassador. This was the cause which prevented Prince Danilo from going to London.

The moderation of the Princess' expressions regarding Montenegro was remarkable. When talking of a sketch of Cettigne, written by Miss Irby and another lady, she complained of it as too much *couleur de rose*, and regretted that the country had not been described without exaggeration in one sense or another.

The Princess had been carefully educated, speaking French, German, and Italian, besides Slav, and understanding English sufficiently for study. She was well informed on all subjects; read a good deal; was shrewd and guarded in her conversation, and had great charm of manner, but was somewhat weighed down by affection for her family. Her character seemed to be a mixture of real patriotism, personal ambition, and disappointment at seeing no immediate prospect by which the two could be combined.

From Corfu she was going in the first instance to Turin to meet her mother and sister, who lived at Paris; thence to Aix-les-Bains. Afterwards she intended to go to some sea-bathing place near Genoa, and to Paris. She expressed herself in very warm terms of the Emperor and Empress of the French, who had personally been very kind to her. She built much on the ultimate assistance of Great Britain, and spoke of her intention of visiting London shortly. I asked her with what passport she travelled. She answered, "With a Montenegrin one in Slav and French," and she went on to say that all countries looked on Montenegro as independent — even Austria and Turkey. Recognition by England was alone wanting.

In pursuance of a promise made at Bowood, Lord and Lady Fortescue came and stayed at Corfu. Lord Seymour paid me a visit too. I had known him well in England. After staying with me for some time he went to Albania, and thence he was summoned back to England on family business. Sir Seymour FitzGerald also passed through the Ionian Islands : he had been Under-Secretary for Foreign Affairs in my time.

One winter, Corfu was fortunate enough to see Sir Rowland Errington and his three daughters. The eldest died not long after : she was very beautiful. The second became Lord Cromer's first wife, and was a guardian angel in Egypt ; and the third married Lord Pollington, the son of the Lord Pollington already mentioned.

Professor Ansted visited Corfu when I was there, and, after a minute examination, wrote a most interesting book on the geology of the Islands. The Duchess of Montrose and her daughter also came, as did Lady Strangford, and, on another occasion, Lord Strangford. The latter astonished the Ionians by his knowledge of Greek, both critical and colloquial. Among other visitors were Lord Beauchamp and Mr. Earle, the father of Mr. Ralph Earle, with two of his other sons, one of whom unfortunately died in Corfu.

On one occasion Mrs. Drummond, widow of Sir Robert Peel's secretary, who was afterwards Under - Secretary for Ireland, with her three daughters, passed a winter in the Islands, where their arrival was warmly welcomed. She was the daughter of the well-known wit called "Conversation Sharpe." It was said that he first attained celebrity by a remark made in the presence of Lord Alvanley. The latter was criticising Scripture history, and observed as to the Ten Commandments that we took them from the Egyptians. Mr. Sharpe, then a young man, replied, " But your Lordship cannot say we kept them."

Amongst our other visitors was Mr. William Eliot, afterwards Lord St. Germans, whom I had known for a long time, and who has been mentioned in a former part of this volume as having been at Bayonne on my return from Madrid. Another was Mr. Edward Herbert, a most amiable and taking young man, who was murdered by brigands in Greece. Later on came Lord Richard Grosvenor—now Lord Stalbridge—and Mr. Stuart-Wortley, of whom more will be heard later.

It would be ungrateful to omit from any account of the Ionian Islands the great advantages and gratification that every one received from the constant visits of the British Fleet. Captain— afterwards Admiral—Clifford, Captain—afterwards Sir Henry—Chads, Admiral Yelverton, and Sir Rodney Mundy, when employed in the Mediterranean Squadron, came constantly to Corfu, and were most successful in conciliating the good-will of all classes.

I recollect a curious circumstance that occurred with regard to Sir Sidney Dacres, when chosen to command the British expedition sent to the West Indies at the time of the differences with the United States concerning the *Trent*. An Ionian lady said to me that, at all events, we should get news of him before they could do so in England. I asked why. She replied, "During the whole of the Indian Mutiny we got information before it arrived in England. Why should we not do so now?"

There was one most interesting lady at Corfu at that time—Countess Valsamachi. Her husband was an Ionian Count, an extremely handsome man, who had been very well received at Vienna at the time of the Congress. She was the widow of Bishop Heber, and a lady very much sought after on account of her kindliness and dignified manner. I believe she had been Miss Spencer by birth, and was often mentioned in Bishop Heber's poems. By her marriage with the Count she had one daughter, who, I think, married a Roumanian.

My most constant companion at Corfu was Sir Charles Sargent, a member of the Supreme Council of Justice. We used to go out together every day, generally taking that beautiful walk leading to what was called the "One Gun Battery." He was a cousin of the Bishop of Oxford, as was his wife, Miss Unwin, who was Sir Charles's first cousin. Lady Sargent had had a brother in the Colonial Office when I was there, and she herself was related to Mrs. Unwin, the close friend of the poet Cowper. Sir Charles Sargent's colleague was Sir Patrick Colquhoun, well known for some time as a diplomatic representative of the Hanse Towns in

England, and also as a Greek scholar. He was cousin to Mr. Colquhoun, our Agent and Consul-General in Egypt.

Another remarkable man connected with the Ionian Islands was Mr. Sebright, who generally went by the name of Baron d'Everton. He had originally been in the service of the Duke of Lucca, who had conferred the title upon him.

# CHAPTER XXXIII

Political agitation—Letters from the Lord High Commissioner—Greek
Revolution—Ionian Islands to be ceded to Greece

As stated before, there had been a great deal of political agitation for some years past in the Ionian Islands. This excitement had recently been stimulated by the publication of a despatch from Lord John Russell, dated August 16, 1859, in which the following passage occurred :—

The people of Tuscany . . . have the right, which belongs to the people of every independent State, to regulate their own internal government.

Lord John Russell had explained why this doctrine did not apply to the Ionian Islands, the reason being that they were under a Protectorate ; but nevertheless the excitement increased. The effervescence in Italy continued, and an insurrectionary spirit of considerable force was making itself felt in Greece itself. Though the Ionian people were personally very civil and courteous to the subjects of the Protecting Power, they gave it clearly to be understood that their one object was to be united with Greece, and that nothing would deter them from pursuing that course, though

368

they wished to do so by peaceful and legitimate methods.

Excitement in the Islands was still further increased by a famous despatch written by Lord John Russell to Sir James Hudson on October 27, 1860. The Ionian Assembly adopted this despatch as the text of a further demand for union with Greece. It began as follows :—

It appears that the late proceedings of the King of Sardinia have been strongly disapproved of by several of the principal Courts of Europe. The Emperor of the French, on hearing of the invasion of the Papal States by the army of General Cialdini, withdrew his Minister from Turin. . . .

The Emperor of Russia . . . declared in strong terms his indignation at the entrance of the army of the King of Sardinia into the Neapolitan territory, and has withdrawn his entire mission from Turin. . . .

After these diplomatic acts, it would scarcely be just to Italy, or respectful to the other Great Powers of Europe, were the Government of Her Majesty any longer to withhold the expression of their opinion.

Lord John Russell went on to say that they did not wish to pass comments on the conduct of the Powers. The questions which appeared to the British Government to be at issue were these :—

Were the people of Italy justified in asking the assistance of the King of Sardinia to relieve them from Governments with which they were discontented ? and was the King of Sardinia justified in furnishing the assistance of his arms to the people of the Roman and Neapolitan States ?

The motives of the people of those States, said the despatch, appeared to have been that the government of the Pope and the King of the Two Sicilies provided so ill for the administration of justice, the protection of personal liberty, and the general welfare of their people, that their subjects looked forward to the overthrow of their rulers as a necessary preliminary to any improvement in their condition. The Italians required one strong Government for the whole of Italy. According to Lord John Russell, the struggle of Charles Albert in 1848, and the sympathy shown by Victor Emmanuel, naturally caused the association of his name with the single authority under which the Italians aspired to live.

The despatch continued as follows :—

Looking at the question in this view, Her Majesty's Government must admit that the Italians themselves are the best judges of their own interests.

Lord John Russell then quoted the maxim of Vattel, "That when a people from good reasons take up arms against an oppressor, it is but an act of justice and generosity to assist brave men in the defence of their liberties."

"Upon this grave matter," said the despatch, "Her Majesty's Government hold that the people in question are themselves the best judges of their own affairs."

After a minute analysis of current Italian politics, Lord John Russell ended this remarkable despatch by saying :—

Her Majesty's Government can see no sufficient ground for the severe censure with which Austria, France, Prussia, and Russia have visited the acts of the King of Sardinia. Her Majesty's Government will turn their eyes rather to the gratifying prospect of a people building up the edifice of their liberties, and consolidating the work of their independence, amid the sympathies and good wishes of Europe.

Sir James Hudson was instructed to give a copy of this despatch to Count Cavour.

When the Ionian Legislative Assembly met, a long paper was read by M. Baccomi on the subject of union with Greece, and M. Lombardo presented another document which was an appeal from the " Representatives of the Seven Islands to the Representatives of the Peoples, the Governments, and the Philanthropists of Christian Europe." Both papers were laid on the table. Sir Henry Storks therefore sent the following message to the Assembly :—

The Lord High Commissioner has perceived that two documents have been laid on the table of the Most Noble Legislative Assembly, and now stand on the order of the day for discussion ; one inviting the Legislative Assembly to call on the Ionian people to declare, by universal suffrage, the national desire to be united to the kingdom of Greece ; the other purporting to be an appeal from the Representatives of the Seven Islands to the representatives of the peoples, to the governments, and to the philanthropists of Christian Europe.

The Lord High Commissioner is desirous of carrying forbearance to the utmost limits of his duty, as the Representative of the Sovereign Protectress of these states ; his Excellency therefore warns the Legislative Assembly that the proposals now standing in the order of the day are clearly contrary to the constitution, and as such cannot be entertained or discussed.

The Lord High Commissioner hopes that nothing will be permitted to divert the Legislative Assembly from its true functions of useful legislation for the good of the country ; and having now informed that body that these proposals are unconstitutional, his Excellency trusts to its prudence and patriotism to remove them from the order of the day.

Given from the Palace of St. Michael and St. George, Corfu, the 12th day of March 1861.

By order of His Excellency,
H. Drummond Wolff,
*Secretary to the Lord High Commissioner.*

In answer to this message, the representatives of the Government in the House reported to Sir Henry Storks that the proposals were not withdrawn from the order of the day ; but, on the contrary, that the Assembly was determined to address a reply to his message, and retain the order of the day as it stood.   In consequence, Sir Henry Storks reported that he had "reluctantly prorogued the Parliament for six months," adding that the most perfect tranquillity prevailed, and that he saw no chance of it being disturbed; although, if the scene of disorder had been permitted to continue, he did not know to what lengths public feeling might have been stimulated.   "The prorogation," he said, "has been favourably received in Corfu, and has created no sensation."

There had been a great deal of discussion meanwhile in England as to whether our Protectorate over the Ionian Islands should be given up or not. At this time I carried on a correspondence about Ionian affairs with Mr. Chichester Fortescue, the Under-Secretary of the Colonial Office, whom I had known somewhat intimately. To him I explained the reasons for and against our continuance of the Protectorate. On the 18th of April 1861, I wrote to him as follows :—

I told you in my last letter that the Lord High Commissioner had deferred his journey to the Islands, and there is now a probability of his not going till after the Queen's Birthday. The delay is judicious, for a tour at present would only create excitement. The word "excitement" perhaps is misplaced. The nature of these people is not inflammatory, like that of the French. They are the most orderly people, except the Belgians, I ever came across, respectful, courteous, and amenable to authority. I mean excitement of mind, and a disposition to be doing something political, which, in another condition, would be dormant.

Sir Henry Storks wishes me clearly to explain to you—though I think I have already done so—the nature of public feeling in these islands on the question of union. It is one of Religion and Nationality, which responds when an appeal is made to it, but which, without such appeal, is silent. In stigmatising the popular leaders as demagogues, in the base sense of the word, he wishes to define them as leaders who are making the movement and not made by it. If I could make myself clear to my own satisfaction, at the risk of being diffuse I would deduce a hundred instances ; but it is difficult to explain the real state of the case when supported only by facts which cannot easily be brought forward.

If you were to appeal to the country on the cry " Annexation or Protection ? " by universal suffrage and ballot, the majority would be enormous in favour of annexation. . . . The feeling for annexation here is, moreover, sufficiently strong to prevent any one from publicly proclaiming his opposition to it. At present, in Corfu, there are many in all classes trembling at the thought of annexation, a rumour of which is sedulously spread by those interested. Yet, put the country to the vote, and not ten of these men would declare their real opinion. All the upper classes, even those who profess themselves in favour of it, would be the first to vote against it, if they dared. One great inducement to the peasants in favour of it is that they imagine it would deliver them from their *signori*. The priests, as a body, are in favour of it. They contribute towards maintaining the feeling amongst the people. The legislators find the feeling so far predominant that an expression of it secures their return, and they make political capital by agitating it.

In a period of tranquillity, therefore, you hear nothing of annexation ; for the papers are not sufficiently read to keep up the sentiment.

There are 1600 places in the Islands. So long as you cannot give a place to every adult male, you will have an opposition working up this cause, if not for office, at any rate for re-election. Even amongst the employés there are several intriguing with the Rhisospasts (Radicals).

An analogous feeling existed in many parts of Italy. Peasants, and others of that class, lived very happily under Grand Dukes; but when the question was put to them, " Will you be annexed to a national Italian Kingdom ? " they voted in the affirmative, perhaps to their personal disadvantage. One may therefore always bear in mind that universal suffrage would carry annexation.

This letter makes it plain that the whole drift of public feeling amongst the people was for annexation to Greece.

During my stay in London in 1862, where I was hard at work in connection with the Exhibition, I received a series of most interesting letters from Sir Henry Storks, describing the agitation going on in the Islands, from which I will quote a

few extracts, as the letters are too long and too
numerous to be given in full :—

PALACE, CORFU,
*March 25, 1862.*

. . . Thanks for your letter. I am very glad to find
that you had so fine a passage to Trieste. I send you some
letters.

Marcoran leaves to-day for London, and awaits a letter
from you, which he will look for at Paris.

Your people, Vassili and Co., left three days ago in the
Liverpool steamer, but have had to make a small détour
viâ Alexandria. I hope they will arrive in time.

The L. A. goes on much in the old way. Every sort of
insane proposal to catch popularity and to compromise me,
as they propose reduction of duties, without providing sub-
stitutes, and boast that they know the Government will not
pass them; but, at any rate, they have proposed them.
Yesterday came on the discussion on the Address, and it is
likely to last three or four days more. Padovan spoke in
his usual style, saying that the Protection was at an end, as
it only existed *de facto*—a pretty good proof of its existence,
by the way. As P.'s speech was an opening speech only, we
shall have him again. Zervo followed, and spoke for one
hour and a half. They tell me that his speech was most
moderate, advocating prudence and attention to the business
of the country, and leaving the "National Question" to
time, and the progress which it could not fail to make.
The Galleries applauded lustily, but the House was "mum."
The fact is, they are moving heaven and earth to make Z.
resign, in order that P. may gain his place and pocket the
£300. I am sure of the wisdom of having confirmed his (Z.'s)
election as President [of the Assembly] and of the appointment of Caruso as President [of the Senate]. The nomination of the latter in the Islands, and particularly in his own,
has given great satisfaction. I will send the *Procès Ver-
baux*, if they are worth it, but these fellows talk such
rubbish, so like children, that the account of their proceedings is hardly worth reading.

Everything is perfectly quiet, and if we are let alone everything will go well. They want to be prorogued, but they shan't be, I am determined, unless they commit some very gross act.

Don't forget the Consular Question, nor to endeavour to obtain some small sum for me. £1000 a year, or even £500, would be of the greatest assistance.

I have no news to give you. I send you a letter for Fairbairn, to whom give my "complimenti." Poor old Carter dropped down dead yesterday morning from apoplexy, or heart : he is to be buried to-day.

I read an article in the *Post* about Ionian politics. Pray thank Algy Borthwick for his *bon souvenir*, with my kind regards. It is very good indeed of him to give one a lift in this way. Remember me also to Sir Edward, Delane, Hayward, Rawlinson, and all friends.

I miss you very much, but am glad you are on the spot to look after our Exhibition. I reckon on you to fight all our battles for us. I write in great haste. You shall hear from me again next week. Peel and Strahan send their love.

*April* 1, 1862.

I suppose ere this you have arrived in London. I hoped to have heard from you by the mail which arrived yesterday. I have little news to give you. The Assembly are behaving as ill as they generally do, and spend their time in idle discussions and in abusing each other. They have spent the whole week in discussing a project of address presented by Lascari, Condari, Tombro, and another, and after all this debate they finished by throwing aside the project of the Commission, and placing on the order of the day to be discussed to-day a project by Lombardo, which is nothing more than a *réchauffé* of A. Valaoriti's address of last year, with a considerable addition of red pepper. Both these projects are objectionable—Lombardo's particularly so—but I make no doubt it will pass by a large majority. Zervo has made a great speech of the most moderate and sensible description, considering his antecedents and opinions. He has behaved most prudently, and with great propriety ; but take them for all in all, they are as bad a lot as I could have found, and will give me a deal of trouble before I have done with them. I am not yet certain what course I shall pursue. They want to drive me to a prorogation which I am determined shall not be unless some extraordinary circumstances arise, which I cannot foresee. They produce little impression out of doors, and people go to the Assembly to hiss and cheer as they go to the Opera.

I have no news to give you. Think of all our work in London, and fight our battles for us if we are attacked. . . . Peel and Strahan send their love, and I am always, my dear Wolff, yours ever,                                    H. K. S.

Kind regards to Sir Edward, Hayward, Rawlinson, Elliot, and C. Fortescue, and all friends.

*April 8, 1862.*

I have received your letter dated Turin, March 28. I cannot give any information about the municipal land for an establishment, because, without knowing the exact spot which would suit, who can say whether our Municipals would make a concession? I should think there would be no difficulty about it, but with such a body as I have to deal with, I cannot answer for anything. All I can promise is to do the best I can. When Mr. Palmer arrives at Corfu I will see him, and ascertain what can be done.

I send you two copies of the Address, and my answer to it. I wish you would send one *immediately* to John Delane, and the other to A. Borthwick. You might add a few introductory remarks. They have taken a month to give this answer to my most moderate speech, and probably a more impudent and lying document was never penned. It was not the project of the Commission which was rejected, though that was bad enough. This is a *progetto* of Lombardo's, being A. V.'s production of last year, but with more abuse and more bile infused into it. The President behaved very well on the occasion. He did not wish to come up with it, and when he signed, he declared that he did so because he was obliged, and that he dissented from its contents. This is recorded in the *Procès Verbal*. It was

supposed I should not receive it; but I did not hesitate
because I thought it too good an opportunity to lose of
putting them in the wrong. My answer has produced *a
very good impression and is universally approved.* These
gentlemen want to be prorogued, for reasons which you
may guess, but they shall not be. I should be glad if this
document were published as soon as possible, because it is
sure to appear in the *Nord* and the French papers. You
know all about the proceeding, and can make such introductory remarks as you think suited for the occasion. A
worse lot I never had to deal with, but I will have the best
of it with them still.

I have no news to give you. Thank God nearly two
months have passed, and by the end of May I shall be
delivered from these worthies.

I have just received your letter from London. I am glad
to hear that you have arrived safely, and are satisfied about
the Exhibition space allotted to us. I have no news to give
you. I go battling on with these fellows, and shall be
sincerely glad when it is all over. I miss you very much,
but it was quite right you should go. If you hear it said
that I am going to resign or come away, pray give it the
strongest denial. I remain here till the latest moment I am
permitted to do so.

During the summer and autumn of 1862, matters
were going on rapidly in Greece, and, on October
23, King Otho was deposed. He fled from Athens
with his Queen, and arrived at Corfu three days
later. Sir Henry Storks paid his respects to them
in the harbour. He told me afterwards that the
Queen was in a great state of excitement, walking
up and down. When speaking about the causes
of the Revolution she said, " Everybody wants to
be a Minister, and everybody can't be a Minister.
Everybody wants a place, and everybody can't get

a place.    Therefore there was constant discontent, which we were unable to satisfy."

The following letter from the Lord High Commissioner may be considered interesting.    It is dated from Corfu, December 2, 1862 :—

I am not surprised at your having trouble about the account, and in winding up the Exhibition.    We have paid the money advanced by the Ionian Bank, and I have desired Boyd to acquaint you, which I believe he has done.

The Lottery is a good idea, and I think it is very kind in Lady Palmerston to assist.    Pray, if you have an opportunity, give my best compliments to her, and express my thanks and the sense I entertain of her kindness.

When do you start? and what are your plans?    I suppose I shall not see you before January.

We enjoy perfect tranquillity here, although we take an active interest in what is going on in Greece.    Both there and here the feeling in favour of Prince Alfred is at fever point.    There is little doubt of his being elected King of Greece, for the public has declared itself in the strongest manner about H.R.H.    British policy here has contributed considerably towards creating this feeling in favour of England, her institutions, and her honesty.

The weather has been terrible—wind and heavy rain.

Before this letter was written, the British Government had decided on annexing the Ionian Islands to Greece, and was taking the necessary steps by communicating with the other great Powers.

# CHAPTER XXXIV

I HAVE many letters written to me at the time by
Mr.—afterwards Sir George—Dasent. He used
to give the most interesting accounts of what was
going on both in Denmark and England. His
views were generally correct, and the letters were
a pleasant miscellany of current politics and gossip.
The following is an extract from one of them :—

You will have seen, if the telegraph is not lazy, that the
cession of the Islands is settled so far as our Government is
concerned. All now depends upon Greece, who had better
get herself a King without delay.

No one is in town except Hayward, just come from
Bowood, where a lady was so icy as to be very agreeable in
that summer weather [written on January 8]. Till to-day
the air has been a great deal milder than an ordinary English
summer.

What have you done with that delinquent —— ? I saw
during my visit that many of the prizes [the Ionian raffle]
had not been claimed. He seemed delightfully ignorant
about the whole matter. What a fool the man is to be
impertinent to me! So great a fool that I must forgive
him as the Turks do naturals.

I am very busy up to the eyes in Army examinations which will last till well on in February.  Borthwick I have tried to see, but unsuccessfully.  He is a good fellow, though.

I am in a sad state of quarantine, for two brace of my children have got the measles and five more persons in the house have still to take them.  You will be annexed and back before I get a clean bill of health.  That stupid —— who has had the measles ever so many times is afraid to let me go and see her. . . .

Gladstone is going to reduce, so as to get the income tax to 7d.  In that case he will defy Derby and all his works. . . .

To-day I dined with the Royal Society.  We had a very bad dinner, in the course of which, finding that every one round me was telling most terrific scientific lies, I was obliged to draw on my invention for a lot of natural phenomena observed in Iceland—every word of them untrue—which I was asked to embody in a Paper.  Catch me !  After dinner we went to the Society itself, and heard a Paper read to help our digestion " On the marked action of the gastric juice on the coats of the stomach after death," illustrated by diagrams of the stomachs of dogs and rabbits, as well as those of seven persons who had died in a hospital of typhus, stone, diphtheria, apoplexy, and all kinds of illness.  This is literally true.

There was another Paper " On the amatory instincts of Canary Birds," but the gastric juice was as much as I could digest, so I came here thanking God that I am not as other men are, anatomists, geologists, chemists, astronomers, or even as that publican who gave us the bad dinner.

About this time, there were rumours of a conspiracy concocted at Rome for the restoration of Francis II. to the throne of Naples.  This gave me perpetual correspondence with Sir James Hudson.  Letters also passed between us with regard to the conveyance of the post to Corfu, in consequence of the proposed extension of the railway to Brindisi.

With regard to the former matter, I wrote to him on the 1st of June 1863 as follows :—

I think it better to give you some details at length . . . as the Italian Consul does not seem to have complete information. Three days ago he was challenged by the L.H.C. to produce proofs of the alleged conspiracy, but has failed to do so.

As for Malta, of course I cannot answer. For this place, I can safely assert that we are in neither apparent nor real ignorance of anything that goes on.

The real fact of the case was that we had done everything possible to prevent any conspiring against the settled state of affairs in Italy ; and we found that the Consul, who suspected treachery, acted on very imperfect data. His informants were notorious. One of them had assisted the brothers Bandiera in their well-known expedition, and had then denounced them. The Italian Consul accused a certain tobacconist in the town, whose wife was related to a supporter of the Bourbons, of being an agent for that party; but there was no evidence whatever against them. These matters made some stir at the time.

On June 9, Sir James Hudson wrote me a letter in which he said :

There has been doubtless much coming and going, whispering and plotting, on the part of a set of persons who find their account in sucking the unhappy Francesco II. quite dry at Rome.

A Government can, of course, only judge by the evidence

before it as to the value of the Conspiracy in a marketable
sense, and in the present case they [the Italian Government]
most certainly believed that there was something serious—
or rather more serious than usual—for not a week passes
but we have some bantling from that hatching-place of
plots, Rome.

You must therefore not be offended if much is said about
Corfu as a stepping-stone in the Conspiracy.

I have explained more than once that Her Majesty's
authorities cannot overstep the law to please anybody, or
serve any particular interest; that we are just and equal to
all, and for all. . . .

I am of Sir H. Storks' opinion as to this "Conspiracy"
or "Plot," or by whatever name it may be designated or
dignified.

I don't think it was ever more than a shadowy or seedy
affair; for even supposing that there were 500 Bashi Bozuk
Albanians in the flesh, and armed to the teeth, what could
they do, seriously speaking, against Italy or for Francesco
II. ? Why, next to nothing. Morally speaking, they would
render Francesco's cause more odious, and physically and
practically they would be hunted down and shot, and there
would be an end of the great Malta-Corfu Conspiracy.

However, as prevention is better than cure, perhaps the
row that has been kicked up will be productive of much
good, more caution, and less zeal.

It may be interesting to state that, towards the
end of our stay in the Ionian Islands, amongst
the endeavours made to conciliate the inhabitants,
the British Government had determined to allow
Ionians to hold commissions in the British Army.
One was given, but without great success, for, on
the first occasion of a young Ionian officer being in
charge and ordering his soldiers to tell off in the
usual way, they gave the numerals in Greek.

The concluding period of England's tenure of

those States was remarkable, as showing the record
of an almost unique political act. It may therefore
be of some interest to go into detail in describing
this unparalleled incident in history.

The Greeks had had the greatest difficulty in
obtaining a King. They were enthusiastic for our
Prince Alfred. But this was impossible. Several
Powers had been appealed to, but in vain. The
*Charivari* published a caricature of some Greeks
standing like armed brigands on a rock, one saying
to the other : " *Tant pis pour lui.* The first man
who passes, we'll make him King ! " It ended, however, in the choice of Prince William of Denmark,
who accepted the throne, and began to reign on
October 31, 1863, under the name of George I.,
King of the Hellenes. When his election was
announced in the previous June, the Archbishop
of Corfu ordered a *Te Deum* to be sung, at which
he invited the Lord High Commissioner to be
present. Sir Henry Storks made me his representative, and I was accompanied by his *aide-de-
camp*, Lieutenant Baring. We were greeted with
cheers, and on our arrival at the church, "God
Save the Queen" was played. I was placed
between the Consuls of France and Russia. A
prayer was offered for the King of the Greeks, and
this was followed by the Danish National Air, and
cries of Ζήτω. A prayer was next offered for Her
Majesty. "God Save the Queen" was again
played, and there was more shouting. Then came
a prayer for Union, and the Greek Hymn. Vast

crowds, carrying Greek and English flags, marched
to the Palace, where the Lord High Commissioner
was warmly cheered ; and the town was afterwards
illuminated.

Just about then I received an interesting letter
from Mr. Baillie Cochrane, who had always been
an enthusiastic admirer of Greece. I quote it
here, as it shows the feeling in England at the
time :—

I suppose that you are all in a great state of excitement now that we may consider the cession of the Ionian
Islands as almost a *fait accompli*. The strange thing is
that our front bench accept it so quietly, and I think the
session will end without a word of remonstrance.

You were quite right in your views of the Eastern
Question. Gregory's debate elicited strong opinions from
the House, and it must have had a great effect on the
Continent.

I assisted last Monday at the *Te Deum* in honour of
the young King, and a very grand affair it was. The
sermon concluded with an aspiration that the Cross might
soon be planted in St. Sophia, on which the whole con-
gregation exclaimed Ζήτω, but the Greeks must be careful
not to go too fast, or they will alarm even their well-
wishers. I had little doubt of their ultimate success, but
they must learn to gang warily.

Here we are in the middle of June and Palmerston still
sailing on in smooth waters, and I see nothing likely to
ruffle the surface. It is, as Lytton says, a question of
succession. Any attempt to remove him would be fatal to
our party. Meanwhile the young move away. Gordon of
Berwick died yesterday, and I am told that Earle is already
in the field. I hope he will succeed.

Please let me know the state of feeling in the Ionian
Islands. I daresay they begin to regret the transfer,
saddled as they will be with a goodly portion of the Greek

debt. What do you think of the Greek bonds rising to 40, which were down at 13, and at one time, I believe, at 4 or 5.

The story is that Bulwer is to leave Constantinople and be made a peer. I mentioned this last night to Lord S. de Redcliffe, whose face glowed with excitement. . . . I know no man so miserable out of place and pay.

I hope we shall meet soon. It is not unlikely we shall visit Corfu during the winter; but by that time I suppose you will have started.

During the spring of 1863, it had been decided that there should be a special election of Representatives, to ascertain the wishes of the Ionian people with regard to union with Greece. The Parliament then sitting was to be dissolved by an Order in Council; the new Parliament was to vote on the question of annexation to Greece or British Protection, and then to be prorogued.

On July 25, the Lord High Commissioner published the following proclamation :—

His Excellency the Lord High Commissioner is pleased to publish for general information the following Proclamation by Her Majesty in Council, dissolving the present Parliament of these States, which is consequently dissolved from the present date.

The Lord High Commissioner has received Her Majesty's Commands to call the solemn attention of the Ionian People to the reasons which have induced Her Majesty to dissolve the Twelfth Parliament of the Ionian States. Her Majesty the Protecting Sovereign has declared Her readiness to consent to the Union of the Ionian Islands with Greece; and it is with a view to consult in the most formal and authentic manner the wishes of the inhabitants of the Ionian Islands as to their future destiny, that Her Majesty is pleased to dissolve the present Parliament.

The Ionian People will fully appreciate the responsibility which rests on them in choosing their Representatives. They are called upon to decide by this choice on the momentous question now submitted to them, and the only wish of Her Majesty is that they may be guided to a wise decision, by which their happiness and prosperity may be secured on a solid foundation.

By order of His Excellency, etc.

Shortly afterwards, I was instructed to send the following notification to the residents of the Islands :—

You are carefully to abstain from any interference, direct or indirect, in favour of, or against any Candidates, either before or during the forthcoming General Election, and you will also give strict orders in the same sense to the Employés in the different Departments placed by the Constitution under the special control of the Lord High Commissioner,—further informing them that any infringement of His Excellency's injunctions on this point will be attended with instant dismissal from the Public Service.

The foregoing instructions are not intended to restrict any public Employé from the free exercise of the Elective franchise ; but the Lord High Commissioner on this occasion is determined to uphold the principle on which he has hitherto acted, of securing the choice of the people from all coercion on the part of the Executive.

By order of His Excellency, etc.

During August, M. Bræstrup, an old Danish statesman, supposed to have an acute knowledge of character, came to Corfu to await the arrival of the King.

The new Parliament assembled in September. The Lord High Commissioner explained to them the reason for their being summoned, and the procedure that should be followed to record the wishes of the Ionian people. Sir Henry Storks ended his speech with these words :

I now leave you to your deliberations, and in so doing will merely echo the wish expressed by Her Majesty that you may be guided to a wise decision, and that the national happiness and prosperity of the Ionian people may by your suffrages be secured on a solid foundation.

To this speech the President of the Assembly made the following reply :—

My Lord—If it were in my power at this moment to express my own opinion, and that of my fellow-members, I would give you a reply immediately, but prescribed forms do not allow me. I shall therefore in due time request you to hear the reply of the Assembly, and I can assure you that the Assembly, on taking the subject into consideration, will pronounce a decision consonant with their national dignity,—and they reserve themselves to adopt, on that occasion, measures adequate to afford a proof of their sentiments towards Her Most Gracious Majesty and the Protecting Powers.

The Assembly then met with closed doors. The Archbishop was sent for, and mass was celebrated in the body of the Assembly, after which the Archbishop blessed the Legislators. The Assembly then voted an Address to be presented to the Lord High Commissioner, and the President read a Decree announcing that the Ionian Islands "are united with the Kingdom of Greece, in order to form for ever its indissoluble part in a single and indivisible State, under the

Constitutional Sceptre of His Majesty the King
of the Hellenes, George I., and His Successors."

On October 6, the President of the Legislative Assembly, accompanied by all the Members,
attended at the Palace for the purpose of presenting
an Address to the Lord High Commissioner. It
ended with the following words :—

EXCELLENCY—The Assembly, amidst the inexpressible joy
which overflows the hearts of all, must express the gratitude
of the Ionian People to the Gracious QUEEN of Great Britain,
both for the generous decision She has taken, and Her kind
disposition towards the Greek Nation.

The same sentiment of gratitude the Assembly must also
declare towards the other Protecting Powers of Greece, both
for their co-operation and the realisation of the national
restoration of the Ionians, and their kind disposition towards
the Greek Nation.

Christian Europe, capable of appreciating the services
offered to mankind by the Greek race, will consent to assist
the Greek Nation in its full restoration, in the interests of
civilisation and the fulfilment of the Decrees of the Most
High.

In reply, the Lord High Commissioner announced
that he would communicate to the Legislative
Assembly, in due form, the detailed arrangements
necessary for the transfer of the Ionian States from
the Protectorate of Her Majesty the Queen to the
Kingdom of Greece. After this reply was read,
M. Curi, one of the Members for Corfu, advanced
and said in English, "God bless the Queen and the
magnanimous English Nation!"

Rejoicings took place in Corfu for three days:
first, in honour of Union ; the second day, in honour

of the Queen; and the third, in honour of the other Protecting Powers. A mass was celebrated at the tomb of Count John Capo d' Istria, the original author of Ionian independence.

A Treaty was signed at the Foreign Office in London on March 29, 1864, between Great Britain, France, and Russia on the one part, and Greece on the other, for the Union of the Ionian Islands to Greece. It was made a condition of our surrender of those States, that all the fortifications should be destroyed. For some time, therefore, before the annexation I witnessed this destruction being carried out by the British engineers. It had to be done against the protests of the Ionian people. But it was a most absorbing spectacle to witness.

The Greek Envoy, M. Zaimis, arrived in Corfu on May 19, to arrange with the Lord High Commissioner as to the form and manner in which the Ionian States were to be ceded to Greece. On the 24th, a levee and review were held in honour of the Queen's Birthday. Sir Henry Storks' reception was numerously attended.

On May 27, the 13th Parliament was dissolved in obedience to Her Majesty's Order in Council, dated April 7.

On June 2, 1864, the actual relinquishment of the Protectorate took place. The Greek troops had arrived on the previous day, but none were allowed to disembark, except the number required to relieve the guards, until the British garrison should have sailed. Her Majesty's troops embarked early on the morning of June 2. The Municipality of Corfu presented them with an address, ending with these words :

Farewell, brave sons of England! Forget, as we do, whatever may tend to mar our mutual love! Love us, as we love you, and desire that we may imitate your national virtue!

Sir Robert Garrett, commanding the Forces, in his reply, made use of the following expressions :—

In the name of the private soldiers, whom I have the honour to command, I request you will be pleased to make known to the inhabitants of the country round Corfu, and to those of the town itself, how fully they have appreciated the kindly feelings which they have unremittingly exercised towards them.

Again repeating the assurances of our very best wishes for the welfare of you all, I now, in the name of the British garrison, bid you most heartily, Farewell!

After addressing a few words of farewell to the friends assembled at the Palace to say good-bye, Sir Henry Storks embarked on H.M.S. *Marlborough* under the usual salutes. The British Colours were lowered, the Greek Flag run up on the Forts, and the British Flags marched off and embarked with Guards of Honour. The ships then left for Malta, except the *Marlborough*, which took Sir Henry Storks to Catacolo to meet the King of the Hellenes.

Thus ended our connection with the Ionian Islands.

# CHAPTER XXXV

Visit to England—Duke of Newcastle—Sir Edward Lytton—Lord
Carlingford—Islands transferred to Greece

Towards the end of 1863, the Government had
telegraphed to Sir Henry Storks to send me home
to concert a method for giving up the Islands.
This business kept me in England for about four
months. I saw Lord Russell and the authorities
at the Foreign Office, to which I was referred by
the Duke of Newcastle. On the 1st of November
he wrote me the following letter :—

I am very sorry I cannot be in town before Tuesday week
(10th), but as regards Ionian business I hope my absence
will be of little importance, for I consider that all matters
of consequence connected with it have passed out of my
hands and now rest with your old Department—the Foreign
Office.

I think you should at once see Hammond and ascertain
from him whether you should call on Lord Russell.

I do not think the protest against demolition of the
fortifications very powerful, though I have no doubt it is
more sincere than most emanations from the Assembly.

This proved to be almost the end of my connection with the Duke. He was very ill at the
time, and died the following year. He was a

most remarkable man, much beloved by those who served under him. At one time I used to see a good deal of him at the Athenæum, where he spent much of his leisure in the society of the gentlemen mentioned in Sir Henry Storks' letters.

It may be considered interesting here to give a few extracts from letters written to me while I was in the Ionian Islands, which alluded to various political matters. I will, first of all, quote one from Sir Edward Lytton, dated January 25, 1860 :—

Parliament has opened. The Commercial Treaty with France is generally unpopular, and may not pass Parliament.

The Chinese papers I have looked over. I think the Conservatives can make no handle of it.

I still think the Government will get through the Session, but there are more breakers ahead for them than I foresaw ; but their great advantage is that the Conservatives are not ready to take office.

Walpole and Henley do not sit in the front row, but three behind.

Further letters from Sir Edward Lytton show how much interest was taken in what was considered a singular event—the cession of the Islands to Greece. He wrote to me from Nice, on January 7, 1863, as follows :—

I begin to doubt whether Parliament will ratify the Ionian Cession. The affair is much complicated by Elliot's mission, and the request to Turkey to yield Thessaly and Epirus—much complicated also by the breakdown of Don Ferdinand, and the uncertainty as to what Greece may do, while, if she do not make a wise choice, to justify ceding the isles, and dismembering Turkey, the blunder of Lord John will be without excuse—the Islands most difficult to govern, and yet equally difficult to get rid of. . . . I see that some of the old Whigs, such as Ellice, who is here, are very angry with Russell and the whole affair. Lord Stratford denounces them. Roebuck, too, I am told, says the Ministers can't last after the meeting of Parliament, if Elliot's message be truly reported. Of that last I think there is no doubt.

I shall stay here as long as I can, but I expect to be back in time for any party discussions—Ionian or otherwise—and these must come early.

NICE, *February* 3, 1863.

. . . I am asked by Dis to take up the Ionian Question. I have agreed to speak on it, perhaps introduce . . . I think it bad for Greece, bad for the Islands, bad for Turkey, bad for the British Empire. . . .

Judging by Storks' letter to me, he seems to favour the cession, to disbelieve wholly about Thessaly and Epirus being asked, and to go with the Government. . . .

What is to become of all the Protectorate party, the Employés, etc.? Is there any island besides Corfu where a Jacquerie may be apprehended? Qy. Cephalonia? Are the islands all of the same mind? Are they all contented with Athens for a capital, or do they look to Constantinople as the Italians to Rome?

On February 12 he wrote me the following letter :—

I am still at Nice for two or three weeks more. At first I was going back to initiate or join in a motion respecting the Ionian Islands; but Dis informs me that the renunciation of the Duke of Coburg leaves it, in the opinion of both parties, so doubtful that the conditions for resigning the Islands will be complied with, that there is not even a plausible ground for any motion, and the cession of the Islands certainly seems very doubtful after all—at all events, indefinitely postponed. The absurd hash of the Government will, no doubt, render it much more difficult to govern them; will have discouraged, I should think, the friends of

the Protectorate, and alarmed all our officials.   And it may
be only a question of time for cession; but it is clear that a
good King of Greece must be found first.

Dis writes that nothing can equal the apathy of Parliament, and that I need be in no hurry to return.   In fact, I
should think that, with the Prince's marriage, nothing will
get Members together much before Easter, and after then
the Government will be probably quite safe.   The Ionian
Question would have been a bad party fight for us, and I am
glad we are spared it.

Robert is pleased with his transfer at Copenhagen, where
in Paget's absence he acts as chargé d'affaires.

On March 11, Sir Edward Lytton wrote to me
again from Nice :—

. . . I conclude that the Ionian Question is suspended for
the moment, and I doubt whether the Islands will be ceded
for a long time.

Nothing can exceed the wicked precipitation of the
Government in an announcement which unsettled all things
in the Isles before anything was settled in Greece.

I hear on all sides from London that the political lull is
without parallel.   Still there are indications of increased
weakness in the Government.   I should not be surprised if
the Cabinet split into pieces at any moment.   Lord Derby
seems, if he live, certain at all events for next year, though
perhaps not till after the Election.

Poland will prove a most difficult question to solve, and
may lead to wholly new combinations.   But in England no
one thinks of Poles—only of the Royal Marriage.   Robert
writes to me that he saw the Princess, and that all at Copenhagen bear testimony to the sweetness of her disposition.

The following letter was written from Knebworth on July 24, 1863 :—

. . . Delays are inevitable, and not the Duke's fault,
though perhaps the Government's.   1st, Delay from the
new King and his Danish patrons; 2nd, from the Great

Powers. Till these hitches are over there cannot be formal annexation and surrender.

At present I am more and more satisfied, from all I see of the House of Commons, that no step was taken there, and I am more sure of this from further observation of the Duke's character. I see that any appearance of opposition makes him obstinate and hostile. I observed this in a recent instance.

A certain Governor had a most strong claim for a certain thing. The Duke, at the outset, was well disposed to grant it, but he is very slow. My Governor got impatient, resolved to press his claim more urgently. I advised him not. I said, "Wait, and you will have what you want— perhaps in a year. That is better than not having it at all." No! he pressed his case, teased the Duke, and, as I foresaw, the Duke turned round and refused the thing rudely, and altogether taking the *chose* wholly *en grippe*.

The two following letters were at that time written to me by Lord Carlingford — then Mr. Chichester Fortescue :—

*March* 24, 1861.

Many thanks for your letter. I was very glad to have your graphic account of the scenes, which have not only roused to excitement the calm of the Colonial Office, but attracted much attention in Parliament and the Town. You will see the notice taken of them in the two Houses by those kindred spirits, Maguire and Normanby. "Official information" is to be laid before Parliament, but we will be careful what we produce. One of the provoking parts of this provoking business is that we cannot produce all that Storks writes, and all that we think of your precious patriots; and that Europe and Ireland will take them as the exponents and champions of an oppressed nationality.

You talk of some means of satisfying these people, without sacrificing the rights of the Protecting Power. Pray let me have your ideas on the subject, because it sounds like squaring the circle. I heartily wish we were well rid of them. Maguire has moved for Gladstone's correspondence and Papers since that time. It is a question whether to give them, and the Duke and Cabinet have not yet decided. At all events, he will get up a debate on Ionian affairs, for the purpose of embarrassing the Government by comparisons with their Italian policy—not because he loves any liberty except his own, but because he loves the Pope and hates England, especially certain Englishmen known by the names of Palmerston and Russell.

I wish you would write me odds and ends of Ionian information, and of your own views, which may be very useful in case of debate. What would be the effect throughout the Greeks of Turkey, Candia, etc., if the Ionian Islands were handed over to Greece, merely on the principle of nationality? Would it not do more to break up the Turkish establishment than all our efforts have done to preserve it? What is thought about it in Greece, and by the Greek Government? What is likely to happen when the Parliament meets again? and when must the Dissolution take place?

*April* 16, 1861.

. . . I, for one, should feel bound to urge and assist in a revision of the Ionian Constitution, if I could see my way to it without passing through a *coup d'état* on the threshold. But I see no legal opening.

It will be seen from this correspondence how much the question filled the thoughts of the British Government, and how long a time was spent in carrying out the measure of transferring the Islands to Greece. The suspense was very painful to all parties—to ourselves, whose future movements were thus undecided, and to the Greeks, amongst whom there was great divergence of opinion. Some Greeks, especially those of the landlord class, looked upon the annexation as fatal to their interests, even, perhaps, to their lives.

The prolonged suspense was on all sides a great ordeal. At length, however, as has been seen, we did leave the Islands, and a few days afterwards I received, from a commissariat officer who had been left to carry out some details, an interesting account of Corfu :—

The change to us few remaining Britons is painful enough; but nothing can exceed the respect and courtesy with which we are treated by all classes.

The Greek garrison in Corfu consists of 400 men, not ill-dressed and fairly set up. The same number is scattered over the Islands. They are amazed at the beauty and the cleanliness of the barracks, and are already overcoming the latter defect.

As I write, the King is entering the harbour: I hear he will stay a week.

The Exodus went off capitally, and the people behaved very well, and cheered louder than I thought they could have done. Philadelphia is not a more complete city of Quakers, and the Esplanade is the most formidable battery left.

Taylor's [1] signboard came down with the British Ensign on the 2nd, and Courage's [2] receipts have amounted to 18/7d. !

[1] The general shop.          [2] A grocer.

END OF VOL. I

*Printed by* R. & R. CLARK, LIMITED, *Edinburgh*.

# MODERN EGYPT

BY

## THE EARL OF CROMER

With a Photogravure Portrait of the Author and a Map.

### Two Vols. 8vo. 24s. net.

*TIMES.*—"An event of far more than mere literary interest. It is a contribution of first-rate importance to the applied science of statesmanship—a contribution for which it would be hard to find a parallel."

MR. SIDNEY LOW in *THE STANDARD.*—"The book is not only absorbing in its interest, but it is a contribution to contemporary history of the highest importance. . . . To those who want to know how modern Egypt came into being, and to those who would learn what modern Egypt is, the book is invaluable. It may be supplemented ; it cannot be superseded."

MR. SPENSER WILKINSON in *THE MORNING POST.*—"Stands almost alone in literature. . . . Of absorbing interest. It tells from beginning to end a story which is perhaps the most dramatic that has passed before the eyes of Englishmen now in middle life. The story is told by the most competent witness, with rare exactitude, with perfect lucidity, and with comments which reveal an even judgment."

*EVENING STANDARD.*—" It is difficult to turn from the perusal of this great work and then to find words in which adequately to praise without the abuse of hyperbole the magnitude of its achievement. . . . It is, of course, a work that every student of our Imperial life must read, and one that will become a classic. . . . Exerts by a combination of rare qualities an extraordinary fascination."

*DAILY NEWS.*—"A powerful, a discreet, an imposing work, a document which will aid administrators in the work of building, which will help the public to form a fair opinion."

*DAILY TELEGRAPH.*—"It would be superfluous to praise a book which is obviously destined to take high place among the rare volumes of authentic contemporary history."

*WESTMINSTER GAZETTE.*—"A fascinating book—a book through which the central stream of narrative runs broad and clear, and in which our guide is no mere historian piecing together the records of others, but himself the chief actor in the scenes that he describes."

*DAILY CHRONICLE.*—"A narrative that holds and a judgment that convinces. . . . A most fascinating and surprising narrative."

*WORLD.*—"It goes almost without saying that Lord Cromer's book is indispensable for all who wish to understand the question of Egypt and our position in that country."

### MACMILLAN AND CO., LTD., LONDON.

# MACMILLAN AND CO.'S NEW BOOKS

### B. L. PUTNAM WEALE

## THE COMING STRUGGLE IN EASTERN ASIA.

By B. L. PUTNAM WEALE, Author of "Manchu and Muscovite," "The Re-Shaping of the Far East," "The Truce in the East and its Aftermath." With Numerous Illustrations, and a Comprehensive Map. 8vo. 12s. 6d. net.

### F. C. SELOUS

## AFRICAN NATURE NOTES AND REMINIS-CENCES.

By F. C. SELOUS, Author of "A Hunter's Wanderings in Africa" and "Travel and Adventure in South-East Africa." With a Foreword by President ROOSEVELT and Illustrations by E. CALDWELL. 8vo.

### Colonel G. J. YOUNGHUSBAND

## THE STORY OF THE GUIDES.

By Colonel G. J. YOUNGHUSBAND, C.B., Queen's Own Corps of Guides. With Illustrations. 8vo.

### Lieut.-Colonel J. H. PATTERSON

## THE MAN-EATERS OF TSAVO, AND OTHER EAST AFRICAN ADVENTURES.

By Lieut.-Colonel J. H. PATTERSON, D.S.O. With numerous Illustrations, and a Foreword by FREDERICK COURTENEY SELOUS. 8vo. 7s. 6d. net.

### H. FIELDING HALL

## THE INWARD LIGHT.

By H. FIELDING HALL, Author of "The Soul of a People," "A People at School," etc. 8vo. 10s. net.

*In Monthly Volumes from December* 1907.

## THE WORKS OF ALFRED, LORD TENNYSON.

Annotated by the Author. Edited by HALLAM, LORD TENNYSON. Vol. I. POEMS. Vol. II. POEMS. Vol. III. ENOCH ARDEN and IN MEMORIAM. Vol. IV. THE PRINCESS and MAUD. Vol. V. IDYLLS OF THE KING. Vol. VI. BALLADS and other Poems. Vol. VII. DEMETER and other Poems. Vol. VIII. QUEEN MARY and HAROLD. Vol. IX. BECKET, and other Plays. Globe 8vo. 4s. net each. [*Eversley Series.*

### THOMAS HARDY

## THE DYNASTS.

A Drama of the Napoleonic Wars. By THOMAS HARDY. Part III. Crown 8vo. 4s. 6d. net.

### MARTIN LUTHER

## THE LETTERS OF MARTIN LUTHER.

Selected and Translated by MARGARET A. CURRIE. 8vo. 12s. net.

MACMILLAN AND CO., LTD., LONDON.